This book is dedicated to the
memory of Stanley Hall, long term member
of the Crystal Palace Foundation.
It was Stan's articles in Crystal Palace Matters
about the Cup Finals and his early support that
gave me the inspiration to research the
football at the Crystal Palace.

Ian Bevan

Front cover of The Crystal Palace Magazine - April 1904.

"To the Palace for the Cup"

*An affectionate history
of football at The Crystal Palace.*

Research by Ian Bevan, Stuart Hibberd & Michael Gilbert.

Text by Ian Bevan and Stuart Hibberd.

Designed and produced by Michael Gilbert.

Best Wishes

Ian Bevan

Michael Gilbert

REPLAY publishing

Acknowledgements

I would like to express my sincere thanks to Stuart Hibberd for all his efforts in the later stages of this enterprise, particularly in pursuing the amateur football history. Also, to Mick Gilbert for his contribution to the research and the excellent design and production of this publication. Additionally, thanks must go to Gina Gilbert who did the proof-reading, and Penny Bevan for various research and promotional work (even though neither of them likes football).

Our special thanks are due to Andy George whose passion for the Cup Finals at the Crystal Palace has led him to accumulate a vast collection of photographs and memorabilia all of which we were allowed to use. Andy also provided the profile of Bert Freeman, the goalscorer in the 1914 Final.

We wish to express our appreciation to The Crystal Palace Foundation for their support and encouragement throughout this project.

There are a vast number of people whom we have pestered for information and who have freely provided a contribution and support. The following is an attempt to list all these people to whom we would express our thanks. If you have helped us and you are not listed below, please accept our apologies for the oversight and be assured that your help was greatly appreciated.

Our thanks are due to:
Dave Barber (Football Association);
Norman Barrett;
Roger Bing (Croydon Advertiser);
Arthur Bower (Barnsley FC historian);
British Library Newspaper Section;
Bryon Butler;
Richard H Chadder;
Sue Cole (Charterhouse School);
Jonathan Cotten (Museum of London);
Peter Cullen (Bury FC historian);
R Custance (Archivist - Winchester College);
Mark Dickson (Shrewsbury School);
Norman Epps;
Mike Floate;
Andy George;
Melvyn Harrison (Crystal Palace Foundation);
Dave Hayman;
Graham Hughes (Wolverhampton Wanderers);
Simon Inglis;
Paul Joannou (Newcastle United historian);

Colin Kerrigan (Historian of London Schools FA);
Ian King (Crystal Palace FC historian);
Ken Kiss (Crystal Palace Museum);
Peter Lamb (National Sports Centre);
David Lancaster (Christies);
Peter Letts (Photographer);
Grant McDougall (Christies);
the late Rob Marsden;
Russell Muir (Old Reptonians);
Philip Paine;
Brian Pearce;
Andy Porter (Tottenham Hotspur historian);
Rob Pratten (Football Museum, Preston);
Eric Price;
Eileen Pulfer;
Mick Renshaw;
Norman Rosser (Archivist, Malvern College);
Steve Roud (Croydon Local Studies Library);
David Roy (Secretary - Arthur Dunn Cup);
Rev. Nigel Sands (Crystal Palace FC historian);
Jerry Savage (Upper Norwood Library);
Irene Seijo (Parks Project Coordinator, Bromley);
Norman Shiel;
Shrewsbury Town FC;
Ray Simpson (Burnley FC historian);
Eric Spottiswoode;
Peter Stanley;
Mike Taylor (Amateur Football Alliance);
Uxbridge Central Library Local Heritage Service;
David Wavell;
Jon Weaver (Groundtastic);
Colin Weir (Historian of Oxford University FC);
Tony Williams;
Mark Wylie (Manchester United FC Museum);
Zentralbibliothek Zurich.

Our thanks to Bryon Butler for providing the Foreword to this book. Bryon is well respected in footballing, journalistic and broadcasting circles and has written the definitive work on the FA Cup.

We acknowledge Desert Island Books Ltd for the use of material in the Book of Football, first published in 1905.

Finally, we would like to apologise to our families for boring them by constantly discussing the subject and thank them for their forbearance while we disappeared to delve into library archives or huddled in corners to discuss progress.

Ian Bevan

Published by
Replay Publishing Limited,
130 Aylesford Avenue, Beckenham, Kent BR3 3RY.

© Ian Bevan, Stuart Hibberd & Michael Gilbert 1999.

Printed by
Cravitz Printing Company Limited,
1 Tower Hill, Brentwood, Essex CM14 4TA.

ISBN 0 9536663 0 1

The Game plan

Foreword by Bryon Butler

Just imagine. A home for the FA Cup Final which allows people to picnic and parade, a national sporting theatre with grassy banks, little gabled stands and a frame of trees in which those without tickets can perch like crows to get a free, clear view of the big game. All around the ground are gardens full of flowers and ornate work in stone and iron. And in the background is a huge, sparkling palace of glass as well as a rip-roaring fairground.

This was the Crystal Palace a hundred years ago. Here was the South London home of football's showpiece for 20 years before the First World War, a magnet for Victorians and then Edwardians, and the scene of the first final to be watched by a reigning monarch. It wouldn't be right now – as the new Wembley will confirm – but the Crystal Palace belonged to a gentler, more tolerant age and brightly reflected the popularity of football and the aspirations of all who took part in the FA Cup.

Not that the story of the Crystal Palace begins and ends with its "score" of Cup Finals. It has, for more than a century, witnessed the development of football at all levels, international to grass root, by way of the celebrated Corinthians and the birth of Crystal Palace FC.

It is a fascinating tale, full of dreams and charm and defined by many of the game's greatest teams and players. The authors, Ian Bevan, Stuart Hibberd and Michael Gilbert have skillfully, evocatively and lovingly done their subject full justice.

Bryon Butler

Introduction

When I was asked by the Crystal Palace Foundation, some years ago, to take people on walkabouts around Crystal Palace Park, the guide notes I was given contained a sentence to the effect that twenty FA Cup Finals took place at the Crystal Palace. This intrigued me as I knew about Wembley and was vaguely aware of the Oval as venues for the Cup Final – but the Crystal Palace?

It was not difficult to find out more about those Cup Finals; they were already well documented. Then, of course, Crystal Palace Football Club began its life at the place that gave it its name and Rev. Nigel Sands has written extensively on the origins and history of the modern club.

Little did I know then that once I started digging, I would discover over 120 years of footballing history at the Crystal Palace stretching back to the early 1860s and ending formally in 1982. During this period the Crystal Palace has hosted a vast array of football teams from all over England and the rest of the world, including South Africa, Switzerland, Belgium and Ireland. Uniquely, the Crystal Palace was the most accessible of grounds where all could come and watch the greatest players of the day while at the other end of the scale, amateur footballers, schoolboys and Sunday League players could come and enjoy playing the game.

Indeed, football may not be over and as we now hear that this autumn Crystal Palace FC is bringing their football academy (youth team) and reserve fixtures to the Sports Centre for the 1999 – 2000 season.

Researching the history of the Crystal Palace ground has proved a massive task, even with three of us, for, not only were there two football grounds for much of the time, but each might be used on two or three occasions in one day, and on any day of the week (except Sunday – until the modern era). Consequently, there are potentially thousands and thousands of games that could be reviewed and many of these would have never been reported. We have therefore taken the approach of capturing and recording the spirit of the competitions that have been played at the Crystal Palace. In the appendices, we have listed as many of the results of those games featuring the major teams. We do however recognise that there may have been other games that these clubs played at the Palace, for example, Casuals had many teams while they were resident and in many cases we found that games were switched or cancelled to accommodate Cup dates.

What follows therefore is a representation of what the spectator might have seen at the Crystal Palace football grounds over the 120 years. It is also about those spectators – why they came, how they got there and what they experienced. It is worth noting that the period 1895 to 1914 was critical in the development of organised sport, especially football, in this country and during this time the Crystal Palace was the premier football ground.

So let us go back to those far-off days and imagine the sights and sounds of the FA Cup Finals, Varsity matches, England v Scotland internationals, FA Amateur Cup Finals, Crystal Palace FC fixtures, Amateur internationals, the Arthur Dunn Cup, Old Boys' games, and more – it all happened at the Palace. No wonder players, officials and fans trudged up Sydenham Hill and exclaimed "To the Palace for the Cup!".

Ian Bevan
August 1999

THE CRYSTAL PALACE AT SYDENHAM ON OPENING DAY 10TH JUNE 1854 (ILN). INSET: SIR JOSEPH PAXTON, DESIGNER OF THE CRYSTAL PALACE.

BEGINNINGS

Sports of all kinds have been associated with the Crystal Palace almost as long as the building and park have been in existence. The site of the present Sports Arena has been home to various sports from rugby football (both codes), speedway, association football, to athletics. But it is football which sparked off the surge of sports that were tried at the Crystal Palace and of course the name Crystal Palace, lives on in one of the senior football teams in the country.

BIRTH OF THE "PALACE OF THE PEOPLE"

The Crystal Palace was originally built to house the 1851 Great Exhibition, held in Hyde Park. However, when the Exhibition was over and the Park was restored to its former glory, the building was not lost. Joseph Paxton, its designer, had other plans for his masterpiece and formed a company to raise the capital to purchase the building. With the materials in its hands, the company found an imposing location to re-erect the building on - to an extended design.

The site chosen was 200 acres on the side of Sydenham Hill in South London, called Penge Place, which was formerly the home of Leo Schuster. At the top of the hill the Crystal Palace was re-built. Meanwhile, Paxton set about designing a park with ornamental gardens, terraces and fountains. A significant element of the park were two massive fountain basins, each with a jet of water at its centre that rose over 200 feet into the air.

The network of fountains, water-pipes and pumping stations could not be completed for the opening of the Palace on 10th June 1854, so there was a second ceremony in the presence of Queen Victoria and Prince Albert on Wednesday 18th June 1856 when the fountains were switched on.

Unfortunately, the cost of operating these marvels was so large that they were only used on special occasions and it was not long before thoughts were given to other uses for these vast areas.

ABOVE: THE ORIGINAL CRYSTAL PALACE IN HYDE PARK 1851.

LEFT: LAYOUT OF THE CRYSTAL PALACE GROUNDS, SYDENHAM 1854. NOTE THE TWO LARGE FOUNTAIN BASINS IN CENTRE OF ILLUSTRATION.

BELOW: A 'NELSON' ENGRAVING OF THE GRAND FOUNTAINS 1856.

BELOW: THE CRYSTAL PALACE c1857, A VIEW TAKEN FROM THE SITE OF TODAY'S NATIONAL SPORTS CENTRE.

ABOVE: THE SWITCHBACK RAILWAY - ONE OF THE ATTRACTIONS AT CRYSTAL PALACE.

LOCATION OF THE FOOTBALL STADIUM

As we shall see, football was played in other locations within the Crystal Palace Park, particularly in the early days, but the football stadium originated in 1894 when it was decided that the Cup Finals should return to London, and the vast area which had been the southerly fountain basin was turned into a massive arena.

The stands were built by John Aird & Sons who had been involved in the building at Hyde Park.

In 1895, the correspondent of The Sunday Times described the scene at the first Cup Final there:

"As the ground is a new one, a few words may

BELOW: PLAN OF THE SITE 1894 SHOWING THE SPORTS ARENAS (BOTTOM LEFT).

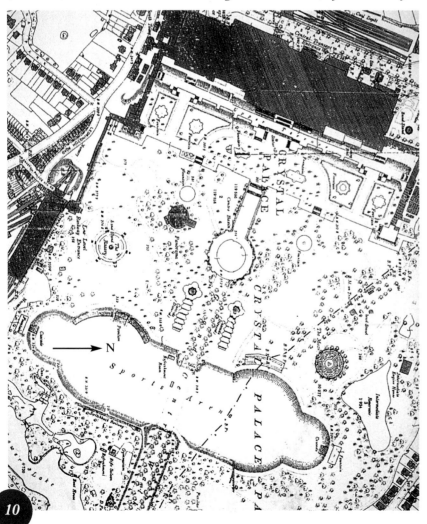

be spared perhaps for a brief description of it. In shape, it is an ellipse, and when finished will measure seventeen acres. It is situated partly on the side of the old lake, which has been filled in and turfed over, whilst the cycle track has been taken in. Yesterday eight acres of the new space were utilised. The goals were pitched on the slant from east to west. At the southern side there was stand accommodation for 3,000 people and provision for over 100 reporters. Another 3,000 reserved seats were placed inside the rails running round the scene of play and beyond these the banked-up sides of the ground formed a natural grandstand for thousands upon thousands. The sea of faces that met one's gaze on all sides presented a sight far easier imagined than described, whilst the excitement and enthusiasm was pulse-stirring enough to be trying to weak nerves".

PLAN OF THE GROUND

In fact, the layout of the ground was somewhat different from this description. It is a common mistake to regard the Crystal Palace as running from east to west. As can be seen from the diagram, the Palace ran its length from north-west to south-east.

It was the same with the football ground. The goals were positioned at the north and south ends of the ground. Around the playing area was a roped-off area known as the ring. On the north side was an entrance with a standing area. This was where the ground was separated from the other fountain basin. In later years, a covered platform with three or four levels was placed here for the convenience of the fans.

On the east side, the ground rose rapidly away from the ring to the trees. At the back of this area, the Crystal Palace Company had already installed a switchback railway as a fairground attraction. On matchdays, spectators would stand on the bank and as the railway was closed, they could also stand on this area. Several thousand could be accommodated there.

Opposite was the Pavilion, which was a small pitched-roofed structure of wooden construction. It was here that guests of honour would sit and where the Cup was presented to the winners.

On either side of the Pavilion, there were two multispan stands bringing the total seating accommodation to 3,000, including space for the Press.

On the southern end of the ground, there was further accommodation for up to 3,000 inside the ring, and beyond, the land rose away into the distance. It was here that the vast majority of the crowd stood; for many, the view was far from brilliant. Only a lucky few could see anything of the game, many had to rely on the roars of the rest of the crowd to know what was going on. The more energetic would clamber up trees or stand or sit on the various tall posts to get a view of the play.

In 1905, when the FA gave the Crystal Palace Company more security with a five year agreement to hold the FA Cup Final, the Company made a number of improvements. The Crystal Palace Magazine described these:

"The aspect of the ground is being entirely changed, huge stands and rows upon rows of small gravel terraces have been built upon the once green banks that surround the field. Very little fault has ever been found with the accommodation generally, but if at previous matches spectators standing on the banks have had now and again to crane their necks to follow every movement of the ball, the splendid terraces which have been constructed should completely obviate any further such inconvenience. They rise gradually from the bottom of the slopes at intervals of about six inches, supported by strong timber, while the surface is sprinkled with a goodly layer of gravel, which, of course, allows free drainage. In all, there will be about nine miles of terracing, and everyone will get an uninterrupted view of the field of play.

As regards the stands, the alterations have been carried out in an even more comprehensive

ABOVE: THE PAVILION.
(SEE ALSO PAGE 54).

manner. The old erections on either side of the Pavilion have been entirely taken away, and two new modern buildings of much greater capacity substituted. For some time past a small army of workmen have been employed in making changes, and the result is gratifying in the extreme. The frontage of the new stands is practically on a level with the Pavilion, and though, of course, constructed on the banks, which, as has so frequently been urged, forms the best of foundations, seeing that none of the seats are above a few feet from the ground – an important factor in the minds of nervous enthusiasts – affords the occupants a perfect view of the game. The increased stand accommodation has in no way interfered with the "ring" seats, which will be laid out as in former years, while it will lessen the congestion around the rails shutting off the actual field of play.

The two new stands will themselves accommodate 5,000 people, which, of course, is considerably in excess of that provided by the old structures...", these are the stands with decorated gables which are so distinctive in photographs of the Cup Finals.

BELOW: CUP FINAL GROUND 1900.
THE PAVILION FLANKED BY FURTHER SEATING FOR 6,000 PEOPLE.

RIGHT: CUP FINAL GROUND 1905
SHOWING THE NEW STANDS UNDER
CONSTRUCTION.

BELOW: CUP FINAL GROUND C1910.

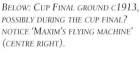

The Crystal Palace Magazine continues:

"Another point – and an important one – is that from the farthest corner in the last row of either of the stands, a perfect view of both goals can be obtained; in fact, with the exception of perhaps two or three seats, even the corner flags can be seen without the slightest inconvenience.

The new arrangements will provide room for over three thousand more people, bringing the total seating accommodation up to just over sixteen thousand. The extra facilities will entail an expenditure of something like £5,000".

By 1911, the Crystal Palace was in a dire financial state and so the whole enterprise was offered for sale. The Sports arena was described in the Sale Catalogue as containing 20 acres, bisected by a Central Avenue. On one side was the Football Ground. This had two covered steel and wood stands, arranged for seating about 5,000, a pavilion containing, on the upper floor, entrance gallery from the ground, and refreshment room, with fitted bars, etc., Committee and Secretary's Room, ladies and gentlemen's cloakrooms, lavatories, and covered seating accommodation for 420. On the lower floor, there were 24 dressing rooms, bathrooms and lavatories, and a store room. The whole building was heated by radiators.

Adjoining the central avenue was a wood and tile building occasionally used as a telegraph office. In the rear was a brick and iron store.

On the opposite side of the Football Ground was an uncovered wooden stand with accommodation for some 3,500 spectators and a refreshment shed with bar and cellar.

BELOW: CUP FINAL GROUND C1913,
POSSIBLY DURING THE CUP FINAL?
NOTICE 'MAXIM'S FLYING MACHINE'
(CENTRE RIGHT).

In 1913, there was a proposal to acquire the Crystal Palace ground for the nation. The FA considered this but rejected it. So, substantially, this was the layout as it existed when football resumed after the First World War. Changes were made to the ring to make space for a speedway circuit in 1928 and in the late 1930s, the arena was used as a paddock for the motor racing fraternity. However, the ground looked much the same in the 1950s as it had always done. This then was swept away to build the athletics stadium and the adjacent National Sports Centre in the early 1960s.

THE NORTHERN FOUNTAIN BASIN

This was also filled in and was used for a number of activities. When the grounds were renovated after the Great War, this arena was also used for football matches. The 1911 Sale Catalogue called the area the Cycle Track consisting of the cement concrete cycle track, one-third of a mile in length and about 30 feet wide, with a curved bank at either end on a timber trestle staging with palisade fencing. Inside, the cycle track was a cinder racing path one mile in length.

On the East side, adjoining the cycle track was a covered stand, wood framed and iron roofed, terraced for seats with accommodation for some 850 spectators with press box and dressing rooms, lavatories and shower baths.

Adjoining this was a Pavilion in brick and wood containing on the lower floor, stores, dressing rooms, shower and Roman baths, lavatories and bar, with covered seats above. The building again was heated by radiators. In the corner adjoining the central avenue was a refreshment stand having open sides and a fitted bar.

With all these facilities, it was not surprising to see many games going on at one time. For instance, Crystal Palace FC might be playing a league match on the Football Ground while say Corinthians were engaged in an exhibition game on the other ground.

ACCESS TO THE GROUND

The Crystal Palace and its Park already had turnstiles at the entrances into the building and at the railway stations. Therefore in the pre-1914 period football supporters paid to enter the Crystal Palace complex and could enjoy all its attractions before and after the big game.

It has been widely reported that at least one of the turnstiles from the Crystal Palace football ground found a new home at Shrewsbury Town. We discovered that there were actually three old turnstiles at Shrewsbury all dated 1884 (which predates the Crystal Palace football ground) and made by Stevens and Sons of Southwark. However, there is no information as to how these turnstiles got there. It may have been that they were acquired after the demise of the Crystal Palace itself in 1936.

EARLY DAYS

The first footballers at the Palace did not have such wonderful conditions in which to play. They probably had to play on Penge Common without even a marked-out pitch. But they were pioneers of the game and their team had the distinction of bearing the name "Crystal Palace".

BELOW: TURNSTILE AT SHREWSBURY TOWN FC. REPORTEDLY PURCHASED FROM THE CRYSTAL PALACE COMPANY.

BELOW: THE 'NORTH BASIN' FOOTBALL GROUND, SURROUNDED BY THE CYCLE TRACK CONSTRUCTED IN 1906.

A Game of Football in the 1400's.

FOOTBALL COMES TO THE PALACE

The game of football was probably introduced to this country by the Romans. At this time, a ball was made by inflating a bladder or skin termed a 'follis'.

The game was first mentioned specifically by William Fitzstephen, in his "History of London" (about 1175). He refers to the young men of the city annually going into the field after dinner to play at the well-known game of *'ball of the day'* (quoe dictitur Carnile varia). This annual event occurred on Shrove Tuesday and by the nineteenth century it was a well-established festival amongst the middle and lower classes.

There were no clubs or code of rules and the sole purpose seems to have been to drive the ball through the opposing side's goal by any means possible. This violent pastime continued until the 1830s.

Meanwhile, football was practised at the top public schools. At Harrow and Winchester they played a kicking game while at Eton there were variations – "at the wall" and "in the field". The other schools played one or other of these games.

About 1860, football became more generally popular, being taken up by old boys' associations of the public schools and also in some of the towns and villages in the South.

THE FIRST CRYSTAL PALACE TEAMS

It is possible that there was a team called Crystal Palace as early as 1861, but certainly around this time they are recorded as playing against other teams being created primarily in the London area, like Barnes, Blackheath and Surbiton.

The Crystal Palace team was possibly formed from the workmen at the Palace or perhaps from men from the local villages of Penge and Sydenham. However, it is more likely that they were Old Boys from the public schools who had played the game at school and wanted to continue. If there is some doubt about this, there is only conjecture as to where they played their matches. At this time, the fountain basins were still in use and there was little unutilised flat ground in the Park. It is likely therefore that football matches were played at the east end of the grounds which adjoined Penge Common – or even on Penge Common itself. This area was already used as a cricket ground in the summer months.

ABOVE: AN ENGRAVING OF FOOTBALL IN THE 17TH CENTURY.

LEFT: CHARLES ALCOCK - BURIED IN WEST NORWOOD CEMETERY, TWO MILES FROM CRYSTAL PALACE.

Evidently, the games were often a shambles with little agreement on the rules and many strived to find some uniformity. One of the prime movers was the young Charles William Alcock and his brother James. Though not present, it is evident that Charles was the 'eminence grise' behind a meeting on October 26th, 1863 at the Freemason's Tavern, Great Queen Street, Lincoln's Inn Fields. Attended by representatives from some of the early clubs, including Crystal Palace, the aim was to form a "Football Association" with the purpose of creating a definitive set of rules. The meeting was attended by the Crystal Palace club secretary, Mr F Day. The club continued to be fully involved in the early development of the Football Association. From 1864 to 1868, one James Turner (from the Crystal Palace club) was FA Treasurer and others were to follow.

Over the next few years, attempts were made to encourage use of the FA rules by a series of representative matches at county level. The first of these took place between Middlesex and a combined team from Kent and Surrey at Battersea on Saturday, November 2nd, 1867. Each of these teams had players selected from the Crystal Palace team and, when the international matches were inaugurated in 1872, players were again selected from the Crystal Palace team.

THE FA CHALLENGE CUP

A historic development came on July 20th, 1871 when the FA discussed the possibility of having a knock-out competition. Present at this meeting was D Allport of Crystal Palace; Mr Allport was one of three members later delegated to purchase the first FA Cup.

RIGHT: THE FIRST FA CUP DESIGNED BY MARTIN HALL & CO.

The trophy, designed by Martin Hall and Company, had two handles and had a figure of a player on the lid. It stood on an ebony plinth and cost about £20.

The first competition was held in 1871-72. There were fifteen teams in all: Barnes, Civil Service, Clapham Rovers, Crystal Palace, Donnington Grammar School, Great Marlow, Hampstead Heathens, Harrow Chequers, Hitchin, Maidenhead, Queen's Park, Reigate Priory, Royal Engineers, Upton Park and Wanderers.

BELOW: FREEMASON'S TAVERN - WHERE THE FOOTBALL ASSOCIATION WAS FORMED IN OCTOBER 1863 AND MINUTES OF THE FIRST MEETING.

It seems that it was a disorganised affair. There were scratchings, defections, refusals to travel and other excuses. Crystal Palace drew 0 - 0 with Hitchin in the first round but they progressed in the competition due to Rule 8 that was then in force, *"whereby in case of a drawn match the clubs shall be drawn again in the next ties or shall compete again at the discretion of the Committee"*. They then easily beat Maidenhead 3 - 0 and drew with Wanderers. This meant that Crystal Palace reached the semi-final but here they met one of the best teams of the day – Royal Engineers. They proved too strong for the Palace side who went down 3 – 0. Royal Engineers went on to

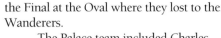

the Final at the Oval where they lost to the Wanderers.

The Palace team included Charles John Chenery who was the only player to play in England's first three internationals.

Another early Palace player was Charles Eastlake Smith who also played for the Wanderers and England against Scotland in 1876. He was the cousin of the famous Corinthian, G O Smith.

The players of that era were dressed somewhat differently from today's designer strips. For instance, the Aldenham School team were described as wearing white jerseys and trousers with a black velvet turban piped in white with a black and white tassel. The Royal Engineers played in blue and red horizontal striped jerseys and stockings with blue knickerbockers and 'nightcaps'. The Crystal Palace team played in blue and white, with blue serge knickerbockers.

In subsequent years, Crystal Palace were not able to equal their success in that first competition, because for the next three years they were knocked out in the first round. However, in the 1875 - 76 season they did go a little further, drawing with the 105th Regiment and then beating them 3 - 0 in the first round only to come up against the Wanderers in the second round – and losing 3 - 0 to them.

At this point, Crystal Palace seem to have disappeared from the football scene. Even the Crystal Palace Company had no record of their demise. One journalist from the Croydon Advertiser in 1945 even consulted Sir Henry Buckland, General Manager of the Crystal Palace, who scanned the archives and made enquiries without finding any record of the club. It may be significant that in 1875 the Crystal Palace Company came to an agreement with Penge Council to take over that part of Penge Common which adjoined the Park. It might be that this affected the area that Crystal Palace used as its pitch, particularly as there was already a cricket pitch in that same area.

The players themselves did not give up though. For years after Crystal Palace had ceased to enter the FA Cup, it is recorded that on occasions they turned out to play other teams. For example,

RIGHT CENTRE: LORD KINNAIRD, THE FIRST PRESIDENT OF THE FOOTBALL ASSOCIATION.

RIGHT: THE HARROW FOOTERS TEAM 1871, NOTE HATS WITH TASSELS.

LEFT: THE FIRST ENGLAND V SCOTLAND 1872 - THE FIRST OFFICIAL FOOTBALL INTERNATIONAL. WOODCUT FROM DRAWINGS BY W. RALSTON.

BELOW: ASTON VILLA V SUNDERLAND, 1893.

in January 1883 a team calling itself Crystal Palace Rovers played a game against the Pilgrims at Walthamstow, the Pilgrims winning 4 - 1. The Crystal Palace team was as follows:

J Aste (capt.); H W Williams, R A Walter; W Leete, P C Muspratt, H Knowles; N Leete, W Pitman, S A Fox, E J Turner, H Reeves.

It was, however, thirty years before another Crystal Palace team was formed.

THE FIRST FA CUP, WON BY ASTON VILLA AT THE CRYSTAL PALACE IN 1895, WAS STOLEN.

THE FA CUP FINAL
THE FA CHALLENGE CUP COMES TO THE PALACE

If the team called Crystal Palace faded into the mists, it was not to be the end of the area's flirtation with the FA Cup. In the 1890s, the FA Cup Final made its home at the Crystal Palace.

The first FA Cup Finals were played at Kennington Oval, they were dominated by the South and the public schools in particular. The first Final was won by the Wanderers, who beat the Royal Engineers. In the next few years, teams like Old Etonians and Old Carthusians lifted the Cup.

As time went by, however, the emphasis moved to the newer Northern clubs. Teams like Blackburn Olympic and Preston took over; Blackburn Rovers won the Cup three times in succession between 1884 and 1886 (a feat that has never been repeated). So, there was a call to move the Final into the northern heartland.

In 1893, at the suggestion of J J Bentley, it was decided to hold the Final at the Manchester Athletic Ground at Fallowfield, and it was there that the Cup celebrated its twenty-fifth birthday. Unfortunately, the arrangements for this game were chaotic and with the rising numbers attending the game, there was a danger of some-one getting hurt, the crowd being so close to the touchlines. This may well have affected the game, indeed Everton were so dissatisfied that they lodged a protest against the result immediately after the game, but later withdrew it.

The following year the Final migrated to Goodison Park where Notts County became the first Second Division club to triumph in a Final, beating Bolton Wanderers. However after only two years up north, the Football Association determined to bring the match back to London, in spite of the fact that no southern club had been in the Final for eleven years. The attitude of the FA was that as London was capital of the nation (and this was a national competition), and was also the home of their headquarters, it was in the London area that the Final should be held.

The decision therefore to create the massive arena at Crystal Palace was most opportune. As Geoffrey Green says in his 'Official History of the FA Cup':

"Here was the very place for the great occasion. An Englishman's home is his castle and most of us associate our lives with the houses we have lived in. So with the Cup Final. Like many of us it has had temporary lodgings, but the main pattern of its life has been built around three great homes. The first was the Oval. Now comes the Crystal Palace and it is here that the scene is set for the next twenty years".

So let us take a closer look at those twenty Finals that took place at the Crystal Palace between 1895 and 1914, for they marked a watershed in the development of the competition. In 1895, 179 teams entered but, by 1914, the entry had risen to 476 clubs. At the beginning, crowds of 40,000 plus were regarded as large but in 1901 over 110,000 came to the Palace, and in 1913 over 120,000 watched Sunderland and Aston Villa compete for the honours.

In the 1890s football was still regarded as a minority sport fit only for working class northerners but when the King attended the 1914 Final and presented the Cup to the winning team, the Cup Final was accepted as being as much part of the establishment as Ascot. New teams got their hands on the Cup – Newcastle United, both Manchester clubs, even a southern club from outside the Football League, Tottenham who won the Cup in 1901. In this period too the highest score in a Final (6 - 0) occurred when Bury beat Derby County in 1903.

Even the trophy itself was to change during this period. The first FA Cup was stolen after the 1895 Final and was never seen again, the second trophy (a replica of the first) lasted until 1911, the third FA Cup was used continuously until it was replaced in 1992 by an exact replica, now in use.

All this happened at the Cup Final ground in the shadow of the original "Twin Towers" which survived after the Cup Finals departed.

BELOW: THE CRYSTAL PALACE WITH ITS ' TWIN TOWERS'.

ABOVE: THE SIGN OF THE TWO TOWERS PUBLIC HOUSE IN GIPSY HILL.

LEFT: FEW OF THE SPECTATORS SAW MUCH OF THE GAME.

1895

ASTON VILLA
v
WEST BROMWICH ALBION

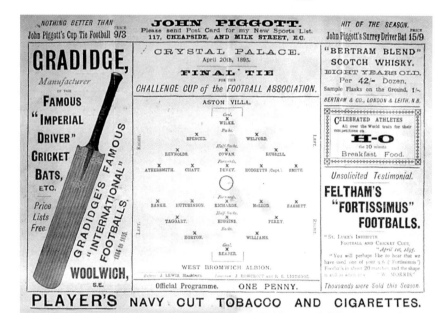

ABOVE: THE PROGRAMME.

ABOVE RIGHT: DEVEY AND HIGGINS CLASH HEADS.

RIGHT CENTRE: THE ASTON VILLA TEAM, CUP WINNERS 1895. (From Association Cup Winners – Player's cigarette cards).

It was quite a coincidence that the two teams that vied for this the first FA Cup Final at the Crystal Palace were the same two teams that fought in the last Final at the Oval in 1892. This was also the third time that they had met in the Final in a nine-year period - and this was the decider! Much of this probably accounted for the massive attendance of 42,560.

Alas, many of the spectators did not get to their positions on the vast slopes until well after the kick off. While the organised ones arrived early and got the bonus of being able to wander in the grounds and enjoy the delights of the great Palace itself, a large number got there at the last minute and were faced for the first time with negotiating the Crystal Palace turnstiles. Consequently, they missed the only goal of the game, for within thirty seconds, Villa had scored what is still the fastest goal in a FA Cup Final.

It was called Villa's "Crystal Palace thunderbolt", in fact it was actually quite a fluke and the height of confusion. Most give the credit for the goal to Chatt but one report reckoned that Devey got the last touch. It was stated that Devey, the Villa centre-forward, started the

BELOW: ACTION DURING THE GAME.

move passing to Hodgetts on the left-wing. Hodgetts put in a cross to Athersmith at outside-right, then Athersmith centred for Bob Chatt to shoot. Reader in the West Bromwich goal parried the shot only for the ball to cannon back into the net off Devey's knee.

The Albion struggled to get on equal terms but despite some sterling performances by their players, Villa came away victorious. Billy Bassett, the greatest winger of his time, played brilliantly in this his last Final. The Albion's troubles were exacerbated when their centre-half, Tom Higgins, was in collision with John Devey the Villa centre-forward and sustained a badly cut head. He returned to play a superb game with his head heavily bandaged. Reader, too, played brilliantly in goal to keep the Villa from scoring again.

So, the Villains came away from the Palace with the Cup in their possession for the second time. Meanwhile, the football ground was not left idle. The manager of the ground, Captain Henshaw Russell, was charged with making the ground ready immediately for *"the East African village, which will be located on the same site. 80 natives of Somaliland and 200 African animals, birds and reptiles are being brought from the interior to Berbera, on the Somali coast"* (Sydenham and Penge Gazette). The exhibition ran from May until 1st October.

THE CUP IS LOST

Villa did not enjoy possession of the *"little tin idol"* for long. On the night of September 11th, 1895, it was stolen from the window of William Shillcock, football and football boot manufacturers, of Newtown Row,

Birmingham, where it was being exhibited. Despite a thorough police investigation and the offer of a £10 reward, the original Cup has never been seen since. Since then a number of explanations have been put forward. In 1958 one Harry Burge *"confessed"* that he had stolen the Cup to melt it down to make counterfeit half-crowns. Later, in 1975, Joseph Piecewright, who had already been jailed for counterfeiting coins, was identified as the perpetrator. More recently, further research has suggested that the Cup had been taken by a team of four people, including John 'Stosher' Stait. Maybe, Burge and Piecewright were the accomplices? Villa were fined £25 by the FA.

When it was clear that the Cup was not going to be returned, the Football Association took steps to replace it. The second FA Challenge Cup, an exact replica of the original, was based on a ten-inch high silver model given to the Wolves team by their Chairman, Sir Alfred Hickman, when they won the Cup in 1893.

VILLA RETURN TO THE PALACE

The second appearance of Aston Villa at the Crystal Palace was even more impressive than the first. However, only a small crowd turned up on December 7th, 1895 to see them take on a team of amateurs selected by Mr N L Jackson. The Londoners were described as the Crystal Palace Football Club but it was really a respectable team of Corinthians. Apparently, the ground was in a terrible state after heavy rain but that did not deter Aston Villa who beat the scratch team by seven goals to three.

ABOVE: MR SHILLCOCK'S LETTER OFFERING £50 REWARD, THE £10 REWARD POSTER, JOHN 'STOSHER' STAIT, THE CUP AND THE SHOP OF W SHILLCOCK, 73 NEWTOWN ROW, BIRMINGHAM.

JOHN HENRY GEORGE DEVEY

John (or Jack) Devey was born in Newtown, Birmingham, on Boxing Day, 1866, and played local football with Excelsior, Aston Unity, Mitchell St George's and Aston Manor before signing for Villa in March 1891.

He made his debut in the opening game of the following season and by the end of the campaign he was top scorer with 29 goals and had appeared in an FA Cup Final - against West Bromwich Albion.

In his career he won five League Championship medals, two FA Cup winners' medals and a runners-up medal. He also won two England caps, in 1892 and 1894, both against Ireland, and was also an excellent cricketer, scoring over 6,500 runs for Warwickshire between 1888 and 1907, including eight centuries.

Devey was a captain who led from the front. An inspiring leader, he did not expect his players to do more than he did himself. He was a skilful individual player - fast and clever and good in the air. He would work the ball through the defence at a greater rate than most men, and he usually made a beeline for the goal. At his best, he could dodge and dribble adroitly and he had a good idea of finding where the posts stood, yet he wasn't selfish. He would draw opposing players to him and then pass the ball to his partner, Athersmith, to finish it off.

After his playing career was over, he ran a sports shop at Lozells, Birmingham and in 1902 was appointed a Villa director.

He died in October 1940.

1896

SHEFFIELD WEDNESDAY
V
WOLVERHAMPTON WANDERERS

*RIGHT: SHEFFIELD WEDNESDAY'S
WINNING GOAL.
Illustrated Sporting & Dramatic News.*

The success of the 1895 Final at the new stadium meant that the next Final was looked forward to with eager anticipation. After the disappearance of the original Cup, there was also a new trophy to be won.

Spectators came to support another Midlands club, Wolverhampton Wanderers, themselves previous winners of the trophy and appearing in their third Final in eight years. Their opponents were Sheffield Wednesday. Visitors came from the North and the Midlands, combining with locals to make this a larger crowd than the previous year; (a new record!). *"The reserved seats were packed to their utmost capacity, and the grassy slopes, which partially bound what was once a lake, afforded accommodation on Saturday last for a crowd both enormous and critical"* (Athletic News).

Not everyone had the same opinion about the new attraction at the Palace. The Crystal Palace concerts on Saturday afternoons had been well attended in previous years but with the thousands coming to the venue for the football, this badly affected attendance at the concert on that day. *"Saturday afternoon has lost its exclusiveness at the Palace, and instead of being the 'thing' to be seen in the well-known concert room the Sybarites of Sydenham think it best behoves their dignity to stay away"* (Sydenham & Penge Gazette).

Evidently, there was considerable preparation of the ground as the Palace authorities had gone to considerable expense in again having the goal drained. The decision of the FA Sub-Committee to have the game played in London for a second time gave general satisfaction to the southern football public who at the time had few opportunities of seeing matches as they were played mainly in the North and the Midlands.

The teams were evenly matched although Sheffield Wednesday had not had a good season in the League. Wolves were described as *"clever, determined and aggressive"* (Football in Sheffield by Percy Young) but the Sheffield poet, James Montgomery described the virtues of the Wednesday: *"science, pluck, resource and unresting energy are the characteristics we are entitled to expect from the men who have vanquished Everton and Sunderland"*. The Wednesday got off to a wonderful start. Almost from the kick off, the ball went into touch. From the throw-in, Crawshaw got possession, passed forward to Brash, who sent across to Spiksley; he forced his way through the Wolves' defence and sent a grand shot which gave his side the lead a minute from the start. As Percy Young in his book on Sheffield football says, Spiksley *"on great occasions, was almost infallible, and he scored"*.

*ABOVE: SOUVENIR MUG MARKING
SHEFFIELD WEDNESDAY'S FIRST CUP
TRIUMPH IN 1896.*

*BELOW: THE SHEFFIELD WEDNESDAY
TEAM, CUP WINNERS 1896.
(From Association Cup Winners –
Player's cigarette cards).*

S.T. DADD.

After a long period when the play went from goalmouth to goalmouth, Black equalised for Wolves. Both sets of forwards did well and Beats got the ball in the back of the Sheffield net only for the goal to be disallowed – the ball had gone over the goal-line.

From the goal kick, the Wednesday forward line went away beautifully, Spiksley running in and shooting a beautiful goal. In the second half, no further goals were scored. So it was Sheffield who were the first to collect the second FA Cup.

Later, Spiksley gave his memories of the Final: *"I have a very vivid recollection of the Final, not so much because of the keenness of the game, but because of a rather funny incident associated with it. I happened to score the winning goal,*

an an Instantaneous Effect.

Sheffield Wednesday's winning goal.

'hitting' the ball with such force that it rebounded into the field, while the goalkeeper, a man named Tennant, was still wondering where the shot had gone. Seeing the ball lying in front of him, however, the Wolves' goalkeeper kicked it up the field under the impression that it was still in play. In the excitement – and players do get excited in Cup Finals – Tennant apparently did not notice the subsequent kick off from the centre, and after the final whistle had been blown said to our captain:

'When do we replay?'
'There's no replay, old man!' our skipper remarked; 'we won by two goals to one, as you will see when we take the medals!' 'You can't have,' said the astonished goalkeeper, 'for only one shot passed me'".

Fred Spiksley

Fred Spiksley was born in Gainsborough, Lincolnshire on 25th January 1870 and after a period playing with Gainsborough Trinity joined Sheffield Wednesday in January 1891. During his period with Wednesday he won his Cup winner's medal, seven England caps (scoring five goals) and made two appearances for the Football League. Evidently a star of that Sheffield Wednesday side, Spiksley was paid a tribute in Ernest Needham's book Association Football (1901):

"I have heard a great deal of criticism levelled at him because he waits for the ball to be put to him, but when you have a player of the style of Spiksley this method pays. When he does get the ball he is fresher and faster than if he had been working hard to fetch it – most likely from close by his own goal".

After leaving Wednesday in 1904, he played for a number of other clubs including Glossop and Leeds City before becoming a coach in Nuremberg, Germany. He was interned when war broke out in August 1914. After the War he coached in Mexico and later with Fulham and again at Nuremberg. In later life he became a bookmaker and died at Goodwood on 28th July 1948.

Spiksley leaves the impression of being a good distributor, excellent crosser and a fine goal scorer.

1897
ASTON VILLA
V
EVERTON

The third Final at the Crystal Palace has been described as the best Final ever played. Aston Villa were at their peak, as they had already taken the League championship by 11 points. Everton were almost as successful – runners-up in the League in 1895, third in the following year and a smooth passage to the 1897 Final by beating Burton Wanderers, Bury, Blackburn Rovers and Derby County.

Firstly, for the favourable atmospheric conditions under which it was played; secondly, for the rapidity and even nature of the scoring, which was all confined to the first half; and thirdly, for the mammoth attendance. The Crystal Palace had many remarkable football gatherings but in its main features we have witnessed nothing approaching to Saturday's function.

Ten minutes before the time fixed for the kick off, Everton, headed by their captain, W.Stewart, entered the field. Their players were in light blue shirts and white knickers". A few minutes later Aston Villa, headed by John Devey, trotted on to the ground. The Villa's colours were claret and light blue shirts, with white knickers. And what a team it was! Howard Spencer, John Reynolds, James Cowan, Charlie Athersmith and John Devey remained from the Cup-winning eleven of 1895. To these had been added Jimmy Whitehouse, signed from Grimsby Town for £200 (a vast sum for the times), had taken over in goal.

All five goals were scored in a devastating period of 25 minutes before half-time, and in that dramatic phase the lead changed hands three times.

At the eighteenth minute, Devey sent Campbell through to put Villa ahead; five minutes later Bell made it 1 - 1 for Everton. Within another five minutes Boyle enabled Everton to lead after a free kick had been given against Cowan of the Villa.

ABOVE: THE PROGRAMME.

The Sporting Life reported that the Villains had been training in Buxton all week but travelled down on Friday to spend the night at the Queen's Hotel, Upper Norwood. Everton on the other hand stayed at the Tavistock in Central London.

RIGHT: ILLUSTRATION OF MATCH ACTION.
Illustrated Sporting & Dramatic News.

" 'All the world and his wife' seemed to be at the Crystal Palace on Saturday afternoon watching the Final tie in the Football Association Cup competition. The official return gives the gate as over 65,000 so that another record was established. It was a fine sight to see so many people placed round the enclosure, and, for once in a way, at a football match, 'Scotch' was not the prevailing dialect...." Not only were the spectators on the slopes but also on the switchback railway, while a few had taken to the trees to get a superb view.

"Interest in the event has certainly reached its greatest development, and the match will be memorable for three reasons.

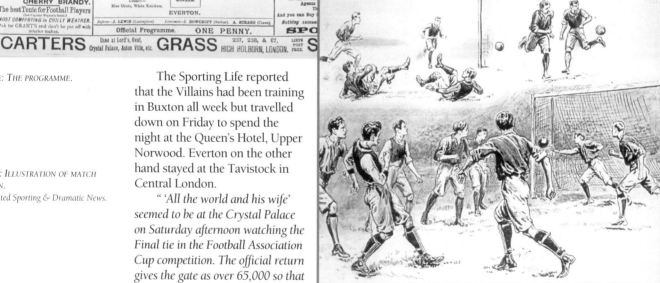

All this happened in ten minutes. But the next quarter of an hour proved decisive as Crabtree, the left-half, sent Wheldon away cleverly to equalise at 2 - 2, and then John Cowan snatched a tremendous victory for the men of Villa Park with a crashing shot.

After that, there were no more goals but the standard of play continued at the highest level right to the end of the game. No wonder the crowd came staggering away at the finish, worn out both physically and emotionally. Sometimes there is nothing more exhausting than watching an exciting match.

"When the last 20 minutes were reached, the teams were still playing at a wonderful pace. Aston Villa attacked for a long time without gaining anything and then the enthusiasm of the spectators were aroused by

PLAYER'S CIGARETTES

SPENCER — EVANS
WHITEHOUSE
REYNOLDS — CRABTREE
COWAN (Jas.)
ATHERSMITH — COWAN (John)
DEVEY — CAMPBELL — WHELDON

ASSOCIATION CUP WINNERS
ASTON VILLA. 1897

several brilliant efforts on the part of Everton to get level. Bell, Milward, and Hartley each shot low, swift and straight, but Whitehouse the goalkeeper, came off with flying colours and each was saved. These were anxious minutes for Villa, but time at last ran out and the victory remained with them. The crowd rushed to the enclosure and the players heartily cheered".

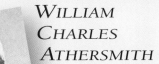

WILLIAM CHARLES ATHERSMITH

Charlie Athersmith was born in Bloxwich, Staffs. on 10 May 1872. At only 12 years of age he joined Bloxwich Wanderers and after playing for Unity Gas Depot in Saltley, he signed for Aston Villa in February 1891.

For the next 10 years he was an outstanding outside-right for the Villa playing in the two FA Cup winning sides of 1895 and 1897. He also gained 12 England caps, scoring three times, between 1892 and 1900.

A mid-nineties writer wrote that Athersmith had "....great pace, is particularly smart and middles well" – a performer to compare with the great Billy Bassett. His pace was a result of all the athletics experience – he gained honours at various levels as an amateur and as a professional runner.

In 1901 he moved across Birmingham to Small Heath before retiring. He later coached at Grimsby Town before his early death in September 1910.

TOP: *THE CRYSTAL PALACE CASTS ITS IMPOSING PRESENCE OVER THE MATCH.*

ABOVE: *A SOUVENIR MATCHBOX KNOWN AS VESTA'S*.*

FAR LEFT: *THE ASTON VILLA TEAM, CUP WINNERS 1897. (From Association Cup Winners – Player's cigarette cards).*

*Vesta - a short friction match, usually of wood.

1898
NOTTS FOREST
V
DERBY COUNTY

RIGHT: ACTION DURING THE MATCH.
Illustrated Sporting & Dramatic News.

BELOW: THE NOTTINGHAM FOREST
TEAM OF 1898.

Henry Gillman, the manager of the Crystal Palace ground, made a special effort to ensure that everything ran smoothly for this Final, expecting a very large crowd. The only time there was a hint of a problem was when the ring-side ticket-holders swarmed the touchlines to mob the Nottingham players on their unexpected victory. The Graphic reported:

"The spectacle of the huge crowd which lined the deep hollow of the Crystal Palace football ground, to watch the Final tie of the Association Cup, was more impressive than the game itself. It is impossible to convey by the pen an adequate idea of the high banks of thousands of faces surrounding the green acres of the football ground,

Notts Forest were therefore the underdogs, but Derby County were supposedly under the handicap of a Gipsy's curse after the eviction of some Gipsies from land that became County's ground. Whatever was the cause, it was to be Forest's day. Capes opened the scoring with a brilliant ground-shot that comprehensively beat goalkeeper Fryer after 19 minutes.

of the swelling volume of the shouts that went up from them as they followed the exciting moments of the game, of their not less impressive silences, and of their swaying movements, comparable to that of a cornfield shaken by the wind as they craned eagerly forward on the sloping ground to watch the players".

Over 60,000 people (another record!) turned up for the East Midlands derby but they were not rewarded with a particularly good game. The team in form were Derby County. They had reached the semi-final in 1897 and on their way to the 1898 Final, they had beaten both Aston Villa and Everton, the previous finalists. Only a week before the great day they had trounced Notts Forest in a league match by five clear goals. In fact, Forest had not been at full strength in that league match as McPherson, the Forest captain, said afterwards:

"Some of our best men were in the stand that afternoon watching for the strong and weak points of our opponents, and they found them out, too".

Derby equalised with a header from the great Steve Bloomer but before half-time, Capes scored again from close range. Then, four minutes from the end, the Forest captain, McPherson made sure of the victory with a remarkable goal from a shot struck while he was flat out on the ground after he had robbed a defender.

So a new name went on the Cup but it was deserved. As a paper at the time stated:

"Few clubs by their long association with the game and its most treasured traditions have better deserved or earned the distinction and we venture to think that the success of the 'Reds' will be heartily and encouragingly welcomed".

That was a fair statement, for Forest had played a major part in the development of the game:

- they were the first to introduce the whistle, experimenting with it in 1878 when playing Sheffield Norfolk. After a successful trial the whistle took the place of the white flag used earlier.

- first to develop the system of 2 backs, 3 half-backs and 5 forwards;
- football shin guards were devised by Sam Widdowson in 1874.

The successful result for Notts Forest helped to ease the discomfort of some of the East Midland journalists at Crystal Palace. One of them wrote:

STEVE BLOOMER

Steve Bloomer was born in Cardley Heath, Worcestershire on 20th January 1874. After playing schoolboy football and a period at Derby Swifts, he joined Derby County at the age of 17. He was described at the time as: "....pale, thin, fragile, ghost-like, almost ill-looking, he caused the Derby crowd to laugh when they saw him.But they didn't laugh for long".

Bloomer was probably the first outstanding goal-scorer. He scored 28 goals for England in 23 internationals, an average of 1.22 goals per game. This remained a record until 1958. He was the first player to hold the record for most goals as well as appearances. He scored in each of his first ten internationals, an England record. He netted five goals in the match against Wales in 1896 and did it again in the same fixture in 1901. It could have been six if Nudger Needham had not taken a penalty (and missed it!). As an inside-right he scored 297 League goals for Derby County and 55 for Middlesbrough from a total of 600 appearances before retiring in 1914.

On retirement, he coached in Germany where he was interned during World War 1. After the War he returned to coach at Derby and later coached in Canada, Spain and Rotterdam.

A measure of the ability of Bloomer has been given by Harry Storer (who later became Derby County manager):

"Bloomer was in his late fifties and employed on the Derby County ground staff. We were chatting together and standing with our backs to a group of players having shooting practice in the goalmouth. Suddenly a ball was mishit in our direction and was hurtling towards our backs. One of the players shouted 'Duck!', I did. But Bloomer turned quickly, sighted the dropping ball and, perfectly balanced, volleyed it into the net. We were all left speechless. He was about 40 yards from goal".

"By the bye, a matter deserves mention which though it may not concern the public directly is still of importance to them in its results. This was the accommodation provided for the provincial Press. Influential papers of an old and high standard had their repeated applications ignored while some of the London journals of far less importance had secured and marked several seats - in one case five".

LEFT: A COMICAL ILLUSTRATION FROM THE GRAPHIC OF NOTTS FOREST'S SECOND GOAL. JACK FRYER, DERBY'S GOALKEEPER, PALMS THE BALL TO THE FEET OF ARTHUR CAPES.

FAR LEFT: THE NOTTS FOREST TEAM, CUP WINNERS 1898.
(From Association Cup Winners – Player's cigarette cards).

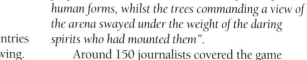

1899

DERBY COUNTY
V
SHEFFIELD UNITED

In the season 1898-99, there were 235 entries for the Cup. The competition was really growing. The list included some names now long forgotten – Oswaldtwistle Rovers, Long Eaton Rangers and New Brompton (later Gillingham) – but it was Derby County and Sheffield United that survived to contest the Final.

The two teams, although still in their infancy, had become leading powers of their day. Sheffield United had been formed as recently as 1889. They had joined the Football League for the 1892-93 season and had brought the first championship to Sheffield in 1898. That same year, Derby, formed in 1884, were beaten Cup Finalists.

Derby County, after preparing at Buxton, stayed on the eve of the game at the Queen's Hotel, Upper Norwood, a short stroll from the Crystal Palace. Sheffield United on the other hand preferred to prepare at Skegness and then stay at The Court Royal Hotel.

On the big day, as the record crowd of 73,833 gathered they were entertained by the Crystal Palace Band. Those arriving on bicycles could leave them at the Low Level, Centre and Penge entrances to the park with

JOHN LEWIS, THE REFEREE. Harmondsworth Magazine.

BELOW: THE SHEFFIELD UNITED TEAM, WITH THE CUP.

the attendants for the sum of 2d (one new penny).

The Sportsman newspaper reported that by 3.15pm *"the crowd had swollen to tremendous proportion, and the banks were literally seas of human forms, whilst the trees commanding a view of the arena swayed under the weight of the daring spirits who had mounted them"*.

Around 150 journalists covered the game and kept the telegraph staff busy all afternoon. The game was also captured for posterity on the cinematograph machine manned by Jasper Redfern, positioned near the players' entrance.

The ground was soft but the game was played at a fast pace, especially at the opening of each half. United won the toss and Needham decided to play with the breeze and the sun at his team's back, defending the Norwood end of the ground. However, Derby were the better side in the first half, Sheffield's defence looking shaky at the outset. In the twelfth minute, Boag scored for County from a goalmouth scramble and, although Morren and Needham for United both had shots go just over the bar, Derby led at half time.

In the second period, Sheffield lived up to their reputation in that season's competition as a strong second half side. The turning point of the game came early in the half. Bloomer, the Derby forward (described by The Sheffield and Rotherham Independent as the deadliest goal-getter in the country), broke free and looked certain to score but shot wide. He then had another great shot saved by Foulke. However, Bloomer, like many great players after him, did not give the Cup Final performance he or his fans would have wished.

Foulke had also earlier been the centre of attention when the 5'4" Macdonald failed in his attempt to charge the 6'2" twenty stone goalkeeper into his net.

A Needham cross and a Bennett header saw United equalise and twenty minutes into the half, Sheffield went ahead. Beers' shot was parried by Jack Spencer Fryer in the Derby goal but Beers followed through to knock in the rebound. Derby were finished by a third goal five minutes later when Almond scored from another goalmouth tussle.

As a result of an injury to May, Derby went down to ten men. Beers had an attempt disallowed for offside and then Priest confirmed the victory with a low hard shot three minutes before the whistle.

HENRY 'HARRY' THICKETT

In 1899 Henry (Harry) Thickett was at the peak of his career, winning two caps for England against Scotland and Wales. The previous season he had been a member of the United side which brought the first League Championship to Sheffield. "Heavy, fearless, speedy, a progressive player who made up for a certain deficiency in tackling by good positioning and scientific kicking, he was a tower of strength" is the description given in Percy Young's excellent book "Football in Sheffield".

United had been taken to two replays in the semi-final by Liverpool. The first attempt at the second replay at Fallowfield, Manchester had to be abandoned due to crowd encroachment. The game did not start until 4pm and the interrupted first half finished at 5.50pm when the match was abandoned. Thickett was injured allegedly with two broken ribs and a ruptured side. For the next game, he was wrapped in nearly fifty yards of bandages with thick pads interspersed.

Thickett and the 'athletes' doctor, Mr Allison, travelled from Manchester on the morning of the game where they were taken to a private hotel in the Strand. Here he was strapped up in 46 yards of specially stiffened bandages, rubbed down and dressed in his football kit over which he put his normal clothes. His team-mates, and more importantly, the opposition did not know the full extent of his injuries. At half-time the doctor administered to Thickett in a private room and in his own words "cut some of the bandages off, strapped him up again, and gave him a bottle of champagne". The local Sheffield paper on the Monday after the game commented that Thickett was rather weak in the first half but improved as the game wore on.

Bloomer had heard a rumour of Thickett's injury but told the doctor that he was not fooled "It's all rot about your cripple. He's alright and he kicks alright". The doctor told the Sheffield and Rotherham Independent: "Had he known, I'm afraid Thickett would not have lasted long". The doctor concluded his remarkable tale:

"A touch on the spot would have laid him out as a dead man. He got into his box and collapsed entirely, and when we cut the wrapping away he was black and blue, with a lump as big as a fist protruding from his side. When he came round he placed his medal into my hand, and said: 'Take it doctor, you have won it! Take it!'. Of course I did not, but the gift of a thousand pounds at that moment would not have given me the pleasure that offer did. Thickett is a splendid fellow, and is typical of the real grit in the United team".

Henry Thickett was born at Hexthorpe near Doncaster in 1873. He also played for Hexthorpe Wanderers and Rotherham Town. He returned to the Crystal Palace in 1909 for the Cup Final, as manager of Bristol City. At the time of his death in November 1920 he was a Trowbridge licensee and his weight had risen from the 14 stones of his playing days to 26 stones, more than his good friend Willy Foulke.

Reports were telegraphed back to Sheffield every ten minutes and when the news of the second and third goals reached the city, hats were thrown in the air.

After the game, Mr Balfour, the Prime Minister, gave a brief speech and presented the Cup. He congratulated both sides and gave Sheffield what he described as *"the proudest trophy for which they can struggle"*.

Needham also spoke to the crowd, standing on the table from which the Cup and medals were presented. The Cup went back into its box and not on a lap of honour.

More speeches followed; one from another Prime Minister Lord Rosebery, who thanked Mr Balfour for attending and the crowd sang

"For he's a Jolly Good Fellow". Mr Balfour, like any good politician, had the last word:

"I can assure you that no better way of spending a Saturday afternoon can be imagined than that we have enjoyed. For my part I am so essentially a peace-loving character that having fought my best for five days in the week, I like to see other people fighting on the Saturday".

TOP LEFT: SHEFFIELD UNITED'S THIRD GOAL.

CENTRE LEFT: FRONT COVER OF THE DAILY GRAPHIC 17TH APRIL 1899.

LEFT: THE SHEFFIELD UNITED TEAM, CUP WINNERS 1899. (From Association Cup Winners – Player's cigarette cards).

1900
BURY
V
SOUTHAMPTON

1900 FA CUP COMPETITION

The twentieth century dawned with the nation concerned about the war in South Africa. In fact, many football clubs were forced to finish their seasons early due to the War, as more and more young men were drafted into the forces.

In South London, fixtures were further affected by the counter attractions at the Crystal Palace. Not only was the Cup Final itself played at the Crystal Palace arena, but also a semi-final as two of the semi-finalists were southern teams.

A week later, the ground was used for the clash between the English League and the Scottish League (see Chapter 6).

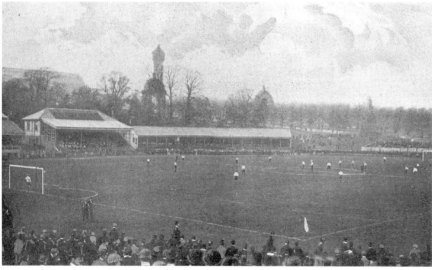

ABOVE: VIEW OF THE GAME FROM THE SOUTH-WEST CORNER OF THE GROUND.

THE SEMI-FINAL – 24TH MARCH 1900

Millwall and Southampton fought their way to the semi-final – still the only two non-league teams to meet in a semi-final! Also, for the first time in 17 years, two Southern clubs at this stage of the competition meant that a team from the South would be guaranteed in the Final.

A large crowd was expected at the Palace; the

official figure was over 37,000. There were many Southampton favours but it was estimated that there were more supporters of the "Dockers" (Millwall), as they were a local team.

In the event, the game was *"a bitter disappointment and one of the poorest and roughest"*. Apparently, both teams were to blame, so much so that after the match, some spectators reproached the players for their tactics.

"No reference to the match would be complete without a word of sympathy for the unfortunate Pressmen, who were 'stabled' in the open, and, with no protection from the biting nor'easter, had to pencil with numbed fingers and shivering limbs" (Athletic News).

The game ended goalless so both teams went to Reading the following Wednesday where Southampton came out the winners by 3 – 0.

THE FINAL – BURY V SOUTHAMPTON

The climax of the season was on April 21st when the FA Cup Final took place. This was also to mark the first of three years in a row that Southern teams got to the Final – but with limited success. Southampton were a strong side from the rapidly growing Southern League. Their opponents were yet another side from the north-west. This time it was Bury, in those days leading lights in the Football League First Division – but it was their first Final as well!

Though it was only late April, London was basking in a heatwave. *"A blazing hot sun poured down upon the greensward, and incidentally also upon the perspiring tens of thousands of excited partisans of the rival organisations who sat, stood, and sweltered long before the match was advertised to commence. An hour before the match there were fully 30,000 spectators present, and when the game started the attendance was quite up to that of the last few years – in fact, officials even declared greater than ever before"* (Sporting Sketches).

Even after five successful Finals at the Palace, it seems that the use of the ground was not guaranteed and was not totally supported. However, The Sportsman newspaper stated:

"Each spring we hear of the probability of the Cup Final leaving Sydenham, but it never does,

RIGHT: ROBINSON EFFECTS A SAVE.

and here again we fancy a plebiscite of the football community would be found to heartily endorse the action of the governing body. Not only is the arena unsurpassably adapted for such an encounter, but a visit to London, even in the expiring days of the nineteenth century, has unmistakable attraction for the average provincial".

THE GAME ITSELF

Unfortunately for the uncommitted spectators and the Southampton supporters (another large crowd of nearly 69,000 came to the Palace that day), it was a one-sided Final. Bury won the toss and decided to play with the bright sun behind them. In the first ten minutes, there was little between the sides but then Chadwick sent in a long shot which went just over the bar. From the goalkick, Bury quickly got the ball back to the Southampton goal area and forced a corner. McLuckie scored from the corner kick.

After the first goal, Bury were in complete control. Wood got a second goal and then, just before half-time, McLuckie got his second, Bury's third.

Even after the teams had turned round for the second half, there was little change. Though Southampton made a brave effort to put the Bury defence under pressure, they could not break through. Pray blasted another long shot to test Robinson who tipped it over the bar. From the resultant corner, Richards crossed the ball and Plant scored with a lightning shot.

That goal proved decisive. Try as they might, Southampton did not have the ability to get back into the game. Bury romped home by four goals to nil.

OTHER INCIDENTS

Wanderer reported in 'The Sportsman' that ten minutes from the end a group of spectators invaded the pitch when referee Kingscott blew the whistle rather loudly. *"Mr Kingscott subsequently admitted that in blowing for a foul he had rather let himself go, but happily there was no harm done. I only wonder that after his exertions, under a tropical sun, he had as much energy left".*

The papers also noted some events that occurred off the pitch, notably the collapse of the cane seat of a chair on which a prominent member of the FA was standing and *"the relieving of a member of the Fourth Estate of a valuable presentation watch by one of the light-fingered gentry"*.

ABOVE: A STOPPAGE OWING TO AN INJURY TO PRAY.

LEFT: A BURY THROW-IN.

BELOW FAR LEFT: THE BURY TEAM, CUP WINNERS 1900.
(From Association Cup Winners – Player's cigarette cards).

FOLLOWING PAGES: PLANT SCORES BURY'S FOURTH GOAL WITH A LIGHTNING SHOT.
Illustrated Sporting & Dramatic News.

ARTHUR KINGSCOTT

Arthur Kingscott was a highly respected referee who at the turn of the century was called upon to officiate at the top games. In 1900 alone he refereed the southern FA Cup semi-final and the replay, followed by the Final itself. Indeed, he was called on again to officiate the following year at the Final which also went to a replay.

After his retirement, Kingscott joined the Football Association and rose to become its Honorary Treasurer (1918 – 1933) and Chairman of the prestigious Final Tie

committee. Meanwhile, his two sons followed in his footsteps and themselves became referees. His elder son, Cecil, was the referee at the 1931 Cup Final, making a unique record of a father and son both refereeing a Cup Final.

Unfortunately for Kingscott, his career went sour when, in 1933 as the representative of the FA, he determined to deal with the issue of referees allegedly taking backhanders from football manufacturers to use their ball in the Final. Kingscott's action was to go to the referee's dressing room on match day and present the referee, Wood, with an appropriate football. Wood objected claiming that his honour had been put in doubt.

The matter dragged on and resulted in a FA tribunal at which Kingscott was found to be at fault. He was sacked and spent the rest of his days trying to clear his name.

1901
SHEFFIELD UNITED
V
TOTTENHAM HOTSPUR

The 1901 Final was a remarkable one. Once again, a southern club, and this time a London club from outside the Football League, reached the Crystal Palace. Tottenham's success generated a great deal of interest in the capital and guaranteed a large crowd. It was reported that 75 railway specials were laid on to bring supporters from the North; which meant at least 75,000 people. But on the big day, the official attendance was 110,820. 'Grasshopper' in Athletic News reported:

TOP: *A TICKET FOR THE FINAL.*

ABOVE: *PERCHED SPECTATORS.*

BELOW: *THE KICK OFF.*

"It was a wonderful sight that Palace enclosure around which the crowd assembled. One vast mass of humanity was closely packed around a big saucer-shaped circus whilst trees, roofs of buildings – indeed every point from which a view of the game could be obtained – were availed of by eager enthusiasts".

It was a lovely warm day which probably pleased the spectators, many of whom had taken up their positions before midday (three and a half hours before kick off). Others spent the time exploring the delights of the Palace and the grounds. But as the time for kick off approached, the crowds grew denser and denser.

At times, there was a surge forward which could have been dangerous, but when the start came the crowd steadied themselves and generally the behaviour of the crowd was admirable. *"Hooting of the referee – and there was a deplorable amount of this – not to be commended, but fortunately it did not take the form of personal violence, and if that official did blunder a feeling of irritation was scarcely to be wondered at, seeing that* *the large majority of those present were anxious to see Tottenham win"* (Athletic News).

The caterers seem to have anticipated the large attendance. The Athletic News records the preparation of:

"2,500 sandwich loaves, each weighing 8 lbs, 1,000 bread and butter loaves each weighing 5 lbs, 1,000 household loaves, 12,000 batons, 21,000 rolls, 120,000 slices of bread and butter, 30,000 pats of butter, 45,120 portions of best cake, 16,000 portions of lunch cake, 1,000 sponge cakes, 1,000 pieces of shortbread, 20,000 French pastries, 10,000 bath buns, 10,000 plain buns, 24,000 scones, 6,000 sixpenny pork pies, 2,000 smoked sausages, 1,728 gallons of milk, 200 rumps of beef, 250 chines of mutton for chops, 150 best ends of mutton for cutlets,

ABOVE: A SECTION OF THE LARGE CROWD AROUND 'THE RING'.

*OPPOSITE PAGE: FRONT COVER OF
THE DAILY GRAPHIC, 22ND APRIL
1901.*

*RIGHT: SHEFFIELD UNITED DEFEND
A CORNER.*

*BELOW: A NEAR MISS FROM
TOTTENHAM WITH THE SCORE AT
TWO ALL.*
Illustrated Sporting & Dramatic News.

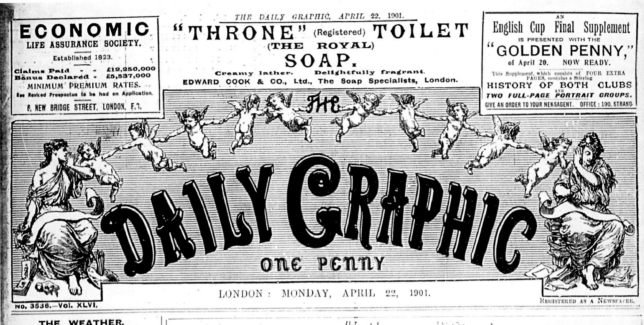

THE DAILY GRAPHIC
ONE PENNY

LONDON : MONDAY, APRIL 22, 1901.

NO. 3536.—Vol. XLVI.

REGISTERED AS A NEWSPAPER.

THE WEATHER.

"FINE AND WARM GENERALLY."
(See page 3.)

Sun rises (at Greenwich's) 4.53; sets 7.5.
Moon's age at noon, 3 days 14 hours.

THE ENGLISH CUP.

FINAL TIE AT THE PALACE.

A GOOD GAME AND A DRAW.

More than two army corps of the British public joined General Sir Redvers Buller at the Crystal Palace in watching a struggle that, for a day at least, obliterated the sterner interest of the fight which still harries South Africa. From Yorkshire, from the Midlands, from the great towns which make up the greater town of London, the army of footballers streamed along the lines of communication which led to Sydenham on Saturday, until 114,000 of them were gathered round the big green board of turf where Sheffield United and Tottenham Hotspur were to play their great Kriegspiel. Without exception, the days for final Cup ties at the Palace have been fine, but Saturday was the warmest and finest of them all, and this fact, added to the other that, for the first time in nearly twenty years, a London club's presence in the arena was giving ground for the hope that the Cup might come back South, made the numbers greater than have ever watched a final tie—or any football match—before. The nearest comparison to the numbers and the appearance of the crowd as it made its way through London would be the multitude that streams southwards on Derby day. No railway carriage that set out from Victoria or London Bridge or Holborn Viaduct held fewer than fifteen enthusiasts, and thousands of people—among them, no doubt, many who had suffered the tedious discomfort of the railways on previous occasions—went by the road. A long stream of brakes and 'buses, carriages, hansoms and coster-carts churned up the dust through Tulse Hill, Herne Hill and Dulwich; their progress making the resemblance to Derby day more marked than ever. Most of the brakes sported colours—blue

(Continued on page 3.)

FOULKES IS MARVELLOUSLY AGILE FOR HIS TWENTY STONE

NEEDHAM FINDS TOM SMITH A GREAT HANDFUL

BROWN HEADS THROUGH AFTER A TUSSLE ROUND THE SHEFFIELD GOAL

GREAT SAVE BY CLAWLEY

TOTTENHAM'S SECOND GOAL

LITTLE WILLIE'S LITTLE PUNCH WITH ALL HIS WEIGHT BEHIND IT

AN UNEQUAL GOAL

A DRAWN GAME: THE FINAL TIE FOR THE ASSOCIATION FOOTBALL CUP BETWEEN SHEFFIELD UNITED AND TOTTENHAM HOTSPUR AT THE CRYSTAL PALACE.

301

ABOVE: A TOTTENHAM SHOT AT GOAL.

60 fore-ribs of beef, each weighing 40 lbs, 40 whole lambs, 300 quarters of whitebait, 500 lbs of soles, 22,400 lbs of potatoes, 2,000 cabbages and cauliflowers, 400 fowls, 200 ducks, and 120,000 bottles of mineral waters".

In the game itself, the junior side were not in the least overawed by their Football League opponents and it was not surprising that the game ended in a 2 - 2 draw. Sheffield United supporters went to London full of confidence but after a keenly contested game they felt lucky to have come away with a draw. In fact, the equalising goal caused a sensation. Spurs had scored their second goal five minutes after the interval but two minutes later Bennett shot and followed the ball into the goal charging into Clawley. There was some doubt as to whether Clawley saved the ball or whether it crossed the line. Mr Kingscott the referee had no doubts and awarded the goal but there were many who doubted his judgment.

"There was the usual rush to the pavilion rails at the close and much cheering, interspersed on this occasion with some unmistakable hooting of the referee. Sir Redvers Buller, it had been arranged, should present the Cup to the winners and the medals to the various players. The draw in which the struggle ended prevented this programme being carried out, but, being promptly recognised, the General was enthusiastically cheered, and had to say a few words" (Athletic News).

THE REPLAY

Surprisingly, it was decided to hold the replay at Burnden Park, Bolton. This was because there was difficulty in agreeing terms for the use of the Crystal Palace and a Liverpool objection to the match being played at Goodison Park. Not many made the trip from London and the crowd only amounted to 22,000. Those who made the trip saw Tottenham beat Sheffield 3 – 1, the only time a team from outside the Football League (or Premier League) has won the Cup. One of the goals was scored by Sandy Brown to maintain his record of scoring in every round, the first player to achieve this.

RIGHT: THE CUP WITH TOTTENHAM'S 'COLOURS' TIED TO THE HANDLES. THE SAME RIBBONS WERE USED WHEN SPURS BEAT WOLVES IN THE 1921 CUP FINAL.

BELOW: THE TOTTENHAM HOTSPUR TEAM, CUP WINNERS 1901. (From Association Cup Winners – Player's cigarette cards).

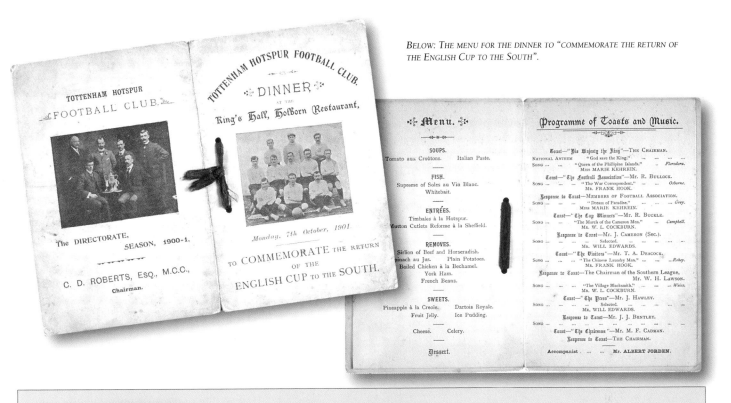

WILLIAM HENRY FOULKE

Willy Foulke, nicknamed "Fatty", was a giant goal-keeper for England, Chelsea and Sheffield United. At 6 ft 2in and weighing in at over 20 stones, he was a star of the Sheffield United team that reached three FA Cup Finals at the Crystal Palace. He played once for England (against Wales on 29th March 1897). He also played county cricket for Derbyshire.

Numerous legends surround Foulke. He was reputed to be able to carry a man under each arm and to punch a football as far as the halfway line. On one occasion, a match had to be stopped after he snapped the crossbar. During another game he was injured but proved too large for the stretcher and had to be carried off the field by no fewer than six men.

His agility made him a great keeper and he was famed as a specialist in saving penalties, although cunning opponents learnt to aim at his ample stomach.

Foulke was also well known for his mercurial temper, which often led him to give away penalties in the most remarkable fashion. In one match, he picked up the Liverpool centre-forward George Allan, whose persistence had become irritating and planted him head first in the mud outside his goal, giving the Reds the penalty they needed to win the match. Foulke's

subsequent meetings with Allan were much relished by the crowds, notably the series of replays of their semi-final match in the 1898 – 99 season that eventually ended with victory going to Sheffield United.

After the drawn Final at the Palace in 1902, Foulke took particular exception to the decisions made by the referee Tom Kirkham and the linesmen and determined, as he lay in the team bath after the game, that he would have to put things right. A few moments later, a steaming, naked 23-stone keeper was sighted scouring the Crystal Palace for the luckless officials. Kirkham was obliged to evade the irate goalkeeper by hiding in a boot cupboard, the door of which Fatty Foulke set about wrenching off until restrained by various onlookers, who included the Secretary of the FA himself.

In 1905 Fatty transferred to Chelsea (as keeper and captain) where his enormous appetite created more legends. Once, he got into the dining room before the rest of the team and polished off all 11 breakfasts. In response to the remonstrations of his team mates he only replied:

"I don't care what you call me, as long as you don't call me late for dinner".

Fatty Foulke once excused himself for his notorious antics explaining:

"Ask the old team if a bit of little Willy's foolery didn't help chirp them up before a tough match".

Chelsea made the most of the psychological advantage of having a huge obstacle in their goalmouth by positioning two small boys behind the goal to emphasise Fatty's bulk (the original ballboys). He ended his career with Bradford City (making a career total of 347 League appearances) and finished up somewhat sadly earning small change saving penalties from holiday-makers on Blackpool sands.

Ultimately, in 1916 he caught a chill while doing this and died of pneumonia, aged 41.

1902

SHEFFIELD UNITED
V
SOUTHAMPTON

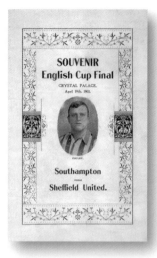

The 1902 Final gave Sheffield United an immediate opportunity to right the wrong of the previous year. But they must have come to the Crystal Palace with some trepidation because they were up against another of those audacious Southern League teams. This time it was Southampton who had got to their second Final in three years. And they had beaten the previous year's winner, Tottenham, in the first round of this year's competition.

At right-back, Southampton fielded C B Fry, a superb athlete who played cricket for England and also held the world record for the long jump. Sheffield United included eight of the side that had beaten Derby County so convincingly three years earlier. One of the newcomers,

Alf Common, who was later to be the first player transferred for a four-figure fee, gave United the lead. Robinson appeared to be distracted by Lipsham rushing in and the ball passed across the goalkeeper into the far corner. But Southampton were not to be denied. With two minutes to go they forced a replay when Wood, who apparently looked offside, put the ball past "Fatty" Foulke.

By the time the Crystal Palace hosted its eighth Final, the authorities had become quite experienced in dealing with a large number of spectators arriving for the big game. At the time, the ground was also used for polo matches. The fence which normally enclosed the ground was removed thus opening up the slope on the southern side for the accommodation of the spectators. The Sheffield Daily Telegraph reported:

"Dozens of extra turnstiles have been arranged, and the Palace people expect that practically instantaneous admission will be had, no matter how great the number. Visitors arriving at the Low Level station will be admitted directly into the grounds, and thus saved the trouble of making their way through the main building. To prevent delay in checking, the railway companies will not this year issue tickets including admission. The entrance fee of one shilling must be paid at the turnstiles, and no change will be given, save the change boxes. The shilling admission of course covers the match as the removal of the enclosing fence has made the park part of the public grounds.

It is almost unnecessary to say that everything has been done to secure the safety of the crowd and non-interference with play.

TOP: A SOUVENIR PROGRAMME.

ABOVE: THE SHEFFIELD UNITED TEAM.

RIGHT: SHEFFIELD ATTACK THE SOUTHAMPTON GOAL.

OPPOSITE PAGE: FRANTIC ACTION.
The Sphere.

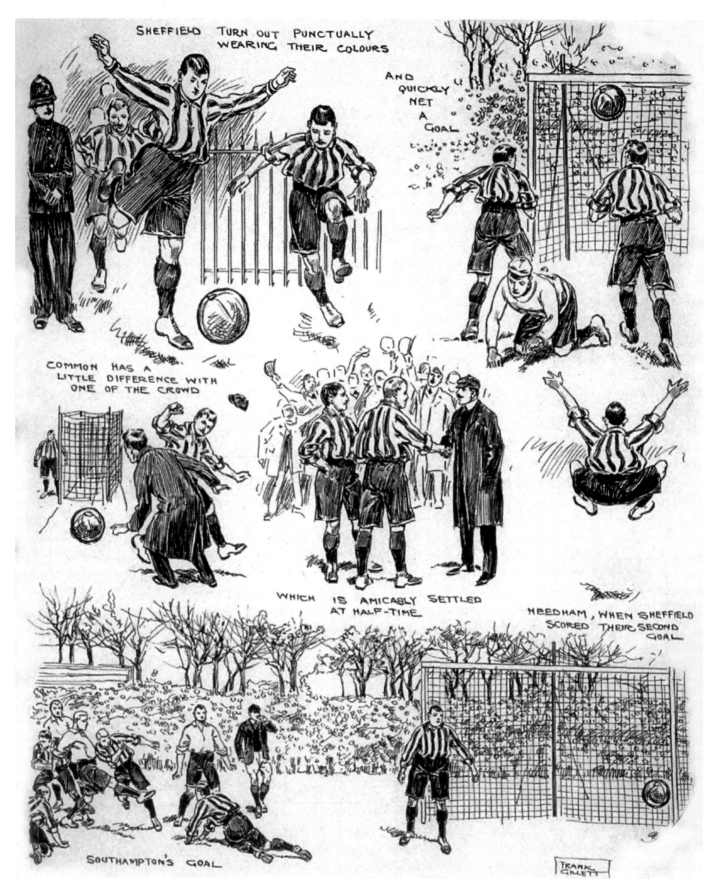

SHEFFIELD TURN OUT PUNCTUALLY WEARING THEIR COLOURS

AND QUICKLY NET A GOAL

COMMON HAS A LITTLE DIFFERENCE WITH ONE OF THE CROWD

WHICH IS AMICABLY SETTLED AT HALF-TIME

NEEDHAM, WHEN SHEFFIELD SCORED THEIR SECOND GOAL

SOUTHAMPTON'S GOAL

FRANK GILLETT

ABOVE: A CARTOON FROM 'THE GRAPHIC', OF THE REPLAY.

OPPOSITE PAGE:

TOP LEFT: ACTION AROUND THE SHEFFIELD GOAL.

FAR RIGHT TOP: THE SHEFFIELD UNITED TEAM, CUP WINNERS 1902.
(From Association Cup Winner's – Players cigarette cards).

CENTRE RIGHT: FOULKE MAKES A SUPERB SAVE JUST BEFORE HALF TIME.
Illustrated Sporting & Dramatic News.

The highest of the stands is not more than 7 feet above the ground. Barricades, whose props sink 3 feet into the ground, break the slopes, and, to further prevent any swaying forward on to the pitch, things have been so arranged that between the slopes and the playing ground there is a sward of considerable extent, actually part of the level on which the match will be played, but separated from it by specially strengthened iron railings. Thus, in the event of a break-in, the impetus will probably be expended on this grass, which, owing to its billiard table levelness, is unlikely to be occupied, and, in any case, the iron railings will prove an effective final barrier to any interference with play".

And this year, the Crystal Palace officials had to do it all again a week later. The replay was attended by a much smaller crowd – only 33,000 – but it was a game of some quality. Again Southampton showed tremendous resilience in their efforts to keep the Cup in the South. Sheffield United went into an early lead – after only two minutes – with a goal from Hedley, but in the second half Southampton got an equaliser from Brown. The killer blow however came eleven minutes from time when Barnes scored Sheffield's second goal and the Cup was on its way to Sheffield.

The Norwood News reported that Alf Common would not easily forget this Final. Not only was he the best forward on the field but *"once in the first half, he ran the ball over the goal-line, and, no doubt, inadvertently punched a spectator in the face, after which he was subjected to the bitterest hostility, a volume of hooting going up every time he touched the ball until at the interval he went over to the crowd and put matters right".*

CHARLES BURGESS FRY

C B Fry was the supreme example of the all-round sportsman. Though born in Croydon (25th April 1872), his family hailed from Sussex. He was educated at Repton and gained a first at Oxford. Fry also has the distinction of being a triple blue – for football, athletics and cricket, and would have got a fourth, in rugby had he not been injured. He appeared for the Barbarians in 1894-95 and an injured thigh caused him to miss the University match after he had played in all the season's fixtures.

He was a fine cricketer. Despite occasional problems with his home county, (he and Ranjitsinjhi once went on strike) he was outstanding for Sussex. He is one of only a handful of batsmen to make six hundreds in successive Innings. His performances for England were mixed but he did eventually become captain of the side, his 287 against Australia at Sydney in 1903-04 remains the highest score by an Englishman in a Test in Australia. It was his first Test match.

He played football for Corinthians and represented his country in the England v Ireland International at the Dell in 1901. The following year he played for Southampton in the FA Cup Final. In athletics, his best event was the long jump and in 1892, while still at Oxford, he equalled the world record with a jump of 23 feet 5 inches, a record that was not broken until 1913.

Fry became a master at Charterhouse before turning to journalism and later taught at the training ship H M S Mercury (1908-1950).

He tried several times to become a member of Parliament but was unsuccessful. However, his involvement in politics led him on one occasion to be offered the throne of Albania, which he turned down as he felt he could not afford it.

He died in Hampstead on 7th September, 1956.

1903
BURY
v
DERBY COUNTY

This was the ninth Crystal Palace Final. Yet despite the evident success of the arena as a venue, its use was still subject to annual review and the negotiations between the FA and the Crystal Palace authorities were often lengthy. The nature of the dispute was never made public though the financial arrangements might have been the reason. In fact, the Crystal Palace Company benefited based on the number of people that entered the grounds up to 5pm on the appointed day. With the massive attendances, this must have been a lucrative event for the Company. The rest of the receipts went to the FA who allocated them amongst the participating clubs.

On this day in 1903, as early as eleven o'clock a few enthusiasts made their way to the football arena, and took up their positions, but as the day wore on the benches and banks took a long time to fill. Indeed, at one o'clock there were still only about 2,000 in the ground – normally there would have been eight to ten thousand. However, when the match began, well over 60,000 were present – not quite as good as previous years.

As both clubs normally wore white shirts, it was agreed that the Shakers (Bury) should wear Cambridge blue shirts and navy shorts and the Rams (Derby) should have red shirts and black shorts.

This must have been the most one-sided Final ever. Bury, who had taken the Cup in 1900, were supremely successful in the 1902-03 campaign. Not only did they reach the Final without conceding a goal, thus equalling Preston North End's record of 1888-89, but they then proceeded to thrash Derby County by six goals to nil.

The game itself was a bitter disappointment. J J Bentley stated:

"Make every excuse you can possibly find, and you are bound to regard the Final of 1903 as about the worst. All you can say is that Bury were

The programme

Final Cup Tie===Crystal Palace.

BURY v DERBY COUNTY.

Sat. April 18, 1903.   Kick-off 3.30.

BURY

Right Wing		Goal		Left Wing
		H. MONTEITH		
		Backs		
	J. LINDSAY		J. McEWEN	
		Half-backs		
	J. JOHNSTON	THORPE.	G. ROSS, (Capt)	
		Forwards		
RICHARDS	WOOD	SAGAR	LEEMING	PLANT

O

		Forwards		
DAVIS	RICHARDS	BOAG	YORK	WARRINGTON
		Half-backs		
	MAY	GOODALL	WARREN	
		Backs		
	MORRIS		METHVEN	
Left Wing		Goal		Right Wing
		FRYER		

DERBY COUNTY

Referee Mr. J. ADAMS.
Linesmen, Messrs. G. W. SIMMONS & F. STYLES.

TOP: THE PROGRAMME.

RIGHT: THE VICTORIOUS BURY TEAM.

decidedly the superior team, express your regret for unfortunate Derby, and wish them better luck another time".

Despite six goals being scored, they were all by Bury. Derby were completely overawed by the occasion and never really got going. The inspiration for Bury was their captain, Ross. He scored their first goal after 20 minutes and saved a certain goal when the full-backs and Monteith had been comprehensively beaten. If Derby had scored, it might have been a very different game.

The Derby faithful would argue that they were hampered by injury. Steve Bloomer had been declared unfit with an ankle injury sustained at Newcastle on Good Friday. Fryer was also doubtful due to a leg injury but he took the field. Many would argue that he should never have done so.

Tityrus in the 'Athletic News' said:

"I never saw Derby County play a poorer game than in this match, for they were weak all round and people wondered what they had come out to see and how ever did they beat Millwall".

Some might also claim that the state of the ground did not help. *"....the surface was studded with little protuberances that proved awfully trying to the men as they tried to manipulate the ball, and it was through striking these self same protuberances that the ball performed all sorts of unexpected manouvres and frequently caused the players to be at fault".*

It was only 1 – 0 to the Shakers at half-time but the spectators were all disappointed at the raggedness of the display and the absence of scientific work by the teams. Of the two, it was the Derby side that went into the pavilion the more tired and when the second half began, the Bury team set off at a blistering pace. Before the half was 25 minutes old, Bury were five goals to the good. Fifteen minutes later, an attack by Derby was broken down and the Bury forwards burst through all opposition and Leeming receiving from Thorpe dashed forward and beat Morris with one of the finest shots of the match to make it 6 – 0.

So, once again Ross received the *"little tin idol"* from Lord Kinnaird while Derby could only rue that gipsy's curse!

ABOVE: THE DERBY DEFENCE.
Illustrated Sporting & Dramatic News.

"THE BALL"

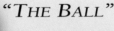

BELOW: THE BURY TEAM, CUP
WINNERS 1903.
(From Association Cup Winners –
Player's cigarette cards).

(68 – 71 cm); it must weigh no more than 453 grams and no less than 396 grams at the start of the game.

In 1900 a football was made from strips of leather sewn together, containing a rubber bladder which was inflated to the correct pressure. All was held together with a threaded lace.

All-in-all this was a dangerous piece of equipment, particularly for those faced with heading the ball. Even in dry weather, the ball was heavy and contact with the lace could give a nasty jolt. In wet weather, the leather absorbed moisture like a sponge and became extremely heavy, making it difficult to control and pass on the wet ground, and mind-numbing when headed.

The footballers in the 1903 Final did not have to contend with a wet ball and the Bury team made expert use of it, scoring six goals without reply, which is still the highest Cup Final margin. After the game, the ball was presented to the Bury club and it sits proudly at Gigg Lane to this day, suitably inscribed with the date and the score.

The footballs used a hundred years ago were very different from those used today, albeit that the dimensions of the ball have remained the same as that set in 1872. The ball should be spherical with a circumference of 27-28 inches

1904
BOLTON WANDERERS
V
MANCHESTER CITY

The 1904 Final was not the most exciting seen at Crystal Palace. It has been eloquently if in a biased way described by J J Bentley, the Secretary of Bolton Wanderers, who made contributions to Athletics News and Football Field:

"Another Cup Final has been played and won, and for the first time the great trophy of the year has gone to Manchester. It could not have been sent to a more enthusiastic football district, unless it had found its way to the opposing town, only ten miles away.

OPPOSITE PAGE TOP: THE REFEREE MR A J BARKER FOLLOWS THE ACTION.

BELOW: THE MANCHESTER CITY TEAM AND MANAGEMENT.

We had typical Cup Final weather – fair and bright, and there was a much better crowd than most people anticipated, over 62,000 being present. They were mostly in favour of Bolton, probably owing to them being considered the weaker side. At any rate, anything the Boltonians did was heartily cheered and better play on the part of Manchester was received in comparative silence. Yes, there is little question about it – Bolton were the popular side, and had the Cup been taken to Bolton, the victory would have been most popular.

There was no mistaking the feeling of the crowd from the time the teams came out of the pavilion to the final whistle sounding, and the Hon. Alfred Lyttleton, in his admirable little speech, opened in capital fashion by expressing sympathy with the Wanderers.

With the exception of Boyd, the Bolton half-back, the teams turned out at full strength, all the Manchester injured players being able to take part in the game, which was not a very good one, but better than the majority of Finals. It was always interesting, for both sides fought strenuously.

OPPOSITE PAGE BOTTOM: A MANCHESTER CITY CORNER.

In the first half, Manchester had a lot of the best of it, and more than deserved the single goal but to my mind the goal – that all-important goal – ought not to have been allowed. From the pavilion we had a splendid view, and Meredith seemed to be waiting behind Struthers and quite a couple of yards offside. The majority about me favoured this view, but such a good judge as John Lewis agreed with the referee, who personally had not the slightest doubt about the matter. But to me it seemed a clear case of offside, and it is a pity that the result should have been decided by what at the best must be considered a doubtful point. On the play it was well earned, but seeing Meredith, as I can still see him, standing, and then making a dart for the ball well behind Struthers, I cannot but think it hard lines on the Wanderers to lose the match by a goal which was open to so much question. But on the play the City fully deserved to lead by that odd goal.

WANDERERS' FINE DASH

Immediately on resuming the Wanderers set about their work as if they meant business, and if the City deserved the goal they had secured the Wanderers were certainly entitled to an equalising point. They showed splendid dash, and for twenty minutes played the game they did against Southampton, Sheffield United and Derby County, with the exception that they seldom shot. Indeed, all through the shooting on both sides was poor, and the only decent shot on the part of the Wanderers in the first half was that by Taylor, who, after a careful run, gave Hillman a thorough teaser from long range.

During the first half-hour after the interval the Bolton men were simply all over their opponents, and had they followed up their energetic work by having a drive for goal the Cup would not have been located in Manchester for the next twelve months, for the City backs were by no means faultless, and afforded every opportunity for scoring. Then for ten minutes the City seemed to realise that it was time they did something, and the Boltonians had an anxious time of it, for Manchester attacked in fine style, and but for sound defence must have added to their score.

Then to their credit be it said, Bolton came over once more, and their opponents were sorely tried during the last five minutes. White sent in a shot which only missed by inches – but miss it did, and Manchester City won by 1 goal to 0....."
(Birmingham Gazette, April 25th, 1904).

Unfortunately, Manchester's celebrations of their first win turned to dust. An FA investigation found that illegal bonus payments had been made to players. Their secretary and some directors were suspended; Meredith and many of the players moved across the city to join Manchester United.

A NORTHERN
IMPORTATION
COLOURED UMBRELLAS
USED AS PARTY BADGES

THE RT HON A.J. BALFOUR
PRIME MINISTER PC LLD DCL M.A. MP
DL — FIRST LORD OF THE TREASURY
BUYS A PENNY
PROGRAMME!

AN EXCITED INDIVIDUAL
GIVES VENT TO HIS FEELINGS
BY TACKLING A POLICEMAN

EVERTON SCORES
THE ONLY GOAL.

THE FRUIT OF
THAT FORBIDDEN
TREE

THE HON A LYTTELTON
PRESENTS
"T'COOP"

WHITE RETIRES
TEMPORARILY. HURT.

BILLY MEREDITH (THE WELSH WIZARD)

Billy Meredith was something akin to a God to his fellow Welshmen, revered the length and breadth of the country but he had to leave Wales to achieve greatness. He began his career in first-class football in 1894 and played regularly for 31 years. Altogether he scored 470 goals in no fewer than 1363 matches and played 48 times for Wales in international matches. Meredith is still the most capped player against England with 20 caps (1895 – 1920) and also the oldest (aged 45 years 230 days). He is one of only two players who have won FA Cup winners' medals for both Manchester clubs.

Born in Chirk, North Wales, he was recruited by Manchester City in 1894 – a sullen and frail-looking youth with little hint of the genius that was to appear as he matured. He rarely had much to say, but "those ninety minutes of consummate ball control and trickery every Saturday afternoon, to the roars of an adoring multitude, were Meredith's one means of communion with his fellow men. For the rest he was as silent as a Trappist". He was constantly toying with the

ball, spinning it, trapping it, juggling it, until his feet developed the tactile sensitiveness of an ordinary person's hands. His mind persistently dwelt on the problems of the game. Nothing was too small to escape him.

"Take corner kicks in wet weather, for example. He placed the ball with laces underneath, to raise it a little from the mud, elementary of course, but such things count. When a penalty rule was enforced, allowing a goalkeeper to advance to the six-yard line, Meredith killed it by walking to the ball and hooking it, gently but irretrievably, over the goalkeeper's head. When his playing days were over, he observed the conventions and 'took a pub'. The story goes that during the Manchester blitz a bomb exploded at the back of the pub and a shower of Welsh international caps descended on the neighbourhood. They took some time to collect again, for there were 48 of them".

(Don Davies – the 'Old International' of The Guardian).

TOP: BILLY MEREDITH SCORES THE ONLY GOAL.

ABOVE: THE MANCHESTER CITY TEAM, CUP WINNERS 1904.
(From Association Cup Winners – Player's cigarette cards).

OPPOSITE PAGE: DRAWING BY RALPH CLEAVER.
Illustrated Sporting & Dramatic News.

One way to see the action.

OOP FOR T'CUP

By the time the Cup Final came to the Crystal Palace it had become an institution in its own right, mainly for the fanatical supporters of clubs from the Midlands and the North, but for others as well.

THE SOCIAL CHANGES

As we have seen, when over 42,000 people turned up for the first Final at Crystal Palace, it was regarded as a massive attendance. Yet six years later, over 110,000 made the trip up Sydenham Hill. Even so, some thought football would be a passing fad – a temporary phenomenon. The following year (1902) when a smaller crowd watched Sheffield United win the Cup, it was claimed that football was *"past its meridian"*. However, this assessment ignored the facts that the 1901 Final had included a London club (Tottenham), and two other events that had occurred since then – the Ibrox disaster when 25 people had lost their lives at a Scotland v England game, and a smallpox scare which deterred people from mingling in crowded areas.

No, football as a mass sport was here to stay. In the second half of the nineteenth century there had been dramatic changes in people's lives and in their leisure time. For the first time, ordinary people from the mill towns and mining villages had free time outside work – by 1847 the building trades had secured a 'four o'clock Saturday' in some towns; in 1890 the engineering trades on Tyne and Wear demanded a complete half-holiday on Saturday. By the end of the century, the Saturday had been generally accepted as an industrial holiday.

And where better to go but to the football ground – the fresh air, the thrills and spills and the reflected glory of one's local team winning a League or a Cup?

The railway companies, not missing the commercial advantages, added to the possibilities by offering excursions to follow teams to away matches and of course to the Cup games.

Not that everyone was enamoured with the new craze. Some members of the religious community particularly, regarded it as a pastime of the evil-minded. And on occasions, footballers themselves were not always welcome at away venues, being denied access to some hotels.

ATTENDANCE AT THE FINAL

The Final was the highlight of the footballing year. So who were the people who came to the big event?

Of course, supporters would come from those towns that were competing, but a trip to the Cup Final would be looked forward to by many others from all over the country. For many, it required a deep long-term commitment throughout the year leading up to the Final.

"The Blackburn operative, the Fazakerley labourer, or the Oldhamite who boards the train at Mumps is not, as a rule, so flush with money that he can walk off to his local station, put down his eleven or twelve shillings, as the case may be, and board the train that is to bear him to the Metropolis. There is little or none of 'the spur of the moment' business about the excursionist from the North".

ABOVE: THE PACKED CROWD AT THE 1905 FINAL.

LEFT: BEER WITH A FOOTBALL LABEL.

ABOVE: NORTHERN FANS SETTING OUT FROM THE KINGSWAY FOR THE JOURNEY TO CRYSTAL PALACE FOR THE 1906 FINAL.

ABOVE: ARRIVAL OF A FOOTBALL SPECIAL AT PARK ROYAL 1908.

OPPOSITE PAGE: GREAT NORTHERN RAILWAY CUP FINAL POSTER, 1904.

RIGHT: THE GREAT CENTRAL RAILWAY'S 8 FT. BY 7 FT. POSTER - DISPLAYED OUTSIDE ONE OF THEIR AGENCIES IN MANCHESTER, 1904.

BELOW: LONDON & NORTH WESTERN RAILWAY POSTER ADVERTISING TRIPS TO THE 1909 FINAL.

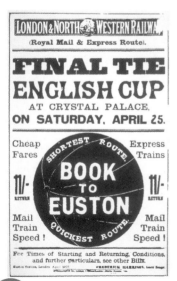

Typically, a local publican would act as treasurer and collect the threepences, sixpences and shillings every week and would arrange the transport with the railway company. With that degree of forward planning, the trip would go ahead even if the local team did not get through to the Final.

For Londoners, it was sufficient to look at the weather on the morning of the match and decide there and then whether to make the short trip to the Crystal Palace. When a London or Southern club managed to get to the Final, it is not surprising that Londoners flocked to Sydenham.

However, football was not only a working class sport. A number of the members of the upper classes would also attend. For instance, in 1899 among the crowd of 73,000 were Lord Rosebery who drove over from Epsom with his two sons, Mr Balfour, the Prime Minister, Mr Cecil Rhodes, the great South African statesman, Lord Kinnaird and the Mayors of Sheffield and Derby. Rosebery was evidently a regular attendee being as passionate about football as he was about racing.

Even royalty were invited – the Prince of Wales was asked on a number of occasions but declined. It was not until 1914 that the King himself came and presented the Cup to the captain of the victorious Burnley team. At last, football was accepted by the establishment.

EXCURSIONS ORGANISED BY THE RAILWAY COMPANIES

Of course, the railway companies were not in the business for their philanthropy but they did make a number of concessions to the public by arranging football specials at reduced rates. For instance, in 1912 "The Locomotive" announced that for the Cup Final that year (between Barnsley and West Bromwich) the London and North Western Railway Company ran 29 special services; the Midland Railway, 16; the Great Western, 15; Great Northern, 12; Great Central, 6; and Great Eastern, 1.

In some cases, the railway companies also supplied a breakfast at a reasonable price on the way to London and a supper on the return

journey. But very often, the organiser (the innkeeper) would lay on barrels of beer and *"provender galore"*. Though strictly no luggage was allowed to day trip passengers, the railway companies turned a blind eye on Cup Final specials. *"That the Cup-tie enthusiast pays a good deal of attention to his 'nosebag' by the way, can be gathered from that one party from Birmingham on a recent Cup-tie day brought with them in the saloon five large hampers filled with roasted and boiled joints, sandwiches and liquid refreshment, the whole weighing several hundredweight. They do not call that kind of thing 'luggage' in Birmingham – rather do they describe the cumbrous cases as ' light refreshments' "*.

This mobility gave people the opportunity to follow their team all over the country. It was reported that when Plymouth Argyle were drawn away to Newcastle United in 1906, a hardy 700 supporters made the trip. They left Plymouth at eight o'clock on Friday evening arriving in Newcastle at nine o'clock on the Saturday morning, having covered a distance of 470 miles. Then, having watched their team draw with the Magpies, they returned to Plymouth, which they reached in time for church on Sunday morning, after an excursion of not far short of a thousand miles.

PUBLICITY

The railway companies were keen to publicise football specials and handbills appeared offering excursions of varying length. On one occasion, the Great Central Railway commissioned a poster which depicted Billy

Meredith kicking a goal with the words *"Billy Meredith secures the Cup"*. Luckily for the Railway company, it proved to be an accurate prophesy as Manchester City won the 1904 Cup Final with Meredith scoring the only goal. Whether the fact that the Great Central Railway were the landlords of the Hyde Road ground where City played had anything to do with the choice of subject it is impossible to say!

THE FOOTBALL ASSOCIATION PICTURE, (Key).

BY CHARLES H. PARKER. 17, NEW OXFORD STREET, W.C.

FINAL TIE.   CRYSTAL PALACE PAVILION.

THE ASSOCIATION FINAL, CRYSTAL PALACE PAVILION, 1910. HANDCOLOURED ENGRAVING BY CHARLES BARKER WITH KEY.

The Fans' weekend

So a grand weekend was in store for the thousands who made the trip to the Crystal Palace. When Newcastle got to their first Final in 1905, almost 10,000 Geordies made the trip. For some, the journey started at midnight, having taken on board the train, *"beer, bottles of whisky and whole hams with loaves of bread and pickled onions in great jars"*. One organised trip included a match ticket and meals for 22s.6d. For an extra 4 shillings, fans could obtain a stand seat.

Some enterprising organisers even brought additional provisions which were left in a hired room at St Pancras to be collected for the return journey.

The Geordie Navy joins the Toon Army

It was not only the railways that offered transport to London. Again in 1905, some chose to go to the game by boat. A ticket for the 24-hour trip down the North Sea from Newcastle could be purchased for 12s or 8s (20s or 15s with food included).

ABOVE: THE ANTEDILUVIAN MODELS IN CRYSTAL PALACE PARK.

sighted that magnificent glass building glistening in the sunlight at the top of Sydenham Hill.

Those that took the London, Chatham and Dover service came to the Crystal Palace High Level station. On getting off the train, the spectator was treated to a walk through the glorious vaulted subway (built in 1865 by Italian cathedral craftsmen) that conveyed the traveller underneath the roadway straight into the heart of the Crystal Palace building full of statues, exhibits and greenery. From there, one could emerge onto the formal terraces and then wander down through the park to the football ground.

FAR LEFT: CRYSTAL PALACE HIGH LEVEL STATION.

That year, there was even a Ladies Outing Club – *"limited to Newcastle enthusiasts of the fairer sex alone"*. They had their own lady secretary and paid their own subscriptions and headed for London in a special saloon on the train, and without the assistance of a single male – a rarity in Edwardian Britain.

Having arrived in London, the enthusiasts still had to get across the centre by 'tube'. A two and a half minute service was maintained taking spectators from Baker Street to the southern termini of Waterloo and Victoria. Others preferred to enjoy the sights and sounds of the city before making the next stage of the journey.

Arrival at the Palace

Then the two southern railway companies – the London, Brighton and South Coast and the London, Chatham and Dover – moved into action, laying on extra ticket booths at the railway stations to speed people onto the trains. Crammed into suburban carriages, thousands were conveyed to one or other of the Crystal Palace stations. And for most of the journey into this alien land, excitement would grow as they

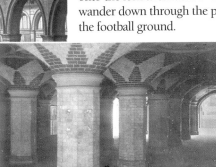

LEFT: THE GLORIOUS VAULTED SUBWAY WHICH LED FROM THE STATION INTO THE PALACE.

BELOW: ENTRANCE TO CRYSTAL PALACE LOW LEVEL STATION.

BOTTOM: AERIAL VIEW OF LOW LEVEL STATION, (FOOTBALL GROUND IS PARTLY VISIBLE CENTRE LEFT OF THE PICTURE).

Passengers on the London, Brighton and South Coast railway arrived at the Low Level station and did not have so far to walk to reach the ground. To prevent delay (which of course was a problem at the 1895 Final),

the railway company cut out the joint travel and admission tickets. For the 1902 game, the entrance fee of one shilling had to be paid at the turnstiles and no change was given, except at special change boxes. *"The shilling admission, of course, covers the match, as the removal of the enclosing fence has made the park part of the public grounds"*.

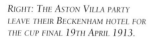
ABOVE: THE W H SMITH STALL IN THE HIGH LEVEL STATION SUBWAY.

Some came under their own steam. In 1899, it was reported that cyclists could leave their bikes with the attendants at the Low Level Station and at the Penge entrance to the Park – the charge tuppence per cycle.

Many spectators would arrive early. Armed with trumpets, drums and rattles, bedecked in their club's colours, they would pay their shilling to enter the grounds, and a penny or tuppence for a programme, and then explore the park with its funfair, the dinosaurs and boating lake – truly a wonderland, a nineteenth century Disneyland! But as the time approached, they adjourned to the arena ready for the kick-off at four o'clock.

Some never made it! One member of the Press, who was leaving the ground some three minutes before the end of the 1911 Final, came across a poor soul wandering in an obscure corner of the Palace. He wanted to know where the football ground was, having just arrived – too late!

THE TEAMS' WEEKEND

For the teams and officials the weekend had a different character. Not for them the crowded trains with their supporters. On the Friday before the 1911 Final, Bradford reserve players left the Midland station at a quarter to ten in the morning, in a crowded train with their wives, and friends and others with an interest in the club. The 15 players from whom the final 11 would be chosen left by a special train at three o'clock that afternoon. They arrived in London at a quarter past eight, and the players enjoyed an evening of entertainment at the Euston Empire Theatre, which is close to the St Pancras Hotel, their headquarters for the weekend. The following morning they went on a drive to Hyde Park returning to the hotel for lunch and the drive up to the Crystal Palace, arriving an hour before the kick-off.

Other clubs were reluctant to let their players spend too much time in the capital. West Bromwich were typical. Even though there was a general rail strike at the time of the 1912 Final, it was still decided to travel on the day of the game *"as we have always done for Finals"*. Inevitably, the players had a terrible time getting out to the Crystal Palace ground, and had to fight their way to get to the dressing-room.

Clubs took different views on accommodation before the game. Some preferred to stay in central London where entertainment was on hand. Others opted for getting to the Crystal Palace area where there were ample hotels – the Queen's, the White Hart, The Royal Crystal Palace Hotel, even Beckenham was within easy reach.

For all, however, it was a nervous time. Some players travelled down with the team but were

RIGHT: THE ASTON VILLA PARTY LEAVE THEIR BECKENHAM HOTEL FOR THE CUP FINAL 19TH APRIL 1913.

not guaranteed a place on the pitch. When the Sheffield Wednesday players and officials started their journey to London on the Friday before the 1896 Final, the team had not been selected. Langley discovered by accident that he would play only if the ground was *"on the light side"*; if heavy, Brandon would replace him.

"I shall never forget that Friday night's experience at the Queen's Hotel, Upper Norwood", Langley said. *"Spiksley was my sleeping partner, and he, like me, did not have more than two hours sleep the whole of the night. Coming from the same county as myself, Spiksley was anxious that I should play. First he would get out of bed and look out of the window and see what the weather was like. Then, after he had got back into bed it would not be long before he would nudge me and say, 'You go and have a look, Mick, and see if it's fine'. He used to call me Mick. And so it went on through the night. You may think it ridiculous conduct, but, recollect, a Cup medal was at stake. The ambition of all the players is to get an English Cup winners' medal – the value is beyond price.*

There were one or two other fellows as restless as I was – Jamieson, for instance. I believe he played in nearly all the rounds, and yet, owing to the weather, was denied his chance of a medal. It was hard luck. I played, as it happened. I shall always

think, however, that, when possible, players' minds should be set at rest early; it means a lot".

SPECTATOR CONDITIONS

For the lucky ones – or the rich – there were seats available in the pavilion. But this was for a maximum of 3,000. For the majority the only vantage point was on the vast slopes at the side of the pitch or on the southern side. The switchback railway, normally an attraction in the park, was closed and spectators could stand on the track to look down on the ground.

In later years, the authorities created some grooves into the ground to give additional footing but even so the likelihood of seeing any of the game was fairly remote. For many, the only chance was to take to the trees of which there were many around the arena. This was not without its problems and accidents did happen. In 1899, it was reported that one poor fellow

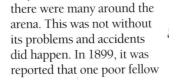

FAR LEFT: QUEEN'S HOTEL, CHURCH ROAD, UPPER NORWOOD.

BELOW: MOST SPECTATORS OCCUPIED THE VAST GRASSY SLOPES.

ABOVE: A BETTER VIEW FOR THE REALLY ENTERPRISING.

LEFT: A PRECARIOUS WAY TO WATCH THE ACTION.

THE CUP FINAL GROUND VIEWED FROM A BALLOON C1913.

fell a distance of 30 feet from a tree, and apparently sustained *"concussion of the brain"*.

Some with iron stamina perched themselves on posts in excruciating positions to see their team perform.

But see the game or not, it was sufficient to be present at this spectacle. To be present as history was in the making – a tale to tell one's grandchildren.

Only one group seem to have been concerned about the spartan conditions at Crystal Palace – or maybe it was just that they were the only ones with the opportunity to express their opinions! The Press were for many years accommodated in

the programme). Eventually, the FA was more prepared to extend the agreement with the Crystal Palace Company and improvements were made to the terraces.

CROWD CONTROL

One of the fears particularly after Fallowfield, and subsequently the Ibrox disaster, was control of the crowd. However, despite the massive crowds – over 120,000 at the 1913 Final – there was never any trouble. It was a carnival day and the policing was kept to a minimum. Even with the massive crowd that attended the 1901 Final, their behaviour was described as *"impeccable"*:

LEFT: SPECTATORS VIEWED MATCHES FROM ALL VANTAGE POINTS.

LEFT: THE CRYSTAL PALACE AND GROUNDS C1920.

uncomfortable conditions in the open stands, exposed to the weather, which was not always clement. They were also some distance from the pitch and not necessarily with a good view of the goalmouths.

"By the bye, a matter deserves mention which though it may not concern the public directly is still of importance to them in the results. This was the accommodation provided for the provincial Press. Influential papers of our old and high standard had their repeated applications ignored while some of the London journals of far less importance had secured and marked several seats – in one case five!" (1898 Final).

THE GROUND

The FA were reluctant to give the Crystal Palace authorities any security that the Final would continue to be held on the ground year after year. But the former fountain basin was a superb arena with its natural bowl effect. The playing surface was lovingly prepared, with Carters providing the seed (as was advertised in

*"The Sydenham slopes are unsurpassed
In their essential fitness
For letting monstrous crowds and vast
The sports arena witness.
But, oh, the wobbling, whelming surge
That ever swayed those masses;
And on your minds this fact I urge –
John Bull's behaviour passes.
All praise, for that good humour blithe
which – in the crush terrific –
Made each crammed
Sydenham slope,
mid writhe and roar, a Slope
Pacific!".*

By 1902, the Crystal Palace Company had installed a number of barricades, with props sunk three feet into the ground, to break up the slopes and prevent any swaying forward on to the pitch. Even if there was a surge, it

BELOW: THE FANS WERE VERY WELL BEHAVED.

59

is likely that the crowd would just flow on to the ring area on the same level as the playing surface but separated from it by strengthened iron railings. However, no trouble was ever reported.

THE WEATHER

In those days, the Final was played at the end of April. There was no guarantee that the weather would be clement and bad weather could so easily have ruined the future of the Cup Final at Crystal Palace. With so little cover for spectators and the muddy conditions that would have ensued on the slopes, spectators might have been deterred and the FA would have looked elsewhere.

But that did not happen. More often than not, the weather was ideal – warm and sunny. In fact, these conditions came to be known colloquially as "Cup Final" weather.

On so many occasions, on the day of the Final there was a blazing hot sun pouring down on the spectacle, which only added to the carnival atmosphere. Even when there had been wet weather in the days leading up to the Saturday, as in 1899, the dawn of the great day brought with it glorious sunshine – even a heatwave (as in 1900). In 1903, there were even snow showers in the week before but true to form on Cup Final day, out came the sun.

FAR RIGHT: CONCERTS WERE HELD IN THE CENTRE TRANSEPT...

For most of the teams, then, that came to the Palace, the worst they had to contend with was the sun shining in their eyes during the late afternoon. Some, however, were not so lucky. In 1908 the weather was particularly poor. Two football matches had been snowed off during April and it had been raining for days before the Cup Final and it continued during the match (it is surprising that it was such a good game!). The spectators must have had an uncomfortable time.

However, the event did generate one lasting benefit. One Gladstone Adams came down from County Durham to support the Magpies. On his journey back to the North-East in a charabanc, his inventive mind turned

BELOW: ... AND INTERNATIONAL BOXING MATCHES.

to the difficulty of seeing through the windscreen in the snowstorm that accompanied their journey home. The result was the invention of the windscreen wiper.

THE QUALITY OF THE FOOTBALL

It was disappointing that the football rarely lived up to the quality of the weather. In later years particularly, though Newcastle promised so much based on their League form, the Final became a dour affair with few goals and necessitating a replay to separate the teams.

There were highlights of course. The 1897 Final was talked about for years after as the best Final ever. That massive attendance at the 1901 Final saw a superlative contest between Tottenham and Sheffield United which ended in a 2 – 2 draw.

But the later Finals were rarely as good as anticipated. Newcastle were the team of the period but when they turned up at the Palace their skill seemed to desert them.

OTHER ATTRACTIONS –
EFFECTS OF THE FOOTBALL

If the spectators were not always pleased at the spectacle which they saw on the great day, there were others who were noticeably disgruntled at the events. Until 1895, a Saturday afternoon at Crystal Palace had been synonymous with music and a selection of music concerts, ballet, etc. The invasion of the Crystal Palace grounds by thousands of uncouth football fans destroyed the genteel atmosphere for the cultured few.

However, this was not the universal reaction from participants in other activities at the Palace. Geoffrey Green, in his book 'Soccer the World Game' tells the story of Herbert Strudwick, the Surrey and England wicket-keeper. Apparently, on Cup Final day in 1902, Strudwick was playing for Surrey against the London County captained by W G Grace at the Palace. The Doctor stopped play so the teams could watch the first half of the

the Cup Final. When play restarted Herbert Strudwick was out first ball. Strudwick had also been out for a duck in the first innings. W G said: *"Had I known that, I would have given you one to get you off the mark"*. *"It's quite all right"*, replied Strudwick who returned to the football ground as quickly as possible to watch the second half.

POST-GAME CELEBRATIONS

After it was all over, for the victorious fans it was a joyous celebration on the journey home. Picking up provisions at the station, the spectators ate and drank their way back home. For those of the defeated team, it was a more sombre retreat, bolstered by the thought that the slate would be wiped clean at the beginning of the following season and hopes could rise again.

For the teams and club officials, there was the possibility of an adjournment to a central London venue, very often the Trocadero, Piccadilly Circus, for a dinner followed by complimentary speeches by the guests of honour. After the 1907 Final, the successful Sheffield Wednesday team was treated to a visit to a London music hall. The star of the show was George Robey who invited the Wednesday team onto the stage. Crawshaw, the captain, was assured that he would not have to speak but Robey announced to the audience *"And now Tom Crawshaw will tell us all about how Wednesday did it!"*. Crawshaw later said *"Honest, I was lost for words but I managed somehow. Mind you, I think they were mostly amused by my Yorkshire accent and probably didn't understand much of what I said"*.

In 1911, there was an added attraction. After the dinner at which Sir William Priestley presided, the team went to the Alhambra to see pictures of the Final on the bioscope.

For the Crystal Palace authorities, there was a clean-up operation to be carried out. However, there was compensation in the fact that each year proved a success and re-inforced the Crystal Palace's right to stage the next gladiatorial encounter the following year.

ARRIVAL OF THE CONQUERORS THE FIRST GRIP.

THE SCENE AT BOLTON ST STATION. WAITING FOR THE CONQUERORS

WORKING UNDER DIFFICULTIES

IN THE STREETS

THE CAPTAINS SHAKE HANDS AT THE START OF THE 1913 CUP FINAL.

LIFTING T'COOP
The coming of age of a national institution

The second decade of the Crystal Palace Cup Finals were dominated by the North-East. However, although Newcastle United and Sunderland took part in six of the ten Finals, neither of them was able to walk away from the Palace with the trophy. Only on one occasion did Newcastle win the Cup during this period and that was after a replay at Goodison Park.

Newcastle were a great side at this time – League Champions on three occasions between 1905 and 1909; fourth, three times; five FA Cup Finals (only once the winner); and appeared in one losing semi-final.

Their neighbours, Sunderland, made it to the Final in 1913 and were described as the "Team of all the Talents" – a team of the best footballers in England at the time. If the First World War had not cruelly taken so many young lives, this team would have created records second to none. But it was not to be!

As it transpired, other teams were more successful in the Cup Final. Clubs that have not reached this stage again – Barnsley, Bradford City – and a certain Manchester club who had recently changed their name from Newton Heath, won the Cup for the first time. Ominously, the newer Merseyside club, Liverpool (now based at Anfield) made it to their first Final in 1914. Despite this, the most successful side in this period was still Aston Villa continuing the run that had started in the 1890s.

Even the trophy itself was changed again. After the second trophy was copied and replicas given to the Cup-winning Manchester United team, a third Cup was commissioned and was fought for at the 1911 Final.

This second decade also brought a change for the Crystal Palace authorities. They had been limited by the fact that the Football Association would guarantee the use of the ground for the FA Cup Final only from one year to the next. At last, in 1905 the FA granted the Crystal Palace Company a five-year deal. This meant that the Company were now disposed to make improvements to the ground to the benefit of all the spectators.

Crowds too continued to be large, but there were dips in the attendance when less attractive sides visited the stadium. Nevertheless, when Aston Villa took on Newcastle in 1905, another six-figure crowd saw the event and when they returned in 1913 to see off the "Team of all the Talents", a world record attendance at the Crystal Palace was reached – 120,081.

The crowning glory came in 1914 when the King himself attended a Cup Final and football was at last accepted as a sport of universal interest. Unfortunately, this was also to mark the end of the Crystal Palace's involvement with senior football – but not the FA Cup.

So let us look at the last ten FA Cup Finals to be held at the Crystal Palace.

LEFT: THE NEW CUP COMMISSIONED FOR THE 1911 FINAL.

BELOW: KING GEORGE V ATTENDED THE 1914 FINAL.

BELOW: SPECTATORS ARRIVE TO WATCH THE 1905 FINAL, SOME TAKING TO THE TREES FOR A BETTER VANTAGE POINT.

1905
ASTON VILLA
V
NEWCASTLE UNITED

When it came to Newcastle's visits to Crystal Palace, their many attributes counted for nothing. As Geoffrey Green says in The Official History of the FA Cup:

ABOVE: NEWCASTLE UNITED LINE UP FOR THE FINAL.

"The ground seemed to exert some strange hoodoo over them and they never showed their true form there. That closely linked, incisive approach work and finishing which carried them past everyone in the earlier rounds of the Cup and kept them season after season at the top of the League championship always seemed to desert them.

It might have been the lush turf at the Crystal Palace which slowed up their game. But the trouble became largely psychological and the harder they tried, the more difficult it became. They could not have had a sterner test than in their first encounter. In 1905 they found themselves pitted against the Cup veterans, Aston Villa. Newcastle were already League champions, but Villa had won the Cup three times (twice at the Palace). That, and the glorious weather on the day, was enough to draw a massive crowd of 101,117 people to Sydenham Hill.

It was such a warm sunny day that over 50,000 had assembled well over an hour before the kick off. But there was plenty to keep them occupied. The Crystal Palace band had been recruited to provide some music and this gave a few, bedecked in 'black-and-white or claret-and-blue top hats and caps and sunshades, in addition to large favours and impressive shades,' the inclination to 'parade to the admiration of other enthusiasts'".

Newcastle were the pre-match favourites - they had already done the double over Villa in the League - though there was strong support for Aston Villa as the team consisted of all English players. Even the Newcastle skipper Andy Aitken was caught by one journalist sitting out

LEFT: THE KICK OFF.

OPPOSITE PAGE: FRONT COVER OF 'THE DAILY GRAPHIC' APRIL 17 1905.

BELOW: THE VICTORIOUS ASTON VILLA TEAM.

on the hotel lawn days before, learning by heart the speech he was to deliver when he received the Cup.

At twenty minutes past three the Newcastle team took to the field in their black-and-white striped shirts and dark blue shorts and were photographed together with their officials in front of the south goal. Two minutes later the Villa team came out. They wore a black band on their left arm out of respect for the memory of the Lord Mayor of Birmingham, who had died during the week. They were photographed under the north goal.

Newcastle won the toss and chose to play with the sun and slight breeze at their backs. But the game was only three minutes old when a shot from Bache was parried by Lawrence in the

THE DAILY GRAPHIC, APRIL 17, 1905.

Player's "NAVY" Mixture

5d. per oz. Mild
4½d. per oz. Medium

John Player & Sons will forward testing Samples to applicants mentioning this paper.

THE DAILY GRAPHIC
ONE PENNY

LONDON: MONDAY, APRIL 17, 1905.

No. 4784—Vol. LXII.   REGISTERED AS A NEWSPAPER

"SOME SHOWERS; IMPROVING LATER."
(See page 3.)

WHAT HAPPENED TO VEITCH THROUGH A COLLISION WITH GEORGE

HAMPTON KICKS A SECOND GOAL FROM A FINE CENTRE BY HALL

HAMPTON SCORES FOR THE VILLA THREE MINUTES AFTER KICK OFF

ALEC LEAKE EXECUTES SOME MARVELLOUS PIECES OF HEADWORK

RUTHERFORD GETS A POINT BLANK FACER

COOL PLAY BY LAWRENCE

FRANK GILLETT

NORTH AGAINST MIDLANDS: PLAY IN THE MATCH BETWEEN ASTON VILLA AND NEWCASTLE UNITED AT THE CRYSTAL PALACE. (See page 9.)

213

ABOVE: HAMPTON, THIRD LEFT, SCORES HIS FIRST GOAL.

RIGHT: ASTON VILLA CELEBRATE AS THE NEWCASTLE GOALKEEPER REMOVES THE BALL FROM THE BACK OF THE NET.

Newcastle goal, only for it to fall in front of Harry Hampton who blasted it home. Play pulsated from end to end with Newcastle coming close through Howie who struck a shot over the bar but Brawn for Aston Villa also had his chances. In the second half, the game continued in the same manner with both sides having opportunities. Villa's tactics were not to Newcastle's liking. They played a fast long ball game, sweeping passes to the wings and in turn their wingers hit long deep crosses. It caught United flat.

With fifteen minutes to go, Villa broke away again and as in the first half, Lawrence saved the first long shot - from the outside-left Hall - but Hampton was there to pick up the loose ball to hammer it home.

So the game ended in a 2 - 0 victory for Aston Villa and the victorious captain was presented with the Cup by Lady Kinnaird.

Colin Veitch said: *"Our tactics were wrong. We went for defence when we should have attacked"*. The early goal rocked Newcastle's pre-match plan.

FAR LEFT: MAGNIFICENT DEFENCE
NEWCASTLE CLEAR WITHIN TWO
YARDS OF THE GOAL.

LEFT: THE NEWCASTLE SUPPORTERS
WERE ENTHUSIASTIC UNTIL THE END.

BELOW LEFT: ANOTHER VILLA
ATTACK.

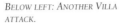

ABOVE: HOWARD SPENCER THE
VILLA CAPTAIN RECEIVES THE CUP.

BELOW: THE ASTON VILLA TEAM,
CUP WINNERS 1905.
(From Association Cup Winners –
Player's cigarette cards).

JOSEPH WILLIAM BACHE AND ALFRED EDWARD HALL

The Villa team which won the 1905 Final had as its spearhead, two friends whose partnership in the Villa forward line became legendary.

Joe Bache was born in Stourbridge in 1880 and as a teenager played for Stourbridge FC. Alf Hall came from Wordsley, Staffordshire, but he too joined Stourbridge. Bache transferred to Villa in 1900 for a fee of £100 and Hall followed in 1903, and it was here that they forged a unique partnership on the left of the forward line. Bache (inside-left) was a goal-scorer but he was particularly brilliant at the angled pass that enabled his team-mates, especially Hall, to run on to the ball and shoot.

Bache gained seven caps for England scoring after 12 minutes on his debut against Wales in 1903. Hall gained one cap against Ireland in 1910.

The partnership continued until 1913 when Hall left to join Millwall Athletic. He subsequently was badly gassed in the Great War and suffered ill-health throughout the rest of his life; he died on 17th October 1957.

Bache went on playing even after the War and after coaching in Germany, he became coach of Aston Villa in August 1927.

He died on 6th November 1960.

PLAYER'S CIGARETTES

SPENCER   MILES
GEORGE
PEARSON   WINDMILL
LEAKE
BRAWN   HALL
GARRATTY   HAMPTON   BACHE

ASSOCIATION CUP WINNERS
ASTON VILLA, 1905

1906
EVERTON
v
NEWCASTLE UNITED

The following season, Newcastle beat all opposition to get to the Palace, only to fail again, this time to Everton. Newcastle were favourites for the Cup having beaten Everton twice in the League. Both teams were referred to as *"the aristocrats of the world"* but evidently, it was not a particularly good match.

Expectations were high. Thousands of *"excursionists"* came down from the North and as usual invaded London . Some of them did not even make it to the Palace

When those fans lucky enough to have tickets arrived at the Palace, the scene became a sea of black and white and blue emblems. The Daily Graphic reported that *"black and white parasols, or blue and white top hats were favoured means of displaying partisanship; and a few minutes before play began a small procession paraded the ground, bearing the popular black and white parasols, and led by an enthusiast garbed as a black and white pitman, with a black and white pick"*. Meanwhile, bands of Everton supporters made their way to their places shouting *"Are we downhearted? - No!"*.

The first half was a great disappointment for the crowd of 75,609 people. Everton actually got the ball in the net early in the second half only to have the goal disallowed as Young was offside. This attempt was started by a cross from Jack Sharp whom the news reports claimed was the one outstanding player on the pitch. And it was Sharp who set up the only goal for Young in the seventy-seventh minute. As it was looking as if the game would end as a goalless draw, the ball was kicked out wide to Sharp, who kicked past Carr and outpaced him. He then centred the ball to Young who blasted it into the goal.

The reporter in the Liverpool Daily Echo had so little to comment on, that when the goal came he compared it to the San Francisco earthquake, which had occurred a week before.

"4:55 - At last a goal. Sandy Young a hero. Fireworks and miniature earthquakes galore - shades of San Francisco. 4:56 - The big glasshouse still shakes at its foundations".

Neither side played to its abilities and apparently did not show any appetite for the game. There was little goalmouth incident and the crowd became restless for some good action. For the non-committed, it might have been tempting to go across to the adjacent arena and watch the replayed Surrey Cup tie in which Dulwich Hamlet beat Croydon by three goals to one.

One correspondent wrote:
"Newcastle were feeble in the extreme. Their halves and backs could do nothing right - Aitken excepted - and the forwards were slow and their

BELOW: THE DAILY MIRROR'S VIEW OF THE MATCH.

EVERTON DEFEAT NEWCASTLE AT THE PALACE.

Curious snapshot of headwork by both teams outside the Newcastle goal. Seven of the men are in the air together.

Typical photograph of football partisans' eager intensity in watching their favourite players.

but instead spent the afternoon at the Zoological Gardens where *"there was a stampede for points of vantage from which to watch the feeding of the sea lions, and the gardens echoed with shouts of delight"* (Daily Graphic).

passes went astray with monotonous
regularity". Colin Veitch admitted that
this was one of the worst games of his
career.

ABOVE: PAINTING OF THE WINNING
EVERTON TEAM WITH CRYSTAL
PALACE BACKGROUND.

Athletic News made the comment
that such a big pitch did not help a
passing game, Newcastle needed a
different approach; "until Newcastle
make up their minds to play an open
game with long passing and plenty of
dash, I cannot see that they will ever
win the English Cup".

LEFT: FANS FROM THE NORTH LEAVE
WESTMINSTER FOR THE CRYSTAL
PALACE.

The Cup and medals on this
occasion were presented by Lord
Kinnaird, president of the Football
Association. In his speech, he expressed the "deep
sympathy of everybody for the American people in
the terrible disaster at
San Francisco".

BELOW LEFT: THE EVERTON TEAM,
CUP WINNERS 1906.
(From Association Cup Winners –
Player's cigarette cards).

There was a
sequel to this game
in that both Everton
and Newcastle were
fined £50 each for
fielding weak teams
in Football League
games during the
run-up to the big day.
Neither side were too
bothered and both
repeated the offence
again but as Newcastle
were to find, the fines
became heavier and
heavier.

JOSEPH WILLIAM HENRY (HARRY) MAKEPEACE

Harry was born in Middlesbrough in
August 1881 but moved to Liverpool at the age
of ten. So it was while playing for Liverpool
Schools that his football career began. Joining
Everton in 1902, he was their wing-half until
the end of the First World War. During this
time he gained a Cup winner's medal (1906),
was a Cup finalist (1907) and earned four
England caps. He was a quiet man off the
field but on it he was capable of putting in
crunching tackles and had a particular skill for precision passing.
Harry also had other attributes. He played cricket for Lancashire
(1906 - 1930) and for England in four Tests against Australia.

After finishing his football career, he went to Holland to coach
and in the 1930s he coached Marine Crosby.

He died on 19th December 1952.

69

1907

EVERTON
V
SHEFFIELD WEDNESDAY

After two defeats in two years, Newcastle must have been acquiring quite a complex about visiting the Crystal Palace. However, this was nothing compared to the events of the 1906-7 campaign. In the first round, Newcastle were drawn at home against a team from the lower reaches of the Southern League First Division. The minnows promptly went up to Tyneside and defeated the Magpies 1 - 0. Ironically, the minor team was called Crystal Palace. At least Newcastle had the compensation of winning the League title again!

BELOW: A SOUVENIR GIVEN AWAY WITH 'THE WEEKLY DISPATCH'.

So the Cup was left for others to fight over. In the end, the finalists were Everton, the previous winners, and Sheffield Wednesday. Everton were third in the First Division and, with ten players from the team that had won the Cup in 1906, they were hot favourites. Sheffield Wednesday were composed of a number of plucky youngsters and some veterans from previous campaigns. Only Crawshaw remained from the side that had won the Cup in 1896. He admitted that it was going to be a tough game, and added: *"Now look here, I'm not going to say we are going to win, and I'm not going to say we shall lose. We are going to try to win. We shall go all the way, and while the ball is rolling you can bet we have a chance. We shall keep going to the end".* As ever the Cup had a mind of its own!

Evidently the game itself did not live up to expectations, Everton did not play up to their usual standards and it was the Wednesday who opened the scoring. They had the ball in the net after nine minutes, only for the "goal" to be disallowed for an offside decision.

This only spurred them on and in the twenty-first minute *"they enjoyed the reward of plucky endeavour. The goal, which originated in a square cross from Chapman on the outside-right, was*

the sequel to a shot which possibly was already "through". Many of the Sheffield players were strenuously appealing for a goal when the ball came out to Stewart, who with a characteristic drive, such as he had signally failed to reproduce in the international at Newcastle, relieved the referee of a difficult responsibility" (Daily Mail).

For the rest of the first half, Everton attacked relentlessly and eventually their efforts were rewarded three minutes from half-time; Sharp, the outside-right, hit an oblique shot into the net.

The second half consisted mainly of Everton pressurising the Sheffield defence but as so often when a side is committed to out-and-out attack, a counter-attack can be devastating. So it was! Five minutes from the end, the Wednesday broke away taking the ball to the by-line. Bradshaw crossed the ball speculatively across the goal only for Simpson to head it into the net.

It was a hard game for both sides. Crawshaw recalled, years later, how Chapman twice had to stop playing while he slipped his cartilage back into place. However, the Daily Mail correspondent summed up the game as follows:

BELOW AND RIGHT: THE DAILY MIRROR REPORTS ON THE MATCH.

The Daily Mirror

THE MORNING JOURNAL WITH THE SECOND LARGEST NET SALE.

No. 1304   MONDAY, APRIL 22, 1907.   One Halfpenny.

SHEFFIELD WEDNESDAY WIN THE CUP-TIE FINAL.

INCIDENTS IN THE CUP-TIE FINAL AT THE CRYSTAL PALACE.

"It was not a day for heroes. Perhaps the chief personal success was obtained by Mr Whittaker, whose refereeing approached perfection. Still, if the game was not worthy of an attendance of 84,594 (the official return), it was a fascinating struggle and an average Final.

The sympathies of the crowd were significantly expressed by the comparative coldness with which the victory was received".

There was only one other notable factor about the match. The referee, Nat Whittaker, went into the match under something of a cloud. The day before, he had been fined one guinea for delaying a match in March after arriving twelve minutes late.

LORD KINNAIRD   LORD   LORD ALVERSTONE
T. CRAWSHAW.   ROSEBERY

THOMAS HENRY CRAWSHAW

Tom Crawshaw was born in Sheffield at the end of 1872 and lived to the ripe old age of 87. After playing for a number of local sides he started at Hillsborough in 1894. The Wednesday were having a good spell at this time and Tom was a stalwart in the Wednesday defence at centre half. During his time there, Wednesday won the Football League twice (1903 and 1904), the Second Division championship in 1900 and the FA Cup in 1896 and 1907. Crawshaw himself won 10 England caps between 1895 and 1904 scoring once.

In 1908 he left Sheffield and joined Chesterfield Town and subsequently had a brief spell as Secretary of Glossop FC.

He retired to run a newsagent's shop in Sheffield.

ABOVE: A POSTCARD SHOWING A SCENE FROM THE MATCH AND THE TEAMS.

BELOW LEFT: LORD ALVERSTONE PRESENTS THE CUP TO SHEFFIELD WEDNESDAY'S CAPTAIN, CRAWSHAW.

BELOW: THE SHEFFIELD WEDNESDAY TEAM, CUP WINNERS 1907. (From Association Cup Winners – Player's cigarette cards).

PLAYER'S CIGARETTES

LAYTON   BURTON
LYALL
BRITTLETON   BARTLETT
CRAWSHAW
CHAPMAN   SIMPSON
WILSON
BRADSHAW   STEWART

ASSOCIATION CUP WINNERS
SHEFFIELD WEDNESDAY, 1907

1908
NEWCASTLE UNITED
V
WOLVERHAMPTON WANDERERS

FAR RIGHT: UNITED'S CUP PARTY START THEIR JOURNEY TO THE CRYSTAL PALACE IN A PROCESSION OF HORSE DRAWN CARRIAGES.

The 1908 Final deserves to go down in FA Cup history as one of the shock results alongside Leeds v Sunderland (1973) and Liverpool v Wimbledon (1988). Newcastle, the League champions in 1905 and 1907, met Wolves, a mid-table Second Division side. The Sporting Life on the morning of the game felt *"there is no comparison on paper and...Newcastle should win in handsome style"*.

BELOW: MATCH DAY TICKET FOR ONE OF THE BEST SEATS IN THE STADIUM.

Newcastle were a team of international stars and the hottest favourites for years. Wolves had beaten Fulham 6 - 0 in the semi-final (still a record score) but they were made up of mainly local lads, strong and workmanlike - yet surely no match for the mighty Magpies. Newcastle were the rich club, their annual income being four times that of the Wolves

£4,500 turnover. Newcastle were a team of *"science, skill and artistry... many members of the team are jugglers of the ball, and of every subtlety in the game"* as The Sporting Life reminded its readers. Wolves by contrast were gritty and stubborn but these were valuable commodities on the day.

Not only was the result shocking but so was the weather. *"Rain in torrents and pitilessly driven sleet, alternated with heavy snow showers"* made the banks around the ground slippery and the playing surface heavy. *"The most sensible dress of the freak variety was wolf-skin"*. On the same day, the games at Southampton and Reading in the Southern League were postponed because of snow.

Newcastle, in the opinion of The Sporting Life on the Friday before the game, should have won handsomely unless Wolves could *"worry the Novocastrians off the game"*. In fact, this is what happened. Newcastle had sufficient chances in the first half-hour to take the initiative. Rutherford hit wide from a good position after 18 minutes. *"The pace became warm, the Newcastle middle line forwarding pass after pass to their comrades in front who dodged and dribbled with captivating skill"*. Appleyard of Newcastle hit a 30 yard shot three feet wide and in one ten minute spell the ball did not leave the Wolves' half.

The turning point came in a short spell just before half time. With seven minutes to the break, the game was goalless but when Newcastle went to the dressing rooms they were two goals down. First, Harrison beat two men, put in a cross which McCracken, the Newcastle captain, cleared but only straight to the Rev. Hunt. He advanced a few yards and hit a chest-high bender past Lawrence who reached the ball but could not stop it. Then, three minutes later, Hedley, the Wolves

RIGHT: THE DAILY MIRROR'S MATCH REPORT.

centre forward, dummied past Veitch, slipped around McCracken and hit in a low drive to send the Wolves' fans wild.

Newcastle started the second half in a more direct manner and the Wolves' defence showed some signs of weakening. Veitch moved up to become a sixth forward while Wilson, the Newcastle winger, was troubling Hunt. Rutherford put in a difficult corner and when the ball broke free, Howie hit the ball into the corner of the net.

Wolves were only bowed not broken. Harrison, their right winger and the man of the match, defended well and gave Pudan, his marker, and McWilliam, the right half, a terrible time. Just after being denied by Lawrence, he beat McCracken and Pudan ran in from 40 yards and beat the keeper from the edge of the box. Wolves had beaten the biggest favourites for many years; 3-1.

Newcastle had ninety percent of the game but they were well beaten. Nevertheless, their captain, Gardner, was philosophical about it:

"Never mind. We shall come again, and our turn will surely arrive some day".

ABOVE: ACTION FROM THE 1908 FINAL.

LEFT: NEWCASTLE UNITED'S FA CUP FINAL SPECIAL JERSEY.

ABOVE AND RIGHT: ILLUSTRATIONS FROM 'THE WOLVES STORY'.

BELOW: THE WOVERHAMPTON WANDERERS TEAM, CUP WINNERS 1908. (From Association Cup Winners – Player's cigarette cards).

ABOVE: THE VICTORIOUS WOLVERHAMPTON TEAM.

BELOW: 'A WOLF IN SHEEP'S CLOTHING'.

REV. K R G HUNT

Kenneth Reginald Gunnery Hunt was born in Oxford on 24th February 1884. He truly represented the Corinthian spirit and epitomised the "sporting vicar" - described by Sporting Life as a "superb tackler and placer". After playing for Trent College (1901-04) and then Oxford University (1905 - 08), he played for a number of professional and amateur clubs - Leyton, Wolverhampton Wanderers, Crystal Palace, Oxford City and, of course, Corinthians.

Hunt was ordained in 1909 and taught at Highgate School from 1908 to 1945. Yet he still managed to participate fully in sporting activity. He won a footballing gold medal in the 1908 Olympic Games. He was capped twice for England in 1911 - against Scotland and Wales, as well as making 20 appearances as an amateur international. In 1913, he played for Oxford City in the Amateur Cup Final and replay and in 1908 he was at right-half for Wolves in the FA Cup Final. He holds the distinction of being the only, and no doubt the last, amateur in the twentieth century not only to play in a Cup Final on the winning side but also to score a goal. In later life, he was a distinguished member of the FA Council until his death in April 1949.

1909

BRISTOL CITY
V
MANCHESTER UNITED

The conclusion of the 1909 FA Cup campaign brought together two newcomers to the Palace – Manchester United and Bristol City. There was great anticipation from the fact that at last there was to be another north versus south tussle. The two teams were also neck-and-neck in the League; Manchester United leading Bristol by just one point. Unfortunately, as so often happens the game itself did not live up to the expectation.

Nevertheless, the crowd were described in The Daily Graphic as *"happy and hopeful to the last. It was a particularly well-dressed crowd, too, and a better behaved one it would be impossible to bring together. While the players were in the arena the crowd was all of a stir and quiver; and when the fighting passion got into its blood it roared and swayed and surged unceasingly. That mighty sea of faces underwent all the barometrical changes from stormy to set fair".*

RIGHT: THE FANS WELCOME HOME MANCHESTER UNITED.

BELOW: THE ONLY GOAL OF THE GAME.

"Let him play. He might get a goal and if he does we can afford to carry him".

Bristol City were also hampered by the loss of Rippon and Marr before the game and Hayes, the Manchester United full back, played with a broken rib.

Though many expected Manchester United to romp to victory, the issue was decided by the single goal – in the 22nd minute. Halse's shot rebounded off the crossbar and Turnbull guided it into the net. On a couple of occasions, the Bristol forwards were presented with an open goal but failed to exploit the situation.

RIGHT CENTRE: MOGER OF MANCHESTER UNITED FALLS IN MAKING A SAVE.

As both teams normally wore red, they both decided to wear an alternative strip. Manchester United chose an all-white kit with a thin red line at the neck and wrists, the red rose of Lancashire on the breast and a distinctive red chevron from shoulder to breast bone. Bristol City wore royal blue shirts and white shorts.

Billy Meredith had been the hero of the victorious Manchester City team in 1904, while his team-mate, George Wall, had been to the Palace only weeks before, scoring two goals in the England victory over Scotland.

Nevertheless, although Meredith mesmerised the Bristol defence, it was Sandy Turnbull, who had also played for Manchester City in 1904, who scored the only goal of the match. Yet it was only by chance that he played because he was suffering with a knee injury, but his captain Charlie Roberts said:

We tend to think of fixture congestion as a modern phenomenon but the 1909 United team were just as hard-pressed. After the Final, they stayed in London until the Tuesday afternoon, returning to Manchester to play Woolwich Arsenal at 6 o'clock that evening. On the Thursday following, they played their last league game of that term at Bradford City.

One consequence of the 1909 Final was the loss of the second FA Cup trophy. This time the perpetrators were not robbers but well-wishers in Manchester. They wanted to have a lasting reminder of the great victory and so they commissioned a silversmith to make a replica.

ABOVE: GOALMOUTH ACTION.

CHARLIE ROBERTS

Charlie Roberts was born in Darlington on 6th April 1883 and after a brief spell at Grimsby Town he joined United in April 1904 for a fee of £700 at the age of 21.

As centre-half and captain of United he was the pivot around which the whole of their game revolved. He directed play and was brilliant at reading a game. Under his stewardship, United won the League Championship in 1908 and 1911, and of course the FA Cup in 1909. Roberts also picked up three England caps (all in 1905) and should have got more but was possibly ignored because of his union activities (he was a founder member of the Players' Union and later its Chairman).

In 1912 he moved to Oldham for £1300 where he retired from playing and was manager at Boundary Park from July 1921 to December 1922. He died in August 1939.

On the 9th July 1910, the FA Council met in Cromer and decided that *"the present Football Association Challenge Cup, having been duplicated without the consent of the Association, be withdrawn from competition and a new cup offered, the design of which shall be registered"*.

Following the Cup Final victory, John Davies gave United the then huge sum of £60,000 to purchase a site and build a new stadium, Old Trafford, to which United moved in February 1910.

BELOW: THE MANCHESTER UNITED TEAM, CUP WINNERS 1909. (From Association Cup Winners – Player's cigarette cards).

1910
BARNSLEY V NEWCASTLE UNITED

After a Final where the participants were newcomers, the 1910 Final was a return to normal business. Once again, Newcastle fought off all opposition to reach their third Final. This was getting to be a habit. One fan even remarked:

"Well, if Newcastle can't win the Cup, they ought to be given it for good attendance".

This time, it was another Second Division team that stood in their way. But Barnsley were a dour, battling side that were unlikely to yield easily.

This was a new experience for the Barnsley faithful. To come south to the Crystal Palace was apparently a very strange experience for the supporters of Barnsley. When the train arrived at Balham on the return journey to Victoria, one of them was heard to remark:

"Ba-laam. Why I thowt it were in Egypt".

London was like a foreign city to them and

Londoners were foreigners. *"Why can't they be neighbourly? They stare at us like we were pot-cats"* (ornaments normally found on the Northern mantelpiece).

The crowd was a particularly happy one. It included fifty trippers who had won a competition organised by the Sheffield Independent. Their prizes were free tickets to the match. However, it was not only a partisan crowd. Thousands of southerners came along just to see what they hoped would be a good game.

Newcastle approached this game somewhat differently. They abandoned their silky footballing style and instead hustled the Tykes. They had the wind behind them in the first half and attacked Barnsley constantly. The Tykes, for their part, seemed prepared to defend in depth and catch Newcastle on the breaks.

Then in the 38th minute, they broke again and with a number of passing movements, the ball reached Lillycrop on the left, who touched it to Tufnell. He shot past Lawrence in the Newcastle goal with ease. Despite further Newcastle attacks, the teams turned round with Barnsley still in the lead.

In the second half, Newcastle changed their tactics. Wilson and Higgins swopped places on the left of the forward line and they played a more open game. Attack followed attack and the

BELOW: THE MATCH PROGRAMME.

RIGHT: MEARNS SAVES FOR BARNSLEY.

BELOW: THE NEWCASTLE UNITED TEAM, CUP WINNERS 1910. (From Association Cup Winners – Player's cigarette cards).

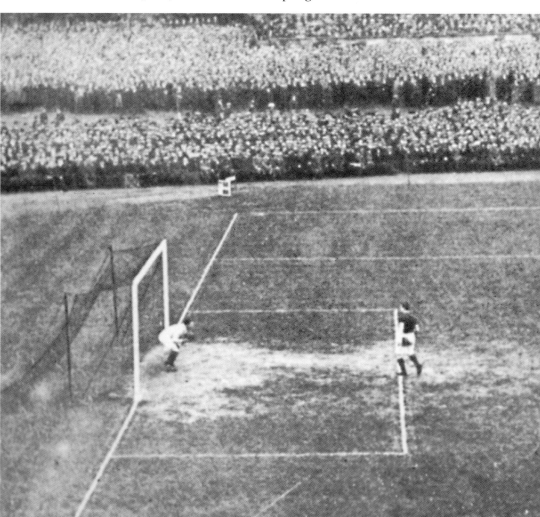

question in everyone's mind was whether Barnsley could hold on to that slender lead. The equalising goal when it came (ten minutes from the end), caught everyone by surprise. Barnsley's secretary-manager, Arthur Fairclough stated:

"My wife had removed the red ribbons from her umbrella to tie on the Cup in celebration of our victory, Tufnell having scored. In fact, at the request of Mr F J Wall, the FA Secretary, I had completed arrangements for the Barnsley M P, Sir Joseph Walton, to receive the trophy. Just as I sat down Newcastle equalised through Rutherford to make the score 1 - 1. And we lost the replay!".

In fact, there was a strong suspicion that Rutherford was offside when he scored. But unlike today's commentators, the reporters of the day deferred to the superior judgement of the referee, Mr Ibbotson. Part of the problem was that the Press box was near the halfway line and so it was difficult for journalists to get a good view of the goal areas.

So hostilities resumed the following Thursday at Goodison Park in front of a large crowd. Newcastle seemed happier in a more compact stadium. This time they reverted to their natural game with Rutherford and Howie being particularly brilliant. Two goals (including the first penalty in a Cup Final) by Shepherd were enough to take the Cup to Newcastle - at last!

ABOVE: CARTOON BASED ON A POPULAR SONG OF 1910 - 'SATURDAY-ATTUR-DAY AFTERNOON'.

FAR LEFT: AT THE START OF THE REPLAY THE TOSS, "WIRED FROM MANCHESTER TO LONDON IN NINE MINUTES BY THE THORNE BAKER TELECTOGRAPH".

LEFT: SILVER AND BRASS VESTA (MATCHBOX) COMMEMORATING NEWCASTLE'S VICTORY.

JOCK (JOHN) RUTHERFORD

Jock was a regular in that great Newcastle side that achieved so much in the period before the Great War. He went to St James Park in 1902 and at outside-right won League Championship medals in 1905, 1907, and 1909; and an FA Cup winner's medal in 1910. He also played in those losing Finals of 1905, 1906, 1908 and 1911.

He was a very strong player and was extremely fast with good control and could centre the ball perfectly. He played 11 times for England, never on the losing side, scoring three times.

In 1913, he moved south to Woolwich Arsenal for a fee of £800 later playing for other London teams during and after the War. He finally retired in 1927 and for a while was coach to Tufnell Park FC. Jock then became a London licensee. He died in 1963.

1911

BRADFORD CITY
V
NEWCASTLE UNITED

There was a new Cup to win in 1911 – the third to be used and this was the one used until 1992. The second Cup was given to Lord Kinnaird in recognition of his services to football and, ominously, the new Cup was the work of Messrs Fattorini and Sons of Bradford, Yorkshire.

Following their success in 1910, Newcastle might have been forgiven for believing that they could repeat the feat a year later. Once again, they sailed through the rounds of the Cup competition to get to another Final at the Crystal Palace. Again, they were up against a team from Yorkshire – this time it was Bradford City who, according to the football afficienados, were not expected to provide much opposition, despite the fact that they had conceded only one goal en route to the Final.

Less scientific observers had other views. Some claimed that it was no coincidence that eight teams whose names began with 'B' had won the Cup, and that there were eight letters in the name 'Bradford'. Even Old Moore predicted that this year's winner's name began with 'B'.

By all accounts, Bradford did not play particularly well either – with the exception of their backs, Campbell and Taylor. Newcastle with all their skill could not penetrate the Bradford defence. In contrast, Newcastle had little to do – the Bradford forwards hardly threatened them.

"Newcastle had the wind behind them in the first half and played badly. Against the wind they did better, and their most dangerous attacks came in the second half, when they were facing it. Mellors then had difficult shots to save from Veitch,

ABOVE: THE THIRD FA CUP COMMISSIONED FOR 1911. MADE IN BRADFORD (REPLACED IN 1992).

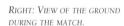

RIGHT: VIEW OF THE GROUND DURING THE MATCH.

Rutherford, Wilson and Stewart". But neither side could score that vital goal.

For the fifth time, United were spellbound by the Crystal Palace. The injured Peter McWilliam, who watched the game from the stand later said: *"We could not play any sort of game. We could not show any kind of form. We were like a lot of beginners and I cannot think of any side that gave such positively wretched displays as we did"*.

Evidently this was a strange Final to be present at. The crowd apparently were muted and showed little excitement. Although there were rosettes and favours in evidence there were not many for the two teams participating. And some were so bored that they wandered off before the game finished to have a look at the exhibits in the Crystal Palace grounds that had been built for the Festival of Empire.

Twenty minutes from the close of the game a voice near the Press seats broke the deadly silence: *"Let's have some football!"*, was the exhortation to the players.

One spectator however was impressed. He was the journalist W T Stead who at the age of 62 attended his first Final with his friend G R Sims. He refers to *"the constant shifting and changing of colours, the zebra-striped Northumbrians and the orange and crimson Yorkshiremen perpetually crossing and mixing on the green of the arena"*. He was struck by the discipline, dexterity and self-control of the players. But what impressed him most of all was the great crowd, an immense sea of faces which *"remind me of nothing so much as a shell-strewn, pebbly beach, rising shorewards"*.

Still, the game ended 0 – 0. A vote of thanks to the Earl of Plymouth was proposed by Lord Portsmouth, who remarked that if the Festival of Empire at the Crystal Palace produced such a truly British scene as that witnessed that afternoon it was bound to be a great success.

So, hostilities had to be resumed four days later at Old Trafford, Manchester, where Bradford won with a scrambled goal. The Newcastle jinx continued.

BELOW: THE NEWCASTLE UNITED TEAM, DRAWN GAME 1911. (From Association Cup Winners – Player's cigarette cards).

ABOVE: THE BRADFORD CITY TEAM, CUP WINNERS 1911. (From Association Cup Winners – Player's cigarette cards).

FESTIVAL OF EMPIRE

In 1911, the year of King George V's coronation, the Festival of Empire was held at the Crystal Palace. For this occasion the British Empire was constructed in miniature in the Palace grounds, complete with three-quarter size replicas of the Parliament buildings of all the Commonwealth countries. These replicas, their exteriors architecturally complete to the smallest detail, were built of timber and plaster. Exhibitions of the products of the appropriate country were on view inside.

On a miniature railway, aptly named the "All Red Route", visitors could tour the Empire and stop off, amongst other places, at a South African diamond mine, an Indian tea-plantation and a Canadian logging camp. Other attractions included a Pageant of the history of London with parts taken by 25,000 London schoolchildren. This was the biggest show ever put on at the Palace but although it attracted hundreds of thousands of visitors from all over the world it did not save the Crystal Palace Company from bankruptcy that same year.

LEFT: THE FAIRGROUND.

RIGHT: THE ALL RED ROUTE RAILWAY.

FAR RIGHT: THE KING AND QUEEN ARE GIVEN 'A GUARD OF HONOUR', AFTER OPENING THE FESTIVAL.

Right: The Canadian parliament building.

Below: Festival of Empire 1911, looking back towards the Palace.

1912
BARNSLEY
v
WEST BROMWICH ALBION

The new Cup stayed in Yorkshire, for in 1912 Barnsley of the Second Division got to their second Final in three years. Evidently, it was not a poor game despite the lack of goals – particularly in the second half.

However, it was a smaller crowd than in previous years – 54,556. Though there were many from the two competing towns, it was a largely impartial crowd, and they were very subdued. One correspondent blamed the languid nature of the crowd on two factors. Firstly, *"the boy scouts were busy with collection boxes for the Titanic fund, and were a reminder of the terrible disaster. The thought of the death cries of hundreds of helpless people was enough to interfere with the joy of the people".* Secondly, the lack of a southern team in the Final reduced the interest in the game. *"Thousands did not care tuppence which side won so long as they saw a good game".*

RIGHT: W H SMITH & SONS SOUVENIR CARD AND PROGRAMME.

RIGHT: THE CLARENCE HOTEL, BARNSLEY FOOTBALL CLUB HEADQUARTERS.

The key to the game was in the two defences. Both sides had skilled and resolute backs who dominated the opposing forwards. Even when the backs were beaten, the forwards of either side, possibly from over-excitement, failed to seize their chances, though each goal had more than one remarkable narrow escape.

For the first twenty minutes, West Bromwich were on top but they failed to take advantage. Then Barnsley got to grips with the game and put together some spiriting attacks from Bartrop and Lillycrop. But the great defence of Pennington and Cook withheld the challenge, and in the last few minutes of the first half, the *"Throstles"* fought back, particularly through their winger, Shearman.

In the second half, Barnsley showed more vigour and speed *"and for the remainder of the match they were quite the equals of West Bromwich at all points".* But the Albion continued to play smart football all round.

There was one occasion when Tufnell hit the upright. *"That one daring dash and fierce fusillade, wherein the Albion citadel escaped by a sheer good fortune, stands out as a prominent incident in the many fierce exchanges of a hotly contested second half".*

In the replay at Sheffield, the score was still goalless at the end of normal time, and so they went on to play an extra half an hour. Only two minutes later, Glendinning, the Barnsley half-back, beat a couple of players and passed to Tufnell at inside right. Away he went, dribbled through the West Bromwich defence and shot past Pearson - into the Albion goal. So Barnsley became the third team from the Second Division to lift the Cup.

Three seasons had now gone by where the Final at Crystal Palace had been inconclusive, with no provision for extra time, and the replay being staged at a northern venue. This led to a public outcry because many had paid large sums of money to get to the Final only to be disappointed not to see a result.

Some wanted the game to be played to a conclusion however long it took. Eventually, the FA Rules Revision Committee recommended that Rule 20 should be altered, to provide an extra half-hour to be played in Final ties which result in a draw. As it happened, this rule did not have to be invoked until 1970, when after the period of extra time, a replay was still necessary.

ABOVE: THE BARNSLEY TEAM FOR 1912.

FAR LEFT: A SENSATIONAL SAVE BY COOPER, FOR BARNSLEY.

LEFT: THE WEST BROMWICH ALBION, DRAWN GAME 1912. (From Association Cup Winners – Player's cigarette cards).

ABOVE: THE BARNSLEY TEAM, CUP WINNERS 1912. (From Association Cup Winners – Player's cigarette cards).

FAR LEFT: A CARTOON ON THE FRONT OF 'THE CHELSEA FC CHRONICLE' (CHELSEA WERE BEATEN BY BARNSLEY IN THE SEMI FINAL).

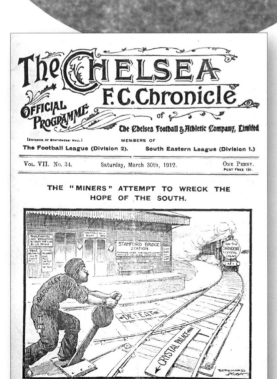

HARRY TUFNELL

Harry Tufnell was born in Burton-on-Trent on 2nd March 1886. He signed for Bury in 1907 and stayed for two seasons. In that period, he only made five appearances in the first team scoring one goal.

In 1909, he signed for Barnsley and made his debut as an inside-forward on 2nd September against Hull City (Barnsley lost 1 - 2). In his eleven years at Barnsley he made 200 League appearances (60 goals) and 29 appearances in the FA Cup (10 goals). Of course, he scored in each of Barnsley's two appearances in the FA Cup Final, scoring the winner in the 1912 Final replay.

Tufnell last played for Barnsley away at Birmingham on 14th February 1920. He then transferred to Wakefield City as player-manager but stayed for only one season, 1920-21, moving on to Doncaster Rovers as player-manager. Harry Tufnell died in 1959.

85

1913
ASTON VILLA
V
SUNDERLAND

BELOW: STEWARD'S BADGE FOR THE 1913 FINAL.

As the Newcastle challenge faded, their north-east neighbours were nurturing a team that was destined to emulate them (until war intervened). Known as the "Team of all the Talents", Sunderland won the League championship in 1913 and made it to their first Cup Final.

Who did they meet there?

Not only the team that had fought them nip-and-tuck for the championship but one of the most experienced Cup fighters, having won the trophy four times - Aston Villa.

This was the first time that the top two League teams met in a Final.

These then were the perfect ingredients to bring a world record attendance at the time of 120,081.

RIGHT: THE VICTORIOUS ASTON VILLA TEAM.

Thousands stood on the southern slopes, on what became a mudslide, and the majority did not see much of the game. When one man professed not even to have seen a blade of grass he was almost envied. Most were happy to be at this monumental event!

BELOW: TOMMY BARBER SCORES THE WINNING GOAL.

By all accounts, it was a good Final in parts. In 'The Only Authentic Record of the Cup' the game was described as follows:

"It was fast and open at the beginning, but the promise of a brilliant start was not kept up - chiefly because the backs on either side soon took to high kicking, and was also anxious to dispose of the remotest possibility of danger by getting the ball away into touch. It was seldom, indeed, that either line of forwards justified their high reputation. There was little or none of the brilliant passing at top speed which had distinguished the Villa in previous victorious years. On both sides too much time was wasted in mere pattern-weaving, and when a concerted attack was delivered the obvious thing was

always done at the critical moment........".

But it certainly had incident. Wallace missed a penalty for Villa early on; then Hardy was forced to leave the field with a leg injury for some ten minutes. With a reserve goalkeeper, this was

THE DAILY MIRROR, APRIL 21, 1913

121,919 AT THE ENGLISH CUP FINAL : RECORD CROWD SEES A THRILLING MATCH.

BOTTOM LEFT: THE EARL OF PLYMOUTH PRESENTS THE CUP TO THE ASTON VILLA CAPTAIN.
(The Graphic).

BELOW: THE ASTON VILLA TEAM, CUP WINNERS 1913.
(From Association Cup Winners – Player's cigarette cards).

PLAYER'S CIGARETTES

ASSOCIATION CUP WINNERS
ASTON VILLA. 1913.

Sunderland's opportunity. But Richardson and Buchan missed some golden chances. Then Hardy came back on the pitch, and Sunderland's chance was gone.

Fifteen minutes from time, the goal that settled it came from a set-piece. Wallace took the cornerkick and it was headed in by Barber, just as Clem Stephenson had forecast. Apparently, early in the game, Stephenson, the Villa inside-left, turned to Barber and said: *"I dreamed last night that we should win 1 - 0 with a goal by Barber"*.

CHARLES WILLIAM WALLACE

Charlie Wallace had quite a connection with the Crystal Palace. He was one of the players that John Robson recruited from the north-east to form the new Crystal Palace team in 1905. He started as a reserve but soon got in to the first team and became extremely popular with the fans. He helped Palace to success in that first season when they won the Southern League Second Division championship. He was spotted by Aston Villa and in the close season of 1907, he moved to Villa Park. For the next nine seasons, Wallace was a regular in the Villa team at outside-right, winning Cup winner's medals in 1913 and 1920 as well as the League Championship in 1910. He made 314 appearances for Villa before moving to Oldham in 1921 where he eventually retired. Later, he was in charge of Villa's junior team and for many years after the Second World War was a steward and dressing room attendant at Villa Park.

Charlie Wallace was the first player to miss a penalty in an FA Cup Final (which he did in 1913). He played for England on three occasions.

1914
BURNLEY
V
LIVERPOOL

RIGHT: COMMEMORATIVE SERVIETTE.

TOP OPPOSITE PAGE : VIEW OF THE CROWD AND THE GAME.

BELOW: THE BURNLEY TEAM LINE-UP IN A MATCH PRIOR TO THE FINAL.

By 1914 the number of entries for the FA Challenge Cup competition had increased to 476 clubs. From these, Burnley and Liverpool, two mid-table sides in the First Division, got to the Final.

Reports of the game talk of it being a somewhat average affair with little good football and that the crowd of 72,000 were subdued most of the time. However, the Sunday Times report of the action describes a number of instances of one goalmouth being threatened and then the other.

On a blazing hot day, Liverpool did a good deal of attacking. Nicholl particularly put in a terrific shot, only for Taylor to get his head to it. The force was so great that the full-back was knocked out for a minute or so. But the several other Liverpool attacks were repulsed by the solid Burnley defence.

FAR RIGHT: PART OF THE 72,000 CROWD ENJOY THE MATCH.

RIGHT: THE LIVERPOOL TEAM PHOTO, TAKEN PRIOR TO THEIR TRIP TO LONDON.

Later in the first half, the pace slackened and Burnley moved on to the offensive and it was Liverpool that had to do the defending. But it was in the fifty-eighth minute that the deadlock was broken. Burnley had a throw-in near the corner flag. Freeman got the ball and kicked it on the volley, well wide of Campbell in the Liverpool goal, straight into the net. Liverpool kept trying to score but it was not to be and the game ended 1-0.

This match was significant in the sense that this was the first attended by royalty. A change was taking place in those who attended matches; it was becoming respectable. *"In the last two or three years League matches at Stamford Bridge and*

ABOVE: FREEMAN SCORES THE BURNLEY GOAL.

RIGHT CENTRE: THE KING STANDS FOR THE NATIONAL ANTHEM.

BELOW RIGHT: THE KING PRESENTS THE CUP TO THE BURNLEY CAPTAIN.

BELOW: THE KING ARRIVES AT THE PALACE TO WATCH THE GAME.

elsewhere have been attended by persons to whom the dangerous epithet fashionable might be applied. Professional football of the best kind is no longer regarded as a spectacle suitable only for the proletariat. The King's presence at the Cup Final, let us hope, will put an end to the old snobbish notion that true blue sportsmen ought to ignore games played by those who cannot afford to play without being paid for their services".

So, just before three o'clock King George V left Buckingham Palace by car, and arrived at Sydenham at 3.20 pm to cheering crowds. He was met by Lord Derby and Lord Kinnaird, and it was the King himself who presented the Cup to the captain of the victorious Burnley team - the last time the Cup was contested at Crystal Palace.

As the storm clouds gathered over Europe, war was declared in August 1914 and the

Crystal Palace was taken over by the Royal Navy and became a training and transit camp - known as HMS Victory VI. There was one more Cup Final before competitive football was abandoned for the duration. This "khaki" Final was held at Old Trafford. The Crystal Palace dominance of the FA Cup was over.

ABOVE: BURNLEY FANS CELEBRATE ON THEIR RETURN HOME.

LEFT: A SECTION OF THE CENTRE SPREAD IN THE DAILY GRAPHIC.

BERTRAM CLEWLEY FREEMAN

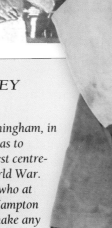

Born in Handsworth, Birmingham, in October 1885, Bert Freeman was to become one of England's greatest centre-forwards prior to the First World War. His first club was Aston Villa, who at the time had the great Harry Hampton at centre-forward. Unable to make any impact at Villa Park, Bert moved on to Highbury signing for Arsenal in November 1905.

Although not a regular in the Arsenal team, he managed to score enough goals to attract the attentions of Everton for whom he signed in April 1908.

It was at Everton that his career blossomed. He ended the 1908 -9 season as the League's top scorer with 36 goals and gained his first England cap (scoring in the 2 - 0 victory over Wales). He stayed at Everton until April 1911 gaining one more cap before surprisingly being allowed to leave - this time for Burnley, then a Second Division club.

In his first season at Turf Moor he helped Burnley to reach third place in the Second Division table - he scored an impressive 32 goals. The following season Burnley gained promotion to Division One with Bert again being top scorer with 31 goals. During this season they also reached the FA Cup semi-final losing to Sunderland after a replay.

The season 1913 - 14 was to be a momentous one for both Bert Freeman and Burnley. The club consolidated its place in the top flight and reached the FA Cup Final for the first time, and who was there to steal the moment as his own - Bert Freeman.

Although he gained three more England caps at Burnley, scoring the winning goal in the 1914 Cup Final was undoubtedly the highlight of Bert's career. He played his last game for Burnley in February 1921 and then joined Wigan Borough, later moving to Kettering Town where he played his last game in 1924. Bert died in August 1955 aged 69.

ABOVE: BERT FREEMAN'S CUP SHIRT.

BELOW: THE BURNLEY TEAM, CUP WINNERS 1914. (From Association Cup Winners – Player's cigarette cards).

ARTHUR DUNN.

A FOOTBALL BONANZA 1895-1914

The period which coincided with the close of the Victorian era and the start of the Great War was a watershed in many ways. In footballing terms, the FA Cup Finals and the expansion of the Football League were a highly visual representation of the growth in popularity of the game. The arenas at Crystal Palace inevitably became an ideal venue for major footballing events and the Crystal Palace authorities were not averse to this trend as it meant additional revenue.

Indeed, on many occasions, both grounds were in use. For example, on 21 November 1896 Old Westminsters fixture with Old Carthusians in the London Charity Cup was booked for the South ground (the Cup Final arena) whilst Clapham Rovers and Mid-Kent were to play on the North ground.

Football of all standards began to be played at the arena. Even the Crystal Palace Engineering School had its own team and a local club, Anerley, were booked to play the First Battalion Scots Guards on Boxing Day 1896 and the First Battalion of the Coldstream Guards two days later.

SCRATCH TEAMS

Scratch teams were put together for exhibition games. As early as December 1895, a team of Corinthians, calling themselves Crystal Palace, took on the Cup winners, Aston Villa, but they were no match for the Villa losing by seven goals to three.

The exercise was repeated on other occasions, notably on March 27th 1897, another team called Crystal Palace (probably Corinthians) took on the 1896 Cup winners, Sheffield Wednesday, but lost 4 – 0.

Just nine days after that glorious Cup Final of 1897 (which gave Aston Villa the League and Cup double), Notts Forest played against Dundee winning 2 – 1.

Prior to the 1908 Cup Final, a team from the London FA took on a team from Brussels. Racing Club de Bruxelles arrived fresh from a victory in an international tournament in Belgium where Old Xavierians of Liverpool had reached the semi-finals; they were also the unbeaten Belgian champions. However, they could not cope with the teamwork and experience of the London team. T S Little of Ilford scored six of the eight London goals, evenly divided between the two halves. Racing Club did not score. The London team that day was:

F Kenyon (Nunhead); J J Bayley (Clapton), C Watson (Tufnell Park); H C Hardy (Wanstead), C S Rance, J E Olley (Clapton); F C Comerford (Woodford Albion), H J Clarke (Deptford Invicta), T S Little (Ilford), N A Wood (Bromley), V T Brennan (Dulwich Hamlet).

BELOW: A CRYSTAL PALACE STAFF TEAM.

BOTTOM: NORTHERN GROUND SHOWING CYCLE TRACK.

ABOVE: CORINTHIANS 1905, MANY OF THIS SIDE PLAYED IN THE 10-3 VICTORY OVER THE CUP HOLDERS BURY IN MARCH 1904. FROM LEFT TO RIGHT: VASSALL, DAY, HEWITT, HARRIS, CRAIG, SIMPSON (CAPT.), NORRIS, ROWLANDSON, MORGAN - OWEN, TIMMIS, VICKERS, HARRIS, WRIGHT.

ABOVE: BILL POSTER 1899.

CENTRE: N L (PA) JACKSON FOUNDER OF CORINTHIANS.

RIGHT: OLD CARTHUSIANS 1889.

OLD CARTHUSIANS

Old Carthusians were another Cup-winning team that used the Crystal Palace for at least three home fixtures in 1896 and six in 1897. These fixtures, like Clapham Rovers, were against Old Boys teams, including Old Brightonians who played locally at the Greyhound ground in Dulwich, using the popular Greyhound pub for their changing rooms.

OTHER GAMES

Other examples of the use of the ground are when the Sevenoaks Charity FA Trophy Final was held on 25 April 1896 between two current Kent League sides, Cray Wanderers and Sheppey United. In January 1897, a team representing London played the Army and in the March played against Sussex. On 15 March 1899 there was a fixture for Players' of England versus Players' of Scotland on behalf of the Benevolent Fund of the Players' Union.

CORINTHIANS

Corinthians (see Chapter 12), too, who were at this stage based at Queen's Club, Kensington took advantage of the Cup Final ground for some matches. Apart from the Finals of the Sheriff of London Shield (see below), they were invited to take part in games against League opposition such as Bolton Wanderers, Everton and others, as an additional attraction at the Easter Bank Holiday.

These matches were often very exciting, high scoring affairs and attracted large crowds. For instance, the match against Bolton on Easter Monday, 11 April 1898, had over 30,000 spectators. Of course, this was not the only attraction during the day. For the price of admission the visitors could enjoy the delights of the park, go to the fair, see the match in the afternoon and then go to the theatre or a concert in the evening. The day would be concluded with a glorious firework display.

CLAPHAM ROVERS

Clapham Rovers played games at the Crystal Palace in the 1890s against various public school Old Boys teams, for example Old Carthusians, Old Foresters and Old Etonians. Formed in 1869, Clapham Rovers were one of the original entrants in the FA Cup in 1872. They won the Cup in 1880 against Oxford University and were runners-up in 1879. Apart from using Crystal Palace, Clapham also played home games at Clapham, Tooting Bec and Wandsworth.

JAMES FREDERICK McLEOD PRINSEP

J F M Prinsep played in the losing Clapham Rovers Cup Final team of 1879 against Old Etonians. As he was born on 27 July 1861, in India, this makes him the youngest FA Cup Finalist in history. He won his one England cap a week after the Cup Final, becoming also the youngest ever international. Prinsep also played for Old Carthusians in the 1881 FA Cup Final, the last all amateur Final.

INTER-LEAGUE MATCH

The Football League too saw the value of using the vast arena and on 31st March 1900 held the annual match against the Scottish League at the Palace.

The game was played on a sunny day in excellent conditions and acted as a trial for the full international between the countries in Glasgow the following week. The English League won the toss and chose to play with the sun behind them. The English team were criticised for weakness in the half-backs whilst the strength of the forwards and backs compensated. Although Bloomer scored after ten minutes the Scots were always in the game and in the verdict of the South London Press deserved to win. They however settled for a draw after twice equalising, the first through Walker from a Smith cross, and later in the final minutes of the game following the English League's second goal from Hedley. The attendance was estimated to be around 12,000 by the local paper.

FOOTBALL LEAGUE: W J Foulke (Sheffield United); H Spencer, J W Crabtree (Aston Villa); H Griffiths (Wolves), W Wigmore (Small Heath), R Norris (Nottingham Forest); W C Athersmith (Aston Villa), S Bloomer (Derby), G A Hedley (Sheffield United), J Settle (Everton), T J Miller (Wolves).

SCOTTISH LEAGUE: H G Rennie (Hearts); N Smith (Rangers), R Glen (Hibernian); N Gibson (Rangers), H Marshall (Celtic), J T Robertson (Rangers); J Hodge (Celtic), R Walker (Hearts), J Campbell, A McMahon (Celtic), A Smith (Rangers).

REFEREE: S Torrans (Belfast).

In this period also a number of new competitions came into existence and where better to hold the Finals than at the Crystal Palace.

SHERIFF OF LONDON SHIELD

One of the first of these new competitions was the Sheriff of London Shield.

When Mr Thomas Dewar, later Lord Dewar, became Sheriff of London in 1898, it was suggested that, to mark his year of office, he should present a trophy, the proceeds of the matches to go to charity. Mr Dewar agreed and asked that the trophy should be contested every year by the best amateur and the best professional clubs of the season.

The first match in the series was set for March 19th,1898 at the Crystal Palace. Sheffield United were the outstanding professional club of the day and the Corinthians were chosen to oppose them. To do this, the Corinthian rules (specifically Rule 7) had to be modified to allow them to enter a competition. The game was watched by a crowd of 20,000.

The game itself was remarkable chiefly for the display of defensive qualities by both sides and, in the end, despite fine attacking from G O Smith and Burnup, the game was goalless. Eventually it was decided to replay the match also at the Crystal Palace on Monday 4th April but the match was drawn again. So it was decided that the honours should be shared.

CORINTHIANS: W Campbell; C B Fry, W J Oakley; B Middleditch, C Wreford-Brown, F M Ingram; R C Gosling, W F H Stanbrough, G O Smith, C L Alexander, C J Burnup .

SHEFFIELD UNITED: Foulke; Thickett, Cain; Johnson, Morren Needham; Bennett, M'Kay, Gaudie, Cuningham, Priest.

REFEREE: Mr E E Stuart.

LINESMEN: Messrs. C Squires, W H Bellamy.

LEFT: THE SHERIFF OF LONDON SHIELD.

ABOVE: AM (LEFT) AND PM WALTERS, FULL BACKS FOR CORINTHIANS IN THE 1880'S. OFTEN KNOWN AS 'NIGHT & DAY' DUE TO THEIR INITIALS.

BELOW: R E FOSTER, C B FRY AND G O SMITH.

GILBERT OSWALD SMITH

It is a sign of true renown for a person to be recognised solely by initials. There is no doubt as to who one is referring when stating the initials W G – it can only be Dr W G Grace, the greatest of cricketers. So it is with G O. He was the finest centre-forward of his day – the 1890s – and some might say the greatest of all time. He had wonderful balance which gave him superb dribbling and swerving powers. He rarely headed the ball because he kept it on the ground, both in dribbling and shooting. Adept at positioning, he made as many goals for his colleagues as he scored himself. He obtained 115 goals for Corinthians in 131 matches and played 20 times for England between 1893 and 1901, scoring 11 goals and captaining the side on 14 occasions.

On the early death of Arthur Dunn, he retired from football and took over the joint headmastership of Ludgrove School with another famous amateur, Corinthian, Oxford and England international, William Oakley .

ABOVE: C B FRY.

RIGHT: THE ARTHUR DUNN CUP.

ABOVE: W J OAKLEY, FULL BACK FOR THE CORINTHIANS. BECAME JOINT SECRETARY OF THE CLUB WITH G O SMITH.

The following year, the Corinthians were out of form and lost to Queen's Park in the two-leg semi-final. So Queen's Park were selected to play Aston Villa for the Shield. Once again there was no decisive result (0 – 0) and so honours were shared.

In the 1899 – 1900 season, the Shield Final was scheduled for November 1899 rather than in the Spring of 1900. There was no doubt this time that Corinthians were the right team to represent the amateurs. Unfortunately, it was not possible to play the game on a Saturday so the crowd at the Palace was only about 7,000.

CORINTHIANS: W Campbell; C B Fry, W J Oakley; B Middleditch, R R Barker, H Vickers; G C Vassall, R E Foster, G O Smith, G P Wilson, B O Corbett .

ASTON VILLA: George; Spencer, Evans; Bowman, Wilks, Mann; Athersmith, Devey, Garratty, Wheldon, Smith.

It was a great game despite the unusually heavy state of the ground. In the very fast and open game the Corinthians played very well even when C B Fry was temporarily off the field. So with goals by Foster and G O Smith, Corinthians won 2 – 1 the Villa goal by Garratty. At last, Sir Thomas Dewar was able to present the trophy to a winning team.

The same two teams met again in the following season (March 2nd, 1901) at Crystal Palace. Again the ground was covered with pools of water and a heavy downpour of rain seemed likely at any moment. However, the teams still put on a good display. This time, Aston Villa took the honours with a superb goal from Athersmith ten minutes from the end.

CORINTHIANS: G E Wilkinson; C B Fry, W J Oakley; B Middleditch, H Thwaites, H Vickers; R G Wright, R E Foster, L J Moon, C F Ryder, B O Corbett .

ASTON VILLA: George; Crabtree, Evans; Bowman, Cowan, Wilks; Athersmith, Devey, Johnson, Garraty, Smith.

REFEREE: Captain Simpson.

It is interesting to note that on this occasion one of the linesmen was a certain A T B Dunn (see profile). The other official was J J Bentley.

The success of the competition led to the Final being held at various grounds in London – Tottenham and Queen's Club. In the 1904 game at Queen's Club, Corinthians took on the Cup holders Bury and trounced them 10 – 3. So it was not until 24th April (Easter Monday) 1905 that the event returned to the Crystal Palace. Corinthians' opponents this year were Sheffield Wednesday.

In front of a 15,000 crowd, the game was played at a fast pace. After only three minutes, the Corinthians went in front when Vassall crossed to G S Harris who scored from close to the goalmouth. However, early in the second half, Wilson scored for Sheffield and got his second fifteen minutes from the end.

CORINTHIANS: T S Rowlandson; O T Norris, W U Timmis; J D Craig, M Morgan-Owen, H Vickers; G C Vassall, S H Day, G S Harris, S S Harris, E G D Wright.

SHEFFIELD WEDNESDAY: Lyal; Layton, Burton; Ruddlesdin, Crawshaw, Bartlett; Davis, Brittleton, Wilson, Stewart, Simpson.

REFEREE: Captain Simpson.

In the two following seasons, the Sheriff's Final migrated to Fulham and then of course, the split between the amateurs and professionals occurred. This meant that the Sheriff of London Shield Competition disappeared from the calendar until it was resurrected in the 1930s.

ARTHUR DUNN CUP

The advent of professionalism edged the amateurs and Old Boys' sides out of the main competitions. It was thought by many that amateur football was doomed to extinction. A famous Old Etonian, Arthur Dunn, commented on this sad state of affairs in a letter to his friend, Norman Malcolmson, as follows: *"Dear N, One might write for ever on this, I think golf is partly responsible. There's nothing for it but an 'Old Boy' association, but who has time to start it? yours, A T B D".*

With Dunn's premature death in early 1902, the idea might have been lost. However, just three weeks later Malcolmson convened a meeting at the Sports Club of Old Boys interested in amateur football. The result was the foundation of the Arthur Dunn Memorial Cup. This decision was later ratified at a meeting chaired by C Wreford Brown, the Corinthian. The actual trophy was donated by R C Gosling and the competition got underway in September 1902. Fourteen schools: Bradfield, Brighton, Charterhouse, Eton, Felsted, Forest, Harrow, Lancing, Malvern, Repton, Rossall, Shrewsbury, Westminster and Winchester took part, resulting in Old Carthusians and Old Salopians reaching the Final at Crystal Palace on March 28th, 1903.

This Final was typically competitive ending in a 2 – 2 draw after extra time. Even the replay at Ealing ended in the same score and it was decided that the cup should be held jointly by these two clubs, six months each. Some famous players participated in this game: the Morgan-Owen brothers for Old Salopians (both full Welsh

internationals; they had been selected to play in an international in Belfast on the same day but preferred to appear for their old school), while Old Carthusians included the Wreford Brown brothers and of course G O Smith. W G Grace, the veteran cricketer, watched from the sidelines.

Salopians were the better side for most of the match and took the lead after 10 minutes when Edwards scored with a long shot. An uncharacteristic error by goalkeeper Wilkinson, deceived by the wind, gave the Carthusians an equaliser. M Morgan-Owen restored the lead before half-time but the Carthusians equalised again 10 minutes from the end. Only 10 minutes each way of extra time was played as both teams were dining at the Cafe Royal in the evening!

In the second season, Old Cholmeleians and Old Cranleighians joined the competition followed by Old Aldenhamians and Wellingburians in 1905 and in 1906 Old Radlians. The competition moved to Queen's Club where the Corinthians were based.

It would be over twenty years before the Arthur Dunn Cup returned to Crystal Palace.

FA AMATEUR CUP FINAL

Despite the popularity of the FA Challenge Cup Finals, only two Amateur Cup Finals were played at the Palace – in 1898 and 1923. Possibly this was due to the lack of success of the first Final on 23rd April 1898.

ABOVE TOP: OLD CARTHUSIANS 1903.

ABOVE BOTTOM: OLD SALOPIANS 1903.

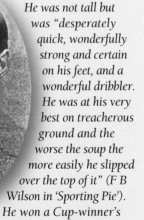

ARTHUR TEMPEST BLAKISTON DUNN

Arthur Dunn was indeed a remarkable man. He was not tall but was "desperately quick, wonderfully strong and certain on his feet, and a wonderful dribbler. He was at his very best on treacherous ground and the worse the soup the more easily he slipped over the top of it" (F B Wilson in 'Sporting Pie'). He won a Cup-winner's medal when Old Etonians beat Blackburn Rovers in the 1882 Final. In 1883 he won his first England cap at centre-forward against Ireland and again played in the same fixture the following year. He disappeared from the scene as professional players took over, until in 1892 when he was recalled as England captain.

He played at left-back in the side that beat Wales 2 - 0 at Wrexham. A month later, he was the sole amateur in the England team that played Scotland in Glasgow, again as left-back and captain. Labelled the "Old Crocks" by the Scottish press, Dunn's side ran out the victors by four goals to nil.

In that year, 1892, Dunn retired and founded Ludgrove School (at Cockfosters) as a preparatory school for his beloved Eton. It was there at the early age of 41 that he died of a sudden heart attack.

MIDDLESBROUGH 2 UXBRIDGE 1
23 APRIL 1898

As Middlesbrough had won the competition four years earlier, against Old Carthusians, they started as favourites. Uxbridge played in red and Middlesbrough in black and white, which mirrored the colours of Nottingham Forest and Derby County who had contested the professional Final at the ground the previous Saturday. However, as the Daily Telegraph reporter pointed out, there the similarity ended:

"Of course, no one expected a huge crowd to assemble for the purpose of seeing Middlesbrough play Uxbridge, but the gathering fell far below the most ordinary anticipations. Probably there were not many more than a thousand people watching the game, and this company on a ground which will accommodate upwards of 60,000 spectators, simply served to emphasise the sparseness of the attendance. A number of people wearing the Uxbridge favours assembled to cheer on the Middlesex players, and Middlesbrough had their set of followers, but the stands were empty, and the huge bank whence so many had witnessed the triumph of Notts Forest over Derby County

ABOVE: THE UXBRIDGE TEAM.
BACK ROW: C J DAVIS,
E BENSTEAD, H SKINNER,
G C GUMBRELL, F BROWN,
H H GAYLARD, A E JACOBS.
FRONT ROW: A R WOODBRIDGE,
W HICKMAN, P BROWNING,
W J KNIGHT, E W WOODBRIDGE.

was scarcely needed, nearly everybody who wanted to see the play being able to do so by standing round the ring... but as four o'clock approached a few hundreds who had been beguiling away their time by watching a game of lacrosse on the neighbouring enclosure slowly wended their way towards the football ground. There may be a time in years to come when the battle for the possession of the amateur trophy will attract its many thousands, but judging by the experience of Saturday that day is still far distant".

The small crowd was nevertheless infinitely larger than the attendance at Middlesbrough's semi-final against Thornaby. The match had to be played behind closed doors due to an outbreak of smallpox.

While public health problems dogged Middlesbrough's preparation, team selection was what troubled Uxbridge. Should Davies or Brown play at right-half? Even after the committee chose Brown, opinions were still divided and to placate Davies' supporters, at the celebration dinner that Uxbridge held on the Thursday after the game, Davies was presented with a medal similar to the one his team mates had collected at the Crystal Palace.

On the big day itself, the Uxbridge club secretary A H Murray arranged for a special train to take their supporters direct to the ground. The return fare from Uxbridge was 3s 1d (about 15p)

and included admission to the game and to the Crystal Palace building.

The game kicked off at four o'clock after the team photographs had been taken by Messrs. Negretti and Zambra, photographers of Crystal Palace. Copies of the pictures were available for 3/- (15p) inclusive of 6d (2 1/2 p) postage.

MIDDLESBROUGH: G Smith; R.Piercy, J Moore; H Allport, R W Jackson, A Nelmes; G Longstaff, R Wanless, J Kempley, W Bishop, W Frost.

UXBRIDGE: G C Gumbrell; H H Gaylard, H Skinner; F Brown, E Benstead, A Jacobs; A R Woodbridge, W Hickman, P Browning, W J Knight, E W Woodbridge.

REFEREE: J Adams (Birmingham).

LINESMEN: C Squire (London), R E Lythgol (Liverpool).

THE GAME

On a bright and fresh afternoon Uxbridge won the toss and chose to play with the wind behind them. Inevitably, the match got off to a controversial start. The referee awarded an indirect free kick for what appeared to be a hand-ball inside the penalty area. Brown took the kick and Hickman hit the post. Middlesbrough counter-attacked, the Uxbridge keeper fisted the ball straight against Kempley's head and without realising it he had put the team from the Tees ahead. Not surprisingly the speeches at the subsequent Uxbridge dinner referred to their lack of luck.

Knight had a good chance to equalise after being put through by E W Woodbridge. Following a period of Middlesbrough pressure Benstead hit a shot over the bar. It was then the turn of the Uxbridge captain Algie Woodbridge to feed Knight who charging through ended in the net instead of the ball.

After half-time, Uxbridge came out strongly. E W Woodbridge had a shot well saved by Smith in the Middlesbrough goal. In the last half hour Middlesbrough showed their superiority. Their second goal was considered doubtful by their opposition who thought the scorer Kempley was offside. The 'Boro centre-forward however *"dribbled in"* and scored with a *"clever place"*.

The Daily Telegraph felt Uxbridge had *"played with some dash at times, but were slow getting rid of the ball and... would not infrequently pass to one of the opposing side"*, while Middlesbrough, *"displayed the better football"*. Another Sunday paper was more critical suggesting *"the marvel is that a combination of Uxbridge's calibre should have gone as far as they did in the competition"*.

It is worth noting that Uxbridge hold the distinction of being the only Southern League club to reach the Final of the FA Amateur Cup.

Though Middlesbrough fans returned to Teesside overjoyed at their team's victory, not all the Uxbridge supporters were downhearted. Returning to Uxbridge station some were shouting *"we've won the Cup"* holding up an egg cup bought as a souvenir of the Crystal Palace.

AMATEUR INTERNATIONAL

Only one Amateur international was played at the Palace before the Great War. The game was played on March 4th 1911 between England and Belgium. This was the fourth match between these two countries. England had won 8 – 2 in Brussels in 1908 and 11 – 2 at Tottenham in 1909. In March 1910 the game had finished level at 2 – 2 in Brussels.

About 5,000 spectators attended the match at the Crystal Palace. The England team was described by The Sporting Life as one of the *"strongest that had ever represented England in an amateur international, there not being a weak spot in it"*. The England captain was V J Woodward. The Rev. K R G Hunt, a Corinthian, who appeared for Wolverhampton Wanderers in the 1908 Cup Final was playing out of position at left-half.

ENGLAND: G R Bancroft (Manchester Univ); R W Cuthbert (Chesterfield), A E Knight (Portsmouth); F C Symons (Nunhead), F V Monk (Southampton), Rev. K R G Hunt (Leyton); S J Hoad (Blackpool), V J Woodward (Chelsea), G W Webb (West Ham), G R Hoare (Woolwich Arsenal), E G D Wright (Hull City).

BELGIUM: H Le Roy (L'Union St Gilloise); E Andrieu (Racing Club de Bruxelles), E Poelmans (L'Union St Gilloise); O Bossaert (Racing Club de Bruxelles), R Schietse (Racing Club de Gand), C Van Hoorden (FC de Bruges); H Goetinck (FC de Bruges), A Six (Cercle de Bruges), R De Veen (FC de Bruges), L Salys (Cercle de Bruges), R Paternostre (FC de Bruges).

The Belgians lost the game according to The Times correspondent because they were *"outclassed mainly because of the forwards inability to do anything to relieve the pressure on their defence. Except for down the wing and a rush by the inside men, attack had practically no part in the Belgians' game. Just at the start the pace of their outside men looked like causing a lot of trouble, but these early and dangerous attacks had scarcely a repetition. England's halves and backs to a large extent controlled the game…"*.

Just three minutes had elapsed when *"Wright broke away from a pass by Hoare, and got in a perfect shot which Poelmans in endeavouring to kick away from under the bar helped into the net"*, according to The Sporting Life. The Times reporter read the incident differently and thought it was a blunder by the defender which turned *"a centre by Wright inside the post"*.

Wright then put a long cross into Woodward who headed on and Webb hooked the ball into the net. Fifteen minutes later Hoare put Webb through the defence for what all journalists agreed was an excellent goal.

Six broke free for Belgium in the second half but he shot straight at Bancroft. De Veen in a good position shot over and it was Woodward who finished the scoring with still half an hour left.

After the game both teams and the guests had a dinner at the Crystal Palace. Lord Kinnaird, the President of the Football Association was in the chair supported by Count Oultremont and M. Max Kahn of the Belgian FA.

VIVIAN J WOODWARD

Woodward was another player who epitomised his era; an amateur who was able to play the game at the highest level. He was, however, something of an enigma. He was a centre forward yet of a frail stature. He scored profusely for England but only once against Scotland.

He was a great dribbler of the ball, had a great shot and was good in the air – the complete forward. However, Gibson and Pickford at the time described him as "a happy blend of G O Smith and W N Cobbold without the genius of one or the other".

He played for Tottenham, Chelsea and the Corinthians. He represented his country at professional and amateur level, 67 times in total.

He appeared for the senior side 23 times scoring 29 goals. Fifteen of the goals however were against Austria and Hungary who had weak teams.

He also gained Olympic gold medals in both 1908 and 1912.

Woodward remains in the record books as England's most prolific captain. He remains top of the list, two ahead of Bryan Robson, with a total of 21 goals during his 13 match reign.

He died in 1954 at the age of 74.

Charles Crump responding to the toast of the Football Association said international football was a means *"whereby people of different countries could get to know each other better and consequently learn to respect each other. Football had already done an immense amount of good in this direction, and there was not the slightest doubt that the more they became acquainted the less likelihood there was that they would take up arms to decide any disputes that might arise at any time"*.

V J Woodward was presented with the Anglo-Belgian Cup. After further speeches they retired to the adjoining skating rink and watched a rink hockey match.

SCHOOLS FOOTBALL

Even the schools took the opportunity to use the new facilities at the Palace. The London Schools Football Association had been founded in 1892 and in the 1893 – 94 season introduced a competition called the Corinthian Shield. The shield itself was donated by N L (Pa) Jackson who paid 30 guineas for it.

As an appetiser for the England v Scotland international in April 1897, the Crystal Palace staged the Corinthian Shield Final. This was between West Ham Schools and South London. In a tight-fought first half, West Ham were the first to score with South London equalising through Fitchie just before half-time. There was no further scoring so the two teams returned to the Palace the following week, this time on the pitch with the Cycle Track. On this occasion, South London won 2 – 1.

Tommie Fitchie later played for Scotland and Wilding, the West Ham goalkeeper, later kept goal for Clapton when they lost the FA Amateur Cup Final in 1904-5 and also when they won it in 1906 -7.

BELOW: THE CORINTHIAN SHIELD.

England v Scotland at the Crystal Palace 1905.

ENGLAND V SCOTLAND

There is one event in the football calendar, now sadly lost due to the excesses of the crowd troubles that marred the 1970s and 1980s, that probably aroused more passion than any other. This was the annual England v Scotland game.

Of course, this is the oldest international fixture of them all. It began in 1872, the same

year as the FA Cup. In fact, it was as a result of Queen's Park's participation in that competition that led to the call for a team to be sent up north. So on 3rd October 1872, six members of the Football Association met and, *"in order to fix the interests of the Association in Scotland, it was decided during the current season that a team should be sent to Glasgow to represent England"*.

Started as it was to encourage the game in Scotland, by the time the contenders met to celebrate the 26th anniversary at the Crystal Palace ground in 1897, the Scots had had by far the best of the results. They had won twelve of the previous encounters with six draws. In fact, up to 1890 England had only won three times.

THE GAME COMES TO THE CRYSTAL PALACE ENGLAND V SCOTLAND – APRIL 1897

As with the FA Cup competition, the match when played in England had been staged at Kennington Oval but latterly had moved a number of times. The creation of the vast arena at Crystal Palace however provided an ideal stage for this spectacle. So at the first opportunity, the England v Scotland game was brought to Crystal Palace and the date was set for the 3rd April 1897.

The Sporting Life correspondent was duly impressed.

"The Crystal Palace has many merits and advantages, and as a venue for deciding important matches is unrivalled. Accommodation was provided on Saturday that could not have been obtained elsewhere, and the Crystal Palace authorities are again to be complimented upon the manner in which they deal with large crowds. Crowds are attracted to

the Crystal Palace for amusement and entertainment. A visitor coming to the great capital, and accustomed to town life, is delighted with the fine open prospect to be obtained at the Crystal Palace. The temple made of glass was the Mecca of the footballer on Saturday, and of the 33,715 spectators who were present, many experienced some difficulty in reaching the rendezvous. Our reporter made one of nineteen in a small compartment on the London, Chatham and Dover Railway. Once on the way to the Palace there were evident signs of the great event uppermost in the minds of the football enthusiasts. Benighted persons who see no fascination in the game should witness one of these

LEFT: ENGLAND V SCOTLAND AT THE KENNINGTON OVAL IN 1878. ENGLAND RECOVERED FROM A 4 – 1 DEFICIT TO WIN 5 – 4. NOTE THE GOALPOSTS WERE VERY FLIMSY WITH ONLY A LIMP ROPE BETWEEN THEM TO MARK THE CROSSBAR.

BELOW: SCOTTISH INTERNATIONAL SHIRT AND CAP IN PRIMROSE & PINK.

contests. All the talk was of football, and the international in particular. The history of each player appeared to be perfectly known, and speculation as to the winner was freely indulged in – principally the opinion was in favour of England".

This differed somewhat from the view of the pundits who regarded *"the Scotchmen as a formidable lot"*.

"Each train to the Palace brought heavy loads of passengers, and one wondered as each train unloaded, how the travellers could possibly have compressed themselves into the compartments. All were anxious to see the game, and the inconveniences were accepted in the best of humour. An hour or more before the time fixed for the game the crowd commenced to muster on the natural sloping bank in front of the Switchback Railway. A number of the Gordon Highlanders lent a little colour to the sombre bank of humanity. The Scotch accent was very pronounced, there were visitors from the far North, the Midlands, the South of England, whilst London completed the complement".

In the stands were prominent people and pioneers of the game – Lord Kinnaird and Mr A J Balfour MP, and a great number of well-known players.

BELOW: CARTOON FROM THE DAILY GRAPHIC, APRIL 5, 1897.

Clever half-back play by Needham

A little difference between Don Doyle and the Referee

Crawshaw being doctored on the field

Reynolds, Ripcasteys

Scotland's First goal – Hyslop scores.

THE WEATHER

Our correspondent was obviously somewhat biased in his reporting for he was not averse to using any excuse for the defeat of the England team. *"....the weather on Saturday gave every promise of moisture and unpleasantness. There was no sun, it did not rain to any great extent, but it was atrociously cold. Had it been a bright day, with sunshine, England would probably have won, but it was a raw, cold afternoon, and eminently suited to the hardy Scots. Not that the weather had any effect upon the game, but we simply mention the circumstance and advance it as an additional theory for our defeat".*

THE TEAMS ENTER THE FIELD

At a quarter to four the police requested everybody to *"take their seats"*, and when this was accomplished, the spectacle was a phenomenal one. Ten minutes before kick off, the England team, led by their captain G O Smith, came onto the playing field for a warm-up. *"The Englishmen wore white shirts and the orthodox blue nicks"*. At two minutes to four o'clock the Scots, *"attired in blue shirts and white knickers"*, emerged from the Pavilion, to loud cheers.

"The Englishmen were of medium stature, whilst Hyslop (about 6ft. 1in.), Allan (5ft.10in.), Miller (5ft 9in.) and Lambie (5ft. 8in.) formed a formidable line of attack, as regards physical superiority, against the English five. What the Englishmen lost in stature they were expected to compensate for in skill. No time was wasted. G O Smith and Lambie, the rival captains, advanced to the centre of the field, the coin was spun, Smith guessed correctly, and at four pm sharp the great struggle had commenced".

THE GAME

The Times suggested that the Scots had the luck with them that day but they were a strong side in all positions. The English team was hampered when Crawshaw, the Sheffield Wednesday centre-half, left the field with a nasty leg injury after ten minutes. He returned to the pitch later but was not back to form.

Nevertheless, the English forwards were very effective in the early stages of the game. The speed and passing of Bloomer, Athersmith and G O Smith caused the Scottish defence all sorts of problems and midway through the first half, Bloomer scored from a cross by Athersmith. However, the Scottish forwards proved much too fast for the English full-backs Oakley and Spencer. The equaliser came five minutes later, when Hyslop provided the scoring impetus in a scramble following a free kick. Only superb goalkeeping by Robinson kept the Scots at bay and the winner came only seven minutes from the end when Robinson could not recover quickly enough from a diving save to keep out a shot from Miller.

ENGLAND: Robinson (Derby County); W J Oakley (Corinthians), Spencer; Reynolds (Aston Villa), Crawshaw (Sheffield Wednesday), Needham (Sheffield United); Athersmith (Aston Villa), Bloomer (Derby County), G O Smith - capt. (Corinthians), Chadwick, Milward (Everton).

SCOTLAND: Patrick (St Mirren); N Smith (Rangers), D Doyle (Celtic); Gibson (Rangers), Cowan (Aston Villa), Wilson (Sunderland); Bell (Everton), Miller (Rangers), Allan (Liverpool), Hyslop (Rangers), W Lambie - capt. (Queen's Park).

ABOVE: THE ENGLISH FULL-BACK HOWARD SPENCER (ASTON VILLA).

BELOW: THE ENGLAND TEAM.

ERNEST 'NUDGER' NEEDHAM

"The prince of half-backs", Ernest Needham was one of the great Sheffield United team that appeared in three FA Cup Finals in four years (winning in 1899 and 1902) and were League Champions in 1898.

A short man, 5ft 5 1/2 ins., he was very fit, tough and a fast player. He was the all-round sportsman also playing cricket for Derbyshire (1901-12).

Born in Chesterfield in 1873 he joined Sheffield United at the age of 18 and stayed with them throughout his career. During this time, he played 16 times for England. He retired in 1913 and became a steel worker.

THE 1901 GAME

The following year, of course, the international moved to Glasgow where it was also held in 1900. In the intervening year, the teams met in Birmingham at Villa Park. And this became the pattern for the next few years. So it was four years (1901) before the England – Scotland game returned to the Crystal Palace.

On this occasion, the weather took a toll on the attendance. The ground was in a deplorable state. Apparently, torrents of rain had fallen that morning and left the turf almost under water. There were large pools everywhere, and it was seriously considered whether to call the match off. As it happened, the rain stopped, the weather gradually improved until the sun shone *"quite brilliantly"*. Yet the weather in the morning was enough to deter spectators. *"With the first signs of improving weather, however, the spectators began to take up their positions, until the crowd reached 18,000 – the numbers given in the official return being slightly above these figures"*.

BELOW: THE BALL COMING FROM BLOOMER ACROSS TO BLACKBURN (WHOM MANY THOUGHT OFF SIDE), THE LATTER KICKS, SLIPPING DOWN AS HE DOES SO. RENNIE, TRYING TO SAVE, FALLS ALAS.
Illustrated Sporting & Dramatic News.

Despite a slippery surface, both teams acquitted themselves admirably and England put up a good performance against a Scottish team that had already proved its ability, they earned a creditable draw and clinched the Championship. Before the game, there had been considerable criticism of the England team following a 4 – 1 defeat in Glasgow the year before and, despite the draw, G O Smith, W J Oakley and Athersmith did not appear for England again.

REGINALD ERSKINE FOSTER (1878-1914)

Reginald Erskine Foster was one of the greatest all-round sportsmen of his or any era. It is truly amazing that he should have been a contemporary of other such outstanding talents as C B Fry and G O Smith.

Foster is unique in being the only man to captain England at both cricket and football.

His cricketing record is exceptional. He scored 287 to win the Test match in Sydney in 1903; this remains the highest score by an Englishman in a Test in Australia. He was also an exceptional slip fielder.

Foster, however, only gained five caps at football due to injuries and work commitments; he was a stockbroker. An old boy of Malvern College, he played for Old Malvernians and later Corinthians.

Tragically, "Tip" Foster died from diabetes at the early age of 36.

The Scots had by far the most of the play, and if it had not been for the English half-backs – Forman, Needham and Wilkes – the Scottish forwards might have run away with the game. In fact, the first goal went to England when Blackburn nudged the ball into the net inches from the goal-line. Sutcliffe had a superb game in the England goalmouth but early in the second half, he made his only mistake – misjudging a high shot from Campbell who scored. Hamilton then headed in the second from a corner kick and England were on the ropes. However, they reckoned without the brilliance of Steve Bloomer, who seized on a clearance by Drummond and gave Rennie in the Scottish goal no chance.

ENGLAND: Sutcliffe (Bolton Wanderers); Iremonger (Nottingham Forest), W J Oakley (Corinthians); Wilkes (Aston Villa), Forman (Nottingham Forest), Needham; Bennett (Sheffield United), Bloomer (Derby County), G O Smith, R E Foster (Corinthians), F Blackburn (Blackburn Rovers).

SCOTLAND: Rennie (Heart of Midlothian); Battles (Celtic), Drummond (Rangers); Aitken (Newcastle United), Raisbeck (Liverpool), Robertson (Rangers); Walker (Heart of Midlothian), Campbell (Celtic), R McColl (Queen's Park), Hamilton, A Smith (Rangers).

ABOVE: ALEC RAISBECK (LIVERPOOL).

THE 1905 GAME

Four years later, on April 1st 1905, the talking points before the game had changed. On the positive side, everyone was very impressed with the new accommodation at the Crystal Palace. The Crystal Palace Company had been assured that the Cup Final would be held there for the next five years, and so felt themselves justified in increasing the accommodation for spectators. New ornate stands were built and terraces were cut into the slopes where most of the spectators congregated.

On the negative side, the critics were back to England's apparent apathy. John Cameron, the Scottish international then with Spurs, wrote:

"English patriotism differs remarkably from the other three home countries, notably that of Scotland. The English regard internationals with interest, never with excitement. To this public, the event of the season is the Cup Final, the England – Scotland match is a secondary affair. Yet tonight in Scotland the rejoicing if the Thistles succeed will be overwhelming and of a national character. The telegraphs will be busy and they will not cease until every village and hamlet has enjoyed the news".

As it happened, there was little joy for either

side that night. England won the game with a solitary goal – by inside left Bache. But it has been described as the worst in the history of the series. *"By the second half the crowd was making little attempt to hide its yawns...."*.

ENGLAND: Linacre (Notts Forest); Spencer (Aston Villa), Smith (Reading); Ruddlesdin (Sheffield Wednesday), Roberts (Manchester United), Leake (Aston Villa); Sharp (Everton), Bloomer (Derby County), V Woodward (Tottenham Hotspur), Bache (Aston Villa), Bridgett (Sunderland).

SCOTLAND: Lyall (Sheffield Wednesday); McCombie (Newcastle United), Watson (Sunderland); Aitken (Newcastle United), Thomson (Hearts), McWilliam (Newcastle United); Walker (Hearts), Howie (Newcastle United), Young (Everton), Somers (Celtic), Wilson (Hearts).

ABOVE: A TUSSLE FOR THE BALL IN MIDFIELD.

FAR LEFT: SCOTTISH TEAM CAP 1905.

LEFT: LINACRE, THE ENGLISH GOALKEEPER MAKES A BRILLIANT SAVE.

BELOW: LYALL, THE SCOTTISH GOALKEEPER CLEARS.

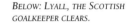

ANDY AITKEN

Andy Aitken was born in Ayr in 1876 and played for Ayr Parkhouse before signing as a professional for Newcastle United. He played at centre-half and was regarded as their best player. Aitken also became the club captain during the period when Newcastle were the leading team in England.

He represented Scotland on fourteen occasions and had the distinction of facing England for eight consecutive matches including the 1905 game at the Crystal Palace.

THE 1909 GAME
THE MATCH THAT NEARLY DID NOT TAKE PLACE

By the time of the 1909 game, a blazing row had erupted between the players and the authorities. The Players' Union had been formed some years earlier but was not recognised by either the FA or the League. Matters escalated when the Union decided to affiliate to the General Federation of Trades Unions; the FA told the players not to affiliate, their Union refused to obey .... deadlock! When, early in international week, it was revealed that the players were considering a collective refusal to play, there was turmoil.

The FA tried without success to tie the players to their acceptance letters of a few weeks earlier in which each player had confirmed his intention to play. On the Thursday, however, the Players' Union issued a statement that after conferring with Federation officials they had decided to postpone action for legal rights of their members until the end of the season, *"not wanting to disappoint the general public"*, and adding *"the public can be assured the players will be in their places and will do their utmost to win"*. These last

RIGHT: THE DEFEAT OF SCOTLAND BY ENGLAND IN THE "SOCCER" INTERNATIONAL AT THE CRYSTAL PALACE WITNESSED BY THE PRINCE OF WALES ON SATURDAY. THE DAILY GRAPHIC MONDAY, APRIL 5, 1909.

1. FLEMING, WHO PLAYED INSTEAD OF WOODWARD, FORCING HIS WAY THROUGH.

2. THE PRINCE OF WALES, WITH LORD KINNAIRD, ON THE ROYAL STAND.

3. HARDY (ENGLAND) STOPS A HIGH SHOT.

4. SCOTTISH BACK HEADS AWAY A CENTRE FROM WALL.

six words only caused more controversy as they implied that the English players might have been prepared to throw the match. There was such an outcry that the FA made each player sign a declaration of their intention to *"play their hardest"* and issued a statement to this effect after the match.

Even so, there was a difficult atmosphere aggravated by the fact that the England captain, Vivian Woodward did not take the field because of injury. Luckily, the situation was partially alleviated by the match itself which England won 2 – 0, taking the international Championship and this without conceding a goal.

The attendance (35,000) was affected by the Boat Race which was held on the same day, but the crowd were joined by the Prince of Wales who asked to meet the captains at half-time. And there was much to occupy spectators before the match. *"Musical selections were rendered by a band, there were the usual entertainers of crowds, and Scotland, whose sons were assembled by the thousand, provided an impromptu procession headed by a piper, who led his followers around the arena to the accompaniment of a martial skirl of the instrument on which he performed so well".*

What of the game itself? By now, Scotland had adopted the racing colours of Lord Rosebery and so took the pitch in rose and primrose hooped jerseys. England of course appeared in their familiar white shirts. Both English goals were scored by Wall of Manchester United, the first after only three minutes came following a corner, when he received the ball and drove it hard, only to see it rebound off one of the backs in the goalmouth straight to his feet. He tried again and this time it blasted into the net. In the fifteenth minute, he got his second with a brilliant individual effort which roared past Brownlie in the Scotland goal. Scotland had a chance to recover when Pennington handled in the penalty area, but Stark hit the lamest of shots that went straight to Hardy.

ENGLAND: Hardy (Liverpool); Crompton (Blackburn Rovers), Pennington (West Bromwich Albion); Warren (Chelsea), Wedlock (Bristol City), Lintott (Bradford City); Pentland (Middlesbrough), Fleming (Swindon), Freeman (Everton), Holley (Sunderland), Wall (Manchester United).
SCOTLAND: Bownlie (Third Lanark); Cameron (Chelsea), Watson (Middlesbrough); McNair (Celtic), Stark (Rangers), McWilliam (Newcastle); Bennett (Rangers), Walker (Hearts), Quinn (Celtic), Wilson (Newcastle), H Paul (Queen's Park).

So the use of the Crystal Palace for the England – Scotland game came to an end. In 1913 the game was played at Chelsea.

LEFT: A CHROMO-LITHOGRAPH OF SCOTLAND'S BOBBY WALKER'S INTERNATIONAL AND LEAGUE CAPS.

BELOW: LORD ROSEBERY.

JESSE PENNINGTON

"Peerless" Pennington was born in West Bromwich in 1883 and it was natural that the able young footballer should sign for West Bromwich Albion (April 1903). During his career with WBA he picked up a Football League Division 2 Champions' medal (1911), Football League Champions medal (1920) and of course an FA Cup Finalist (1912). In all, he played 494 times for WBA which was for many years a club record.

He had the honour of playing 25 times as left-back for England. He was a stalwart in the England defence from 1907 to 1914.

He retired as a player in 1922 and, apart from a brief period as coach to Kidderminster Harriers, was employed in various capacities by WBA until 1960. Pennington died on 5th September 1970.

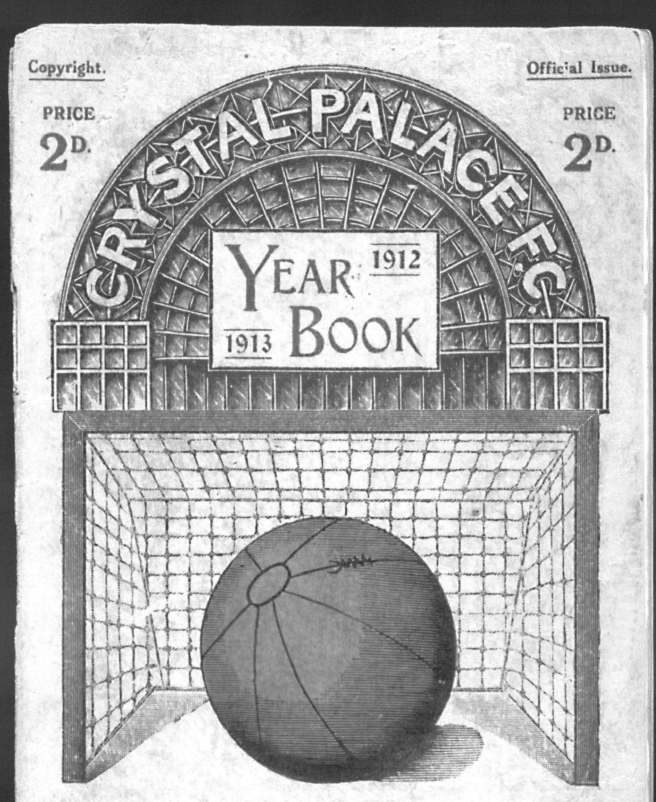

CRYSTAL PALACE FC YEAR BOOK FOR THE SEASON 1912-13.

THE MODERN CRYSTAL PALACE CLUB

The original Crystal Palace club disappeared in the 1870s, but after the Cup Final ground was opened, there were occasions, as we have seen, when teams calling themselves "Crystal Palace" did play matches on the new ground.

With the success of the Cup Finals, particularly when Southern clubs like Tottenham and Southampton appeared and attracted 100,000 plus crowds, the Crystal Palace Company became keen to exploit the potential in South London and therefore decided to form their own club. So in 1904 it was formally proposed that a Crystal Palace football club should be created.

Unfortunately, the Football Association did not much like the idea of the owners of the Cup Final ground having a club that could compete in the competition and they refused permission.

The following year, however, the idea was resurrected – this time a separate company was formed and the ground was rented. Mr J H Cozens, general manager of the Crystal Palace, and his predecessor Henry Gillman, consulted William McGregor, the Aston Villa chairman and founder of the Football League, as to the requirements for setting up a football club. Enthused himself by the idea, McGregor offered them the services of a young assistant secretary at Villa, Edmund Goodman. He became Secretary of the Crystal Palace club and later manager. Aston Villa also bequeathed their colours to the new club, and Palace were to wear the claret and blue for the next seventy years.

Goodman now set about organising the club. He first recommended that a Mr Sydney Bourne be approached to become a director. Goodman had identified Bourne by analysing the Crystal Palace Company receipts for the Cup Finals and noticing that he had consistently bought blocks of tickets for the event. Bourne became Chairman and remained in that post till his death in 1930.

The next step was to appoint a team manager and here again, Goodman made a shrewd selection. John Robson was enticed from Middlesbrough where he had had considerable success and brought with him a number of players who were to become regular members of the team along with a few local lads such as George Woodger.

With the personnel in place, the priority was to obtain entry to a competition. In the first instance, the Club applied along with Clapton Orient and Chelsea to join the Football League but were rejected by one vote.

J. Robson (*Manager*), Mr. T. C. Walters, Mr. A. Daniel (*Director*), J. Thompson, Oliver, Grant, Ross, Astley, Edwards, Mr. A. P Cufflin (*Director*), Mr. S. Bourne (*Chairman*), Mr. E. F. Goodman (*Secretary*), and Birch (*Trainer*).

Thompson, Hewitson, Needham, Watkins, Birnie (*Captain*), Innerd, Walker, and Roberts. Harker. Wallace. [*Read from left to right*

Unfortunately, by the time the decision was made known, it was too late to apply for entry to the Southern League First division. Palace thus had to settle for a place in the Second division where they would have to face the reserve sides of those in the Southern League First division. To supplement the fixtures, Palace also entered the United Counties League (which were mainly midweek matches).

So it was in the United Counties League that Palace played their first match – against New Brompton (now Gillingham). After a resounding victory at Priestfield, the next day the "Glaziers" played Southampton Reserves in their first game at the Crystal Palace. However, after racing to a 3 – 0 lead, fatigue and the loss of Dick Harker resulted in Southampton scoring four goals to win the game with Soy getting a hat-trick.

This setback was only temporary and by the end of September the Crystal Palace Magazine was able to report that Palace had lost only two matches out of nine – a notable feat when it is remembered that eight of those games were played in twenty-three days. The Magazine was however quite critical:

"It is with no intention of depreciating the merits of their opponents that we say they ought to have won every one of the games. Bad shooting on the part of the forwards has been the great fault".

ABOVE: THE CRYSTAL PALACE TEAM FOR 1905.

FAR LEFT: WILLIAM MCGREGOR.

LEFT: EDMUND GOODMAN (SECRETARY, MANAGER).

BELOW: SIR SYDNEY BOURNE (CHAIRMAN).

The magazine was concerned that the club did not get the support that it deserved and pleaded for more people to attend the Cup tie against Clapham on 7th October. The magazine also generated interest by running a football competition where readers were invited to predict the results of the next three fixtures:

October 21st Southern United (Away)
November 1st Swindon (Away)
November 4th Grays United (Home).

For the successful entrant a free season ticket to all Palace's home games was on offer. For the record, Grays went down 9 -1 and Palace recorded seventeen wins to take them to the top of the division.

The Glaziers played their home matches either on the FA Cup Final ground or on the pitch that was surrounded by the Cycle track in what had been the northern fountain basin. It was here on 10th February 1906 that they met West Ham Reserves, and in wretched weather they beat the Hammers 3 – 1, two of the goals coming from young George Woodger.

ABOVE: MR GOODMAN IN HIS OFFICE AT ANERLEY ROAD.

RIGHT: THE CRYSTAL PALACE STAFF TEAM 1912.

To raise funds, the Club made use of the facilities in the Crystal Palace and organised a Smoking Concert on 28th February 1906. *"The General Manager, Mr J H Cozens, with his usual courtesy, granted free admission to holders of tickets to the Crystal Palace, and concessions such as this go far to popularise the Crystal Palace for the holding of gatherings of this sort. Mr Syd. Bourne, the Club's genial Chairman, fitted the task to perfection, and was supported by many well-known Football enthusiasts, Mr Wall, the*

ABOVE: FRONT COVER OF THE CRYSTAL PALACE MAGAZINE, APRIL 1904.

secretary of the Football Association, being among them. He set the ball rolling by the announcement that Messrs. Brown and Bernard had presented, free of charge, the Art Programmes and the assistance of the Ladies to sell them, so as to augment the Referee Children's Dinner Fund. A sum of £5 7s was the outcome of this, and a precedent has been effected that should stimulate other clubs in the future to assist this deserving fund.

An appeal was made for local support by the Chairman, and was readily taken up by some of the visitors, and in view of the numbers who attended the concert, no difficulty should be experienced in assisting the Directors in their laudable efforts to create what was undoubtedly wanted in the district, namely, a first-class Football Club".

The evening was such a success that two months later a *"Great Bohemian Smoking concert"* was held and this time ladies were allowed. *"The opportunity now presents itself for the fair sex to attend in their hundreds ....."*. Tickets were available from Mr E F Goodman, Offices, Crystal Palace – Gents 2s. (10p), Ladies 1s. (5p).

If attendances were not all that had been hoped – Palace regularly attracted between two and three thousand spectators, although four thousand attended the 4 – 0 drubbing of Watford Reserves at the beginning of March – it was a very successful year and they became deserved champions of the Southern League second division.

The club also did well in the other competitions for which they entered. Runners-up to Watford in the United Counties League, they had a good Cup run as well. After beating Clapham 7 – 2 (with Walter Watkins scoring the first Palace hat-trick), later they trounced Chelsea 7 – 1 with another Walter Watkins hat-trick. There was some controversy over this game as Chelsea fielded primarily a reserve side. As they had a Football League fixture that same afternoon it was quite understandable but it led to the FA ruling that any club competing in the FA Cup must in future field its strongest side.

After a further victory over Luton, Palace were drawn against Blackpool, then a mediocre Second Division club. After two draws, at Bloomfield Road

LEFT: THE CRYSTAL PALACE FIRST TEAM SQUAD, SEASON 1907-08, DISPLAYING THE UNITED COUNTIES LEAGUE TROPHY WON IN 1907.

and then at the Palace, Palace lost the second replay at Villa Park by the odd goal.

Crystal Palace thus had good reason to be satisfied with their first season and in the club handbook of 1906-07, Edmund Goodman noted:

"I consider that the Crystal Palace should, in time, get as big as any club in the South, or even in England, that is if our team is fairly successful from the playing point of view. To prove this I would point to the attendance at the various Final ties which have been played on our ground, when from 60,000 to 110,000 persons have attended annually. Now with all due respects to the visiting teams which have from time to time appeared in the Final, we know that they always bring a large following, but at the same time amongst the large crowd there are always thousands of south Londoners, which shows that if you provide them with first-class football they will support it".

Palace's efforts in their first season were rewarded by their election into the first division of the Southern League for the 1906-07 season. The club proudly announced that ticket prices would remain the same for the new season – and this included admission to the Palace for two hours before the game began with free admission to the ground. *"At no other place in the world, we suppose, is such a sixpenny worth offered, as after the matches are over, visitors can see the thousand and one attractions inseparable from the Palace without extra charge".*

Meanwhile, the Club still entered the United Counties League and the Reserves were elected into the London League, Premier division; *"thus a match at the Palace is assured for practically every Saturday in the season".*

To set the club on a firmer footing, the directors made a share offer in the summer of 1906. One pound shares were available and to encourage more investors holders of ten or more of these were granted a free season ticket to the pavilion, while those taking five shares were given a season ticket to the covered stands.

The Glaziers did not find it as easy in the higher division and had a mixed season. However, in the Cup they made history. As has been recorded elsewhere, having progressed through the qualifying rounds of the competition, Palace were drawn in the First round proper against the mighty Newcastle United. Of course, many of the Palace side had come from the north-east as had their manager, Mr Robson. But it was still a shock for a new minor club to go to St James Park and beat the top team in the land. This success was followed by further victories, firstly over Fulham in a replay in front of a 20,000 crowd at the Crystal Palace. An even larger crowd of 31,123 came to see Palace draw 1 – 1 with fellow Southern Leaguers Brentford. Palace won the replay at Griffin Park to set up a quarter-final tie against Everton. More than 35,000 came along to see if Palace could topple another First Division side, but it was not to be. After a draw at home, Palace went out of the Cup at Goodison by 4 – 0.

BELOW: THE CRYSTAL PALACE SQUAD, SEASON 1909-10.

After just two seasons in charge, John Robson left to take over at nearby Croydon Common before the start of the 1907-08 season. Edmund Goodman now took on the joint role of Secretary and Team Manager.

In the season that followed, Palace dropped out of the United Counties League to concentrate on their main objective – to win the Southern League title.

GALLAHER'S CIGARETTES.

GEORGE WOODGER,
CRYSTAL PALACE, 1909-10.

GEORGE WOODGER

George was born in Croydon on 3rd September 1883. After playing for local teams in Thornton Heath and Croydon he joined Crystal Palace as an amateur during the 1905-06 season. He was described as "a player possessing a neat, clever, polished style which has earned for him the peculiar title of 'Lady'...". He later moved to Oldham Athletic where he earned his only England cap, against Ireland in February 1911.

JOSHUA "JOSH" JOHNSON

Josh Johnson was born in Derbyshire and started in football with Ripley Athletic. After brief spells at Aston Villa and Plymouth Argyle he joined Palace in November 1907. Between 1907 and the start of the First World War, Josh made 295 appearances for Palace.

goalkeeper position. But the replacement – Joshua ("Josh") Johnson – proved to be inspirational. He was to give stalwart service to Palace right up to the First World War and played 295 games for the Club.

THE SOUTHERN LEAGUE

Goodman's first season in charge was quite successful. The team finished fourth in the League and this form continued into the next season which started with a 4 – 0 win over Brighton and a 4 – 4 draw with Southampton (in which Palace at one point were 3 – 0 down). Then the season fell apart and after a long string of defeats Palace ended up in 16th position.

Gradually, Goodman changed the side and those that had helped in the early days of the club – Ted Birnie, Bob Hewitson, Wilfred Innerd – left for pastures new. In came new talent like Bob Spottiswood, Jimmy Hughes and Harry Hanger.

These three particularly created a solid defence which gave Palace a platform to achieve better success in the League. When Hewitson left to go to Oldham, Goodman had a major problem in filling the

RIGHT: CARTOON WITH THOUGHTS OF WINNING THE SOUTHERN LEAGUE SHIELD.

BELOW FAR RIGHT: PORTRAIT OF BOB SPOTTISWOOD (PROVIDED BY HIS SON ERIC).

SOUTHERN LEAGUE SHIELD.

SCRAP & SCUFFLIN

ANTICIPATION.
" 'M yes! I think that'd look very well on MY sideboard!"

BOB SPOTTISWOOD

The Crystal Palace Yearbook described Bob Spottiswood as "the fastest right-half in the South. It is always refreshing to watch his alertness, which is just as prominent near the end as at the beginning of a game". Bob came from a sporting family in Carlisle. His father, George, was a famous runner particularly in the quarter-mile. His brother, Joe, played football for Swansea Town, Manchester City and Bury.

Bob played initially for his home club, Carlisle United, but left in the 1908-09 season (age 19) and joined Croydon Common. After one season he joined Crystal Palace at half-back. He played 189 times for Palace (178 in the Southern League; 11 in the FA Cup) and became a great favourite with Palace fans. His abilities were recognised in 1910 when he was nominated for the England tour of South Africa but injury prevented him from making the voyage. Later, Bob moved to Clapton Orient and then Aberdare Athletic in the early 1920s. Eventually, he gave up due to a leg injury and went to Italy where he became trainer at A C Milan (1922-26). Bob loved music and was a regular visitor to La Scala. He was eventually deported by Mussolini.

"Crystal Palace" Football Teams. 1912-13.

In 1909, Innerd left and George Woodger took over as captain. This and those new signings led to a much better season and the Club finished seventh in the table with some memorable victories including a 6 – 0 drubbing of Southend.

In these years there was great rivalry between Crystal Palace and their neighbours Croydon Common. In 1909 Croydon were promoted to the First Division of the Southern League which set up a local derby clash. The game was keenly anticipated and 12,000 came to Crystal Palace to see it. However, the game itself turned out to be a very ill-tempered affair with players accused of kicking and tripping their opponents. Even the crowd became aggressive and abusive. Palace won the game and whereas the Palace team went on to conclude a successful season with another win over Brighton (now managed by John Robson), Croydon were relegated.

Apart from spectacles like this (and big FA Cup games) the attendances at Crystal Palace FC

games were never large – averaging 3,000 to 4,000. Those that came were however well entertained with half-time recitals by the Upper Norwood Prize band and some impressive football from their band of talented players.

To make ends meet, the Club had to get financial rewards from selling some of their best players to Football League clubs. In 1910, Woodger made his move to Oldham for a fee of £800 – a substantial sum in those days. Woodger, known as "Lady" for his elegant ball-skills, was desperate to get international recognition and this could only come if he played for a big club. As replacement

ABOVE: THE CRYSTAL PALACE SQUAD, SEASON 1912-13.

LEFT: THE 1912-13 FIRST TEAM LINE-UP.

BELOW: UPPER NORWOOD PRIZE BAND.

Upper Norwood Prize Band
Conductor: Mr. W. W. GRANT.

WINNERS OF OVER 50 PRIZES,
: : Including 9 CHALLENGE CUPS. : :
HOLDERS of the SOUTH OF ENGLAND QUARTETTE
CHAMPIONSHIP for Two Consecutive Years. Also
CHAMPIONSHIP SOUTH LONDON MUSICAL
: : : FESTIVAL for a similar period. : : :
DIPLOMA of HONOUR, BRUSSELS EXHIBITION, 1910.

HORACE COLCLOUGH

Horace Colclough was born in Meir, Staffordshire in 1890. He signed for Palace from Crewe Alexandra in 1912. Here, he switched from right-back to left-back and took over from Joe Bulcock.

Colclough made history when he became the first Palace player to play a full international (while still at the Club). He replaced Pennington against Wales at Cardiff on 16 March 1914.

He played 82 times for Palace but after being injured in the War he retired from the game.

RIGHT: ONE OF A SERIES OF CIGARETTE CARDS PROFILING POPULAR PLAYERS.

Mr Goodman drafted in a centre-forward from Halesowen, Charlie Woodhouse and he started in fine style with a hat-trick on his debut, in a 5 – 4 win over Leyton in front of the home fans.

Sadly, only a year later Woodhouse was to die suddenly after a short illness. He was buried in Elmers End cemetery, Beckenham. Despite this, the team was bolstered by the arrival of Ted Smith, from Hull. Smith scored a record 111 goals for Palace including, like Woodhouse, a hat-trick on his debut. At the end of the 1911 – 12 term, Palace were placed seventh.

FAR RIGHT: CARTOON FROM CRYSTAL PALACE FC YEARBOOK IN WHICH MR BOTHAM, A DIRECTOR OF THE CLUB PLEADS FOR FA CUP SUCCESS.

The 1912-13 season was another of mixed fortunes. They were joined by a famous amateur and Corinthian, Rev. K R G Hunt, who had already played at the highest level and had confronted Palace in a Cup-tie for Wolves (see below). There were some notable wins especially against Southampton who went down 8 – 0 on a foggy day in November at the Crystal Palace. Hewitt got four of the goals and Williams three.

The Southern League title still eluded them though. As it happened there was to be only one more real chance to do so. In 1914, the First World War broke out but the 1913 -14 season was uninterrupted and Palace made a strong bid for the Championship. They beat most of their rivals. One of the few to win against them was Swindon – and that defeat was to prove critical.

At the end of the season, it was Swindon who were top of the League with Palace second – on goal-average!

THE FA CUP

If Palace did not manage to attract large crowds for their League games, the FA Cup was a different matter. They had already proved their capabilities by beating Newcastle, and this success continued in the following seasons with bumper crowds at the Crystal Palace and at their opponents' grounds.

CHURCHMAN'S CIGARETTES.   H. COLCLOUGH.

A GOOD HINT.
Mr. B-th-m —'' And don't forget, young man, there's another bracket to fill, and you know which Cup will fill it best.''

JOE BULCOCK

Joe Bulcock was born in Burnley. Having played for Exeter City, he moved to Palace in 1909. In all, Joe made 146 appearances at full-back. Described as "strong and sturdy and ideally suited to the tough demands of the Southern League", he became the first-choice left-back and his career went from strength to strength. In his first season he only missed three games. He was selected to represent the Southern League and the Football League at Stamford Bridge in April 1910. He also played for the FA in South Africa.

After four seasons, injury forced Bulcock out of the team. In 1914 he moved to Swansea Town but was killed in France during the Great War.

On New Years' Day in 1909, Palace travelled to Molyneux to take on the mighty Wolves, who were the Cup-holders. But the team were not over-awed and battled to a 2 – 2 draw with two goals by Jimmy Bauchop. Thus, on the the following Wednesday, 30,000 people populated the slopes of the Crystal Palace for the replay. Honours were even at the end of the first half with a goal apiece, and with another goal for each side in the second half, the game went into extra time. Now Palace took control with another goal by Bauchop and finally they won the game with a goal by Archie

Needham that Rev. Nigel Sands describes as *"one of the finest goals in all Palace history. He received the ball in the centre circle, inside our half, and ran at the Wolves' defence, striding through tackles as well as the strength-sapping mud, before lashing it into the net and falling exhausted in the Wolves penalty area and there accepting the acclaim of the fans and the congratulations of his team-mates".*

Another large crowd of over 17,000 turned up at the Palace for the next Cup game. This time the opponents were Burnley but there was to be no fairy-tale ending. In a dour game, there were no goals and so Palace had to visit Turf Moor for the replay. This was an unmitigated disaster for Palace with Burnley netting nine goals without reply.

The big Cup game the following year was against another Lancashire club. Everton were already a club with a long pedigree, Cup and

On 28th June 1914, an assassin shot the Archduke Franz Ferdinand in Sarajevo. The European nations got sucked into war and for four long years the youth of Europe was sacrificed on the fields of Flanders and elsewhere.

Some of the best of British footballers were lost in their prime. At home, the Cup Finals ceased after the 1915 Final.

Crystal Palace Football Club was faced with a number of problems – loss of players, falling gate receipts – and finally in February 1915 the uneasy relationship that they had with the Admiralty (who had taken over the Palace for the duration of the War) came to a head and they were evicted. Palace moved to Herne Hill, to the ground used by amateurs, West Norwood. The connection of the team with its spiritual home was severed temporarily(?).

By the time the War ended, Crystal Palace Football Club had taken up residence at a new temporary home – The Nest, opposite Selhurst Station, the former home of Croydon Common. Then in 1924, Crystal Palace moved again to the disused brickworks off Homesdale Road, to their current home, Selhurst Park.

Meanwhile, the Crystal Palace itself swarmed with military personnel and vehicles for four long years and the banks around the football ground, which had buzzed to the sound of enthusiastic football fans, were left to the birds.

LEFT: THE 1914 SQUAD DISPLAYING THE LONDON CHARITY CUP, CRYSTAL PALACE BEING THE FIRST CLUB TO WIN THE CUP TWO YEARS IN SUCCESSION.

League Championship winners, and participants in that epic Cup Final of 1897.

An excited 35,000 turned up at the Crystal Palace for the David-and-Goliath clash, but there was to be no giant-killing on this occasion – Everton won 4 – 0.

The Glaziers did a little better in the 1911-12 competition. Having worked their way through the earlier rounds, their second round opponents were Sunderland. This team had taken over the mantle for so long held by Newcastle as the premier North-East club and a top First Division club. Their young side was known as the "Team of all the Talents" and were to reach the Cup Final in 1913.

In their first visit to the Crystal Palace in 1912 they found the Glaziers tough opposition and had to settle for a goalless draw but in the replay at Roker Park they scored the only goal that knocked Palace out of the Cup.

CLOSURE!!!!

The 1914-15 season opened as usual but matters elsewhere were now dictating events.

THE *1913-1914* YEARBOOK

Just before the start of each season, the fledgling Crystal Palace Football Club published its Yearbook giving the results and comments on the previous season as well as the fixtures for the new season, also pen pictures of the players and officials.

The 1913-14 Yearbook was particularly optimistic as Crystal Palace had had a reasonably successful season in 1912 – 13 and could look forward to even better prospects in 1913-14, and so it turned out to be.

The Chairman, as always, was keen to implore members to encourage more to come to matches – was it ever different?

Ironically, there was even a comment to the effect that the Football Association was about to agree to extend the arrangements at the Crystal Palace for the staging of the Cup Final. A year later, both the Cup Finals and Crystal Palace FC were gone!

'WASHING DAY' THE ROYAL NAVAL VOLUNTEER RESERVE MAKE CRYSTAL PALACE THEIR HOME.

NAVAL DAYS

The advent of war meant that the Crystal Palace was commandeered by the Royal Navy. In fact, the Palace and the grounds were taken over by the Royal Naval Division. This force was formed in 1914 and gained many of its recruits from the Royal Naval Volunteer Reserve which was disbanded after a disastrous engagement at Antwerp, Belgium in 1914.

So the Palace was transformed to accommodate hundreds of naval recruits. The statues and greenery were pushed to one side and tiers of hammocks were hung up along the exhibition galleries. Here it was that over 8,000 young recruits were taught the elements of signalling and wireless telegraphy. The site then became known as HMS Victory VI but it was commonly called "HMS Crystal Palace". Being on land, the Division was often called the "Crystal Palace Army" and its members "Glass-house soldiers" but they were proud of their naval roots. The Royal Naval Division moved to Blandford, Dorset in February 1915, and HMS Victory VI continued as a preliminary training course for "hostilities only", where the ratings did a three-month course.

It was not all work for the trainees and there was ample time for recreation. The YMCA played a significant role in providing services for the ratings. This began in early September 1914.

Initially, some space was provided in the Crystal Palace building and this was soon enlarged to include accommodation in the Egyptian, Grecian and Roman Courts and part of the Centre Transept. Here, sailors were able to read, write and watch the concerts that were put on. In addition, the YMCA provided refreshments, a library, a savings bank, post office, laundry and much else.

Of course, the football and sports grounds were ideal for the athletic activities provided by the YMCA. In the summer, there was cricket, tennis, and regular field-day sports. In winter, there was basketball, running, jumping, and of course football as well as other sports.

Football was very popular and at times there were up to fifteen teams being run at the base. Serving men were also given free entry to Crystal Palace Football Club's home games. Of course, Crystal Palace had by now relocated to Herne Hill.

ABOVE: ROYAL NAVAL DEPOT CRYSTAL PALACE PASS, 1918.

BELOW: ON PARADE.

Above: Cover of 'HMS Crystal Palace' souvenir.

Top left & right: Physical training class in front of the Cup Final ground stands.

Right: Physical training staff.

Right: RND Cricket Club. YMCA.

Opposite page.

Top: Physical training, on the Northern ground.

Bottom: Physical training class tableau.

Crystal Palace 1928.

A FEAST OF AMATEUR FOOTBALL

THE POST GREAT WAR PERIOD – INTRODUCTION

As the war clouds cleared and the country began the long process of reconstruction, the Crystal Palace was still under the control of the Admiralty. Even when the building and the park were returned to the Crystal Palace Company, the grounds were in a dreadful state.

The football ground was not fit for matches to be played on and the 1920 FA Cup Final migrated to Stamford Bridge as a temporary measure. The FA did consider moving back to the Crystal Palace and came to an outline agreement to do so. In the end, the potential costs were prohibitive. Ultimately, the FA was offered space at the new Empire exhibition site at Wembley.

Meanwhile, Crystal Palace FC continued its travels, eventually settling in 1924 at Selhurst Park, which is still their home.

For the Crystal Palace football ground, the future looked bleak. Then the authorities were approached by the honorary secretaries of two distinguished amateur clubs, Corinthians and Casuals, who were each looking for a new home. Work began on reconstruction and renovation and on September 11th, 1922, Corinthians had the honour of playing the first game (see Chapter Twelve).

The Corinthian Club, the best of the amateur game, could still compete with the professionals while the Casuals battled on in the Isthmian League. Countless other amateur competitions began to use the Crystal Palace as the premier location for their best matches, like the Arthur Dunn Cup, Amateur Internationals, the Universities and many more.

Unfortunately, as the professional game went from strength to strength, the amateurs were left behind. In time, Corinthians could not match the skills, fitness and resources of the professionals and had to settle for being only another amateur side – eventually as a Corinthian-Casuals alliance.

The Crystal Palace ground remained much as it was but rarely echoed to the sound of large crowds as in former years. Both arenas were used for football and often up to four games were played in one day.

By the late 1920s, the Crystal Palace Company was keen to use the arena for other activities and in 1928 were convinced by London Motor Sports to create a speedway circuit in the arena. For six years, amateur football shared the ground with the speedway.

The tragic fire of 1936 marked another watershed. Football and speedway had departed but four days after the fire, work began on the construction of a motor-racing circuit and the ground became a paddock for the parking of vehicles. Two years later, sporting activities were prorogued as the nation was again at war.

Nevertheless there was much good football to enjoy in these inter-war years, so let us look at what was on offer.

ABOVE: THE PRINCE OF WALES SIGNS A FOOTBALL AT A MATCH DURING THE 1920's.

BELOW: TWO PANORAMAS OF THE CUP FINAL GROUND, WHERE A LARGE CROWD WATCH A SPEEDWAY MEETING DURING THE 1930's.

VARSITY MATCHES

Amongst the first to use the ground after its re-opening were the two old universities. The Crystal Palace staged the 45th and 46th varsity games – in 1922 and 1923. The Daily Telegraph thought that this was a much better venue than the Queen's Club *"because of the mists that often hang over West Kensington"* and *"because the new ground for the match is most appropriate to the best-class Amateur Association Football"*.

OXFORD UNIV 0 CAMBRIDGE UNIV 2
13TH DECEMBER 1922

This was the forty-fifth match in this historic fixture and at the time the series was standing all square. Both teams had won twenty games with four having been drawn.

On this occasion, Oxford started the game as favourites not having lost to Cambridge since 1914. Cambridge, on the other hand, were weakened by the loss through injury, with a sprained ankle, of their captain and best player, Claude Ashton. One paper reported that *"Ashton's absence seems to have destroyed all chance of a victory for Cambridge"*.

Cambridge still however had an outstanding keeper and amateur international in H P Bell, who captained the team the following season. Oxford had shown the better form in their games leading up to the match. Their 3 – 2 victory over the Corinthians was seen as a good indicator of their superiority. They also had a forward line which was fast and played a good short passing game.

Cambridge, however, had used 27 players in 13 games attempting to find their best side but were expected to lack cohesion without Ashton and were therefore expected to lose.

OXFORD: H M Warde-Clarke; J S Stephenson, W V Cavill; S W Bayliss, A J E Potts, A Platts; C H Kingsley, A H Phillips, H G Lewis, P H Barnard, J E Fraser.

CAMBRIDGE: H P Bell; F W Wilkinson, R Chalk; D Johnson, F J Mustill, E M Forsyth; D G A Lowe, H Douthwaite, I M Sorensen, M Thomas, E J Capel-Slaughter.

Nevertheless, the day after the match, the Daily Telegraph was explaining why Cambridge had won and why their predictions were wrong. Cambridge were the better team, more inventive, more purposeful and began and finished well. B Bennison, their reporter, said:

"for vigour it was admirable, in the way of speed and tenseness, it was splendidly unlike that which we see on most days; I enjoyed every minute of it.....the game was a sporting one from start to

finish; it was not done to the accompaniment of the referee's whistle. Hard knocks there were galore, of course, which was as a varsity match must always be. In its hardness, if not in skill, it was worthy of the best traditions of the football of Oxford and Cambridge".*

G Wagstaffe-Simmons of The Sporting Life had a quite different opinion. When he reported on the 1923 game, he said:

"As a game it is an improvement on last year when Cambridge won by 2 goals to 0" but *"yesterday's was not a thrilling match"*.

The first half of this game finished goalless. Phillips of Oxford missed an open goal with Bell on the ground. Cambridge might also have taken the lead if their wingers had been more effective; *"these two players were more remarkable for speed than a clear notion of how to arrange their attack so that goals might be got"*, according to Bennison in the Telegraph.

The game was well into the second half when Capel-Slaughter going flat out centred and Sorensen, drove in unsighted, during a goalmouth melee with Warde-Clarke.

Oxford might well have been given an equaliser when Bell, having saved a shot, was charged into the goal. The ball appeared to be over the line but with seven or eight players of both sides on top of the goalkeeper, the referee was unsighted and did not give a goal.

Oxford went close again with Barnard and Lewis both hitting the crossbar. Douthwaite, positioned at centre-forward in place of Ashton, sealed the game for the Light Blues. Yards into the Oxford half, he went forward, dribbling past three defenders before driving a shot hard and beyond the reach of the Oxford keeper. The Sporting Life wondered if Warde-Clarke had even seen the shot.

The 8,000 spectators witnessed a sensational result; The Sporting Life said Oxford had territorial superiority but Cambridge won with their best display of the season....... *"and this sufficed to bring them a very great reward"*.

OXFORD UNIV 1 CAMBRIDGE UNIV 1
WEDNESDAY 12TH DECEMBER 1923

The previews for this game complained of the poor standard of varsity football. Prior to the game, Cambridge had played thirteen matches and only won three whilst Oxford conceded 54 goals in 11 games, winning only twice.

Reports in The Sporting Life were fairly scathing. The game according to Wagstaffe-Simmons was one in which *"there was a marked*

H. M. WARDE-CLARKE.

J.A.MELHAM/22.
Oxford goalkeeper.

ABOVE & CENTRE: CARTOONS FROM THE SPORTING LIFE, 1922.

F. W. WILKINSON

J.A.MELHAM/22.
who will Captain Cambridge To-day

H. P. BELL, England & Cambridge

J.B.MELHAM/22.

LEFT: PROGRAMME FOR OXFORD V CAMBRIDGE, DECEMBER 1923.

AMATEUR CUP FINAL
LONDON CALEDONIANS 2 v EVESHAM TOWN 1 (A.E.T) 21 APRIL 1923

The second Amateur Cup Final to be played at the Palace aroused much greater interest than the first in 1898. The Athletic News reported:

"No Amateur Cup Final since the competition was instituted has aroused more interest than that which is to be played at the Crystal Palace next Saturday between London Caledonians and Evesham Town. The chief reason why this Final is attracting such attention is because the London Caledonians – in their thirty-seventh season – are one of the oldest of London's amateur clubs and Evesham Town only formed in February, 1919, are the babes of the Amateur Cup. While the Worcester League Champions have had to play right through the qualifying rounds to the Final, the Caledonians only came in when the Competition proper began".

The Evesham Standard said:

"Evesham is in a state of bubbling excitement. Everyone it seems is going to the Crystal Palace this Saturday to see the town play the Calies......and nothing but the match is on everyone's tongue. The Budget, the fight in the House of Commons, even such a question as cheaper beer is no more a topic of conversation than the death of Queen Anne. The question is will the Town win: No! Yes! Hurray!".

The Daily Chronicle sent their reporter, Athenian, to Evesham to find out more. He watched the Worcester Cup Final against

LEFT & BOTTOM LEFT: CARTOONS FROM THE SPORTING LIFE, 1923.

HILLEARY (Cambridge).

absence of the finer points of football". Oxford fielded three players from the previous year's meeting at the Crystal Palace – Stephenson, Fraser and Barnard. The only Cambridge survivor was Bell.

OXFORD: Archdale; Stephenson, Ashton; Boddington, Chadder, Morgan; Petersen, Barnard, Seldon, Whitworth, Fraser.

CAMBRIDGE: Bell; de Koven, Fleming; Powell, Robinson, Reid; Taylor, Wright, Hilleary, Lowe, May.

Cambridge started strongly and scored in the fourth minute following a cross from the left to their centre-forward Hilleary. Oxford should have equalised from a free kick given against Bell for 'carrying' but the chance was wasted.

Cambridge were on top until half time but the second half was more even. Barnard and May went close before Chadder beat two men and passed to Fraser who won a corner. Bell in the Cambridge goal could only half clear the difficult corner kick, to Chadder who headed into an open net. The last 20 minutes brought no further goals despite the efforts of both sides.

CHADDER (Oxford).

CLAUDE THESIGER ASHTON

Claude Ashton was born in Calcutta in February 1901. He went to school at Winchester and then on to Cambridge University where he gained blues for hockey and football, and captained the cricket team in 1923. Ashton joined Corinthians in the 1920 -21 season and appeared regularly for them until his retirement in 1933. He appeared in all positions (including in goal for his club) but was at his best at wing-half. Despite the decline of Corinthians, Ashton was considered good enough to be granted a full England cap in 1925.

He also gained 12 England amateur caps and was the last player to captain England on his only appearance.

After retiring from football, he helped Beckenham hockey club and played England trials. He also continued his participation in cricket playing for Essex until 1938. He was a Chartered Accountant by profession and later worked at the Stock Exchange. Ashton lost his life in an air crash while on active service for the RAF in the Second World War (1942).

Kidderminster Comrades. He was unimpressed: *"to be quite frank, Evesham were most disappointing. They did not impress individually or as a team....Now Kidderminster on their showing here should have been beaten by a side still in the Amateur Cup competition at this time of year by anything of ten goals upwards. Evesham merely beat them by three to one"*. However, the defence did catch his eye. *"I cannot recall another amateur defence which consists of such a tall set of fellows. The average from goal to half-back inclusive is practically 5ft. 11in."*.

In the Worcester Cup Final, Bob Jones faced three penalties, saving two of them. Evesham won 3 – 1. Jones was, in Athenian's opinion, *"a useful goalkeeper but not a very powerful one. One longed for a mighty biff approaching that handed out by Hayes of Ilford, who can land the ball two-thirds of the field every time"*. The Evesham Standard countered the criticism. 'Referee' in his column of 21 April 1923 said *"he was rather hard on the Town, but quite possibly he was suffering from a bad liver"*.

London Caledonians were one of the leading amateur clubs in England. Formed in 1886, they won the Isthmian League Championship six times, finally in 1924-25. In the 1912-13 FA Cup competition they reached the first round proper losing to Wolves 3 – 1. In the same season, they went on to claim the Isthmian League title and the London Charity Cup. Their ground was for a time within sight of the Crystal Palace. They played at the old 'Greyhound' pitch in Dulwich Village where among others they entertained Aston Villa. The Midlands side were guaranteed £15 gate money but unfortunately the receipts were only £4 19s 6d. By 1923 they were based at Tufnell Park.

The Calies star was Sloan, a full and amateur international for Ireland. Four English amateur internationals, Basil and Eric Gates, Jimmy McCree and Ian Hamilton; Bobby Noble, an amateur international for Scotland, and Barr who had won a Middlesex cap and badge, all added to a formidable side.

On their route to the Final the Caledonians had played six games scoring eighteen goals and conceding three. Evesham had to start earlier in the competition and had played ten matches scoring thirty times and conceding six goals.

The Caledonians did not have to concern themselves too much with travel arrangements being London-based; Evesham's were more elaborate. The Evesham Standard gave details of special trains decorated in *"red ribbons and other favours"*. Special trains left Evesham for Paddington at 6.40 am, 8.00am and 8.10am returning early on the Sunday morning.

ABOVE: PROGRAMME COVER FOR THE AMATEUR CHALLENGE CUP FINAL 1923. NOTICE THAT CASUALS WERE PLAYING AN ISTHMIAN LEAGUE FIXTURE AT THE SAME TIME.

"Arrangements can be made for parties of 23 to go by special char-a-banc from Paddington to drive round the city and see the sights, to have lunch and go to the football ground, and back to the city after the match at 10 shillings per head".

Memories of the First World War still hung heavily over the country. So, on the morning of the game, Evesham Town FC and the Evesham Ex-Servicemen visited the Cenotaph to place wreaths. The football club's captain Harry Ratcliff placed their wreath.

Evesham commissioned 'a cinema man' whose job was to 'shoot' various parts of the crowd and the ceremony at the Cenotaph, the teams, part of the match, and the spectators, with the film to be shown at the Evesham Grand Cinema after the big day.

Unfortunately, the cameraman missed the ceremony at the Cenotaph as he got left behind at Paddington station.

The Calies mascot was a big, live bulldog dressed in black and white and led up and down by a lady supporter. Apparently the bulldog did not take much interest in the match. The Evesham supporters brought with them a model cock robin. About the size of a swan, *"that cock robin was always in the picture. It was waved about at the match, it was taken to the Palladium to see the show. There it was handed round, and everyone in the dress circle took out a feather as a souvenir, so the poor old bird was feeling a bit undressed towards the end of the day"* (Evesham Standard).

After roaming around London, everyone made for the Crystal Palace and some took time to wander through the war exhibition. The team had lunch in the Palace and then prepared for the match.

Tickets for the game cost between one shilling and five shillings, the most expensive being in the pavilion. The attendance was nearly 15,000 and receipts were over £1,100.

The game itself went to extra time, London Caledonians winning by two goals to one. Some Evesham supporters believed the first Caledonian goal should have been disallowed for off-side. However, the Evesham Standard conceded that the best team on the day won but was not short of praise for its own side.... *"There are many qualities which we admire in this world. We admire cleverness and skill, and scientific methods, which have become a fine art in football. Of such qualities the Evesham team has a share though not to the extent of some of the Clubs which they defeated in the competition. But there are other things. More admirable perhaps than cleverness and skill are the qualities of pluck, grit, courage and doggedness, the good old English characteristic of never knowing when they are beaten, the determination to overcome difficulties, however great, and to battle for victory till the last whistle blows. In those great qualities the boastful or arrogant in victory, and they have shown that they can accept defeat with good temper and with the calm spirit of good sportsmen. So hats off to the Robins, everybody!"*.

*LEFT: THE LONDON CALEDONIANS
TEAM OF 1921.
BACK ROW L TO R:
J MCCUBBIN, R NOBLE,
A M P SLOAN, P J B DAWSON,
R STEWART, H M FINN, C KELSO.
FRONT ROW L TO R:
J C BLYTH, B H GATES, E H GATES,
W BARR.*

*THE EVESHAM TOWN TEAM WERE:
R JONES; F STOKES, H BRIDGES;
T GOULD, R RATCLIFF, G PENNELL;
G HAMPTON, J BUSBY, A MEAKINS,
S JONES, E OSBORNE.*

The president of the FA, J C Clegg, had to leave before the end to catch a train so the Cup was presented by the vice-president Mr A Davis.

After the game the Evesham team officials and dignitaries including the local MP Commander Eyres-Monsell had dinner at the Trocadero. A further reception was held later in Evesham.

There was one unfortunate incident which spoiled the day for some. One party had brought a case of beer and whiskey and left it in the cloakroom at Paddington intending to take it with them on the 11:35 pm train to provide a little cheer. Sadly, the man with the cloakroom ticket failed to make it for the 11:35 so they travelled home without it.

One man however gave a different assessment of the day. He was impressed by:

– the number of things in the street that missed him

– the number of ugly policemen

– the smell of petrol and burnt oil which pervaded everything

– the number of new buildings in the course of construction.

He also thought that people who lived at the Crystal Palace should undress in the dark!

1924 AMATEUR CUP SEMI-FINAL

In 1924, because both of the semi-finalists were local teams, and they had already drawn in their first match, the replay was held at the Crystal Palace on 22nd March 1924. Unfortunately, they drew again 0 - 0 and a second replay was necessary at Stamford Bridge before Erith and Belvedere progressed to the Final.

AMATEUR INTERNATIONALS

Amateur internationals came back to the Crystal Palace in 1923. On this occasion, the visitors were Ireland – a sensitive meeting with the recent tensions and political changes in the Emerald Isle.

ENGLAND 3 IRELAND 0
10 NOVEMBER 1923

The day was windy and 7,000 spectators attended what was only the Irish amateurs second game in England; in 1907 they had lost 6 - 1 at White Hart Lane. The teams for this game were as follows:

ENGLAND: J F Mitchell (Manchester City); Sgt Twine (Army), A G Bower (Corinthians); C T Ashton (Casuals), G H Armitage (Wimbledon), F H Ewer (Casuals); Lieut. K E Hegan (Army), S J T Earle (Clapton), Fusilier Macey (Army), A G Doggart (Corinthians), L J Barry (Notts County).

RESERVES: B C A Patchitt (Corinthians), H Morris (Bromley).

IRELAND: N Adams (Cliftonville); J Bruce (Cliftonville), G Shields (Cliftonville); W Read (Ards), J Robinson (Cliftonville), R Collins (Ards); M McKinney (Larne), J Auld (Cliftonville), A Sloan (London Caledonians), J Harris (Glenavon), J McGrillen (Clyde).

The Irish team included A Sloan who had played at the Crystal Palace earlier in the year in the 1923 FA Amateur Cup Final. England had a strong side who had lost 2 – 0 the previous month in the Charity Shield against the professionals.

Ireland won the toss and chose to play with

the advantage of the wind but they could not convert this into goals. At half time, it was England who led 2 – 0. Fusilier Macey, the England captain scored first. *"For one handicapped by lack of weight and inches as he is he did very well indeed. He certainly has the right idea of what is expected of a centre-forward. Doggart sent the ball over from the left and the laughable little soldier had it in the net in a twinkling"* – Daily Telegraph, 12 November 1923.

Earle scored the second, dribbling through and putting it in from close range.

In the second half, Barry scored after thirteen minutes following the *"most brilliant individual effort of the game.....he received the ball when in his own half of the field, evaded his challengers and dribbled to within a few yards of the goal, when he shot with great force. Adams beat the kick back, but Barry pounced on it again and drove it into the net"*.

Ireland were thought to lack strength in midfield. Sloan had a good game and was unlucky to have a brilliant shot saved by Mitchell just before half-time.

The Daily Telegraph report of the game, by B Bennison, gives a fascinating insight into the growing divide at the time between

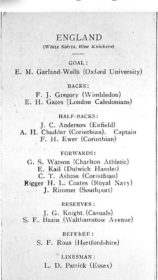

ABOVE & RIGHT: A MATCH DAY CARD ISSUED TO THE PLAYERS FOR THE ENGLAND V IRELAND GAME IN 1929.

THE DAILY TELEGRAPH (18TH NOVEMBER 1929) DESCRIBED ROBINSON AS AN EFFICIENT SUBSTITUTE FOR THE ORIGINAL CHOICE - CHADDER.

the professional and amateur game. It is also interesting to read this in the context of football today. Amateurs and professionals he said have little in common *"one is free to exploit the game for the game's sake; the other must needs do battle for points, by which the worth of his team is appraised. And it is probable that those of the spectators accustomed to watch League games who took themselves to the Crystal Palace on Saturday to see the selected amateurs of England and Ireland were rather out of their element. I suspected that many of them would have been happier had they been of a crowd of white – hot partisans and felt the thrills that come from noise and clatter. But they did see football that told of the individual as distinct from football that has the appearance of being machine-made.*

It is probable that a team made up of the very best of the two sides we saw at Sydenham would suffer to be beaten by a combination of our leading professionals, but if the match did not produce a classic example of association football, the majority of onlookers must have felt that it broke new ground. It was not a match remarkable for speed; neither was it a desperate fight for victory. Of keenness there was, of course, plenty; but the outstanding feature was the wholeheartedness of the players to make their football characteristic of themselves. Passes were not given in the air; they were done as passes should be done – on the ground, and so we saw much delightful and uncommon combination".

ENGLAND 7 IRELAND 2
16 NOVEMBER 1929

Being the first amateur international side to score against England at the Crystal Palace was little compensation to the well-beaten Irish team. England fielded five new caps in Robinson, Watson, Rimmer, Anderson and Garland-Wells. Edgar Kail the local hero who scored 427 goals in his career for Dulwich Hamlet played at inside-right. J Dogherty the Portadown inside-left was regarded as the best Irish player from the previous fixture between the sides. The teams were as follows:

ENGLAND: H M Garland-Wells (Oxford Univ); F J Gregory (Wimbledon), E H Gates (London Caledonians); J C Anderson (Enfield), *Cpl R J C Robinson (R A F), F H Ewer (Corinthians); G S Watson (Charlton Athletic), E Kail (Dulwich Hamlet), C T Ashton (Corinthians), H L Coates (Royal Navy), J Rimmer (Southport).

IRELAND: A Gardiner (Cliftonville); J Crymble (Linfield Swifts), B McGuire (Cliftonville); R Falloon (Cliftonville), J McMahon (Derry City and Bohemians), Cpl Jones (Army); J Quinn (Cliftonville), A Kelly (R A F), J Miller (Cliftonville), J Dogherty (Portadown), W C Kerr (Glenavon).

The conditions were not particularly good. The light was bad, it was bitterly cold and it rained heavily throughout the game. The Daily Telegraph suggested that *"in less dreadful conditions Ireland would perhaps not have suffered such a heavy defeat".*

Claude Ashton was the star for the English and his speed and strength overcame the conditions and the opposition. He scored a first-half hat-trick and his, and England's fourth, early in the second half. Watson scored the fifth and MacMahon then beat Garland-Wells with a long shot. Coates made it 6 – 1 and Kelly then brought it back to 6 – 2. The final scorer was McGuire who put into his own net.

Despite the score, Gardiner from Cliftonville was rated the better of the two keepers.

ARTHUR DUNN CUP

The Arthur Dunn Cup, that had started at the Palace in 1903, returned after the First World War. The 1923 Final was held elsewhere (the "Spotted Dog" at Forest Gate) but in 1924, now that Corinthians and Casuals had settled at the Palace, the Arthur Dunn teams moved in.

The competition was now reduced to 16 teams as more and more schools switched to rugby. However, there were still many games to be seen at the Palace. Not only was the Arthur Dunn Final played at the Crystal Palace ground but many of the earlier games in the competition as well. Old Salopians, for instance, tended to play most of their games at the Palace including a second round match against Old Wellingburians in 1927. (Old Salopians won 3 – 0 and went on to win the Cup again that year).

However, the competition in these years was dominated by two teams – Old Malvernians and Old Wykehamists, each of them winning the Cup three times in a row. Malvernians made the early running (1924 – 26) until Old Salopians defeated them in the 1927 Final.

OLD SALOPIANS 6 V OLD MALVERNIANS 3 2ND APRIL 1927

This turned out to be a remarkable match. Malvernians had dominated the competition for the last three years, and had beaten Old Salopians the previous year. So it was quite a disappointment for the late arrivals from Shrewsbury to know that Malvernians had already scored. Some had been to watch the Boat Race at Barnes and did not get to the Palace until fifteen minutes after the start.

Gradually though Salopians got into the game and equalised before half-time and even went ahead in the second half. Within five minutes, Malvernians equalised. So, when full-time came around the scores were equal (2-2).

Extra time of fifteen minutes each way followed. In this period, another five goals were scored, one each to make it 3-3 and then Salopians scored three times to win the game. Newton scored a hat-

trick but the outstanding player was G S Watson, who was later to play in the Football League for Charlton Athletic, Crystal Palace and Clapton Orient.

It is also worth noting that J M Peterson, who scored the Salopians' second goal, became Headmaster of Shrewsbury School and later Eton College.

OLD SALOPIANS: J D Deuchar; P S Snow, R Heslop; R C Lancaster, L B Blaxland, A T Barber; J M Peterson, H V Newton, H G Lewis, G S Watson, J T Bush.

OLD MALVERNIANS: J H Mears; I Begbie, G L Miller; R N Stone, N W Beeson, S S Fieldon; H C D Abrams, C G Toppin, G B Partridge, C G W Robson, W R T Picton-Warlow.

ABOVE: OLD MALVERNIANS, THE CUP WINNING TEAM OF 1926.
BACK ROW L TO R:
L S EAST, W R T PICTON-WARLOW, H A PRIDHAM, E R T HOLMES, C G W ROBSON, T B G WELCH, D B CAMPBELL.
FRONT ROW L TO R:
R N STONE, C F MORICE, W C STUART-LOW, G L MILLER, G B PARTRIDGE.

BELOW: OLD MALVERNIANS, THE CUP WINNING TEAM OF 1925.
STANDING L TO R:
   E R T HOLMES,
   A E MACKINNON,
   C G W ROBSON,
   H A PRIDHAM,
   W R T PICTON-WARLOW.
MIDDLE ROW L TO R:
   G B PARTRIDGE,
   G F MORICE, N W BEESON,
   W C STUART-LOW,
   G L MILLER.
FRONT: D J KNIGHT,
   N H STONE.

RIGHT: OLD WYKEHAMISTS, WINNERS OF THE ARTHUR DUNN CUP 1931. BACK L TO R: A D GARROW, G S GRIMSTON, G R M RICKETTS, J L T GUISE, G I BARTY-KING. MIDDLE L TO R: A R V BARKER, P G T KINGSLEY, C T ASTON, J F T TOPPIN, C R V BELL. FRONT: M B S BOWER, J W M MANSEL.

BELOW: PROGRAMME COVER FOR THE 1931 ARTHUR DUNN CUP FINAL AND THE OLD BOYS' CUP FINAL.

Old Malvernians returned the following year to meet Old Wykehamists in what even the Winchester correspondent described as *"one of the most exciting well-fought Finals that can ever have taken place in the competition....."*.

Wykehamists reached the Final again in 1929, this time they met Old Carthusians whom they defeated 3 – 0. Claude Ashton put in an outstanding performance and proudly collected the trophy from Mrs Arthur Dunn, who regularly presented the prize to the winning team.

This heralded the beginning of a winning streak for Wykehamists who were successful again in 1930 (Old Salopians 4 – 1) and 1931 (Old Citizens 5 – 1).

The competition continued to be played at the Palace up to 1934, the Corinthians having already moved to pastures new. Throughout this period, four teams dominated the competition – Carthusians, Wykehamists, Salopians and Malvernians. The most consistent were Malvernians, who won the trophy four times between 1923 and 1936.

Then, like the Corinthians, the Arthur Dunn competition moved – in this case to the Hurlingham club, the home of polo.

OLD BOYS CUP FINALS

The Arthur Dunn competition had proved so popular when formed in 1903 that it was eventually decided to limit entry to 24 teams. For the unsuccessful applicants a second competition was proposed but it was the 1913 – 14 season before the Old Boys Cup competition was created under the auspices of the newly-formed Amateur Football Alliance.

In the first campaign in 1914, the Old Hurst Johnians won the Cup but then of course war intervened. However, when the Arthur Dunn Cup was resurrected in the 1920s, so was the Old Boys Cup. Traditionally, it was always played on the same day as the Arthur Dunn Final.

So throughout the period that the Arthur Dunn was played at the Palace, the Old Boys Cup was also contested.

RIGHT: TICKET FOR A LOCAL SCHOOLS' FA CHALLENGE SHIELD, 1929.

BELOW: ACTION IN THE 1936 ARTHUR DUNN CUP FINAL.

> **CRYSTAL PALACE.**
> HENRY JAMES BUCKLAND - General Manager.
> **Crystal Palace Schools' Football Associations'**
> CHALLENGE SHIELD.
> FINAL ON THE SPORTS GROUND
> AT THE CRYSTAL PALACE ON
> EASTER MONDAY, 1st APRIL 1929, at 3.30
> **Lewisham S.F.A.** (HOLDERS)
> v.
> **Beckenham & Penge S.F.A.**
> ADMIT ONE TO STAND or RING SEATS
> PRICE 6D.
> This ticket does **not** admit to the grounds of the Crystal Palace, and the usual price of admission is to be paid at the turnstiles.

SCHOOLS

The Crystal Palace was an ideal venue for local Schools organisations to stage inter-district matches, as evidenced by the match between Beckenham & Penge Schools and Lewisham Schools (above).

It must have been a great thrill for these schoolboys to run out onto the pitches where their heroes of the Cup Finals had played.

ABOVE: A MATCH ON THE NORTHERN GROUND IN 1924.

AFA SENIOR CUP FINAL

This Final was staged at the Crystal Palace on occasions. In 1924, for instance, the Final was held on April 5th when the Bank of England played Eastbourne.

INTER-BANK CUP (DAILY TELEGRAPH CHALLENGE CUP)

This competition was started in 1912. The Cup was given by the Daily Telegraph, through the efforts of Viscount Burnham, to the Banks and the Stock Exchange. The idea was for an annual football match in aid of the Lord Mayor Treloar Cripples Hospital and College at Alton, Hampshire.

Sir William Treloar was Lord Mayor of London in 1911-12 and wished to leave some mark to commemorate his year of office. He had no family of his own (he and his wife adopted a girl, Florence Treloar) and he wished to do something for children who suffered tubercular joints and similar conditions, hence the hospital, which still exists today.

Each year the game was played at the Crystal Palace and a great honour it was. For instance, in 1925, Frank Coles, a respected member of the Amateur Football Alliance was selected to play for the Banks. Unfortunately, he evidently had a difficult afternoon as he was pitted against A G Bower (Chelsea, Corinthians and England) and Freddie Ewer (Corinthians and England).

Eventually, the expenses at the Crystal Palace became too much to yield a good income for charity. At this point, Frank Coles (Honorary Secretary of the London Banks FA) and a representative from Treloars approached the Arsenal Manager, Herbert Chapman, and later George Allison and Tom Whittaker – they were pleased to lend the Stadium at Arsenal for the match, free of expenses wherever possible. The competition ended when the formation of the National Health Service made appeals of this nature unpopular.

LEFT: THE DAILY TELEGRAPH CHALLENGE CUP.

131

THE
CORINTHIANS
and
THE CASUALS
FIXTURES 1924/5
At the CRYSTAL PALACE

1924

Oct. 11	The Casuals *v.* Wycombe Wanderers. I.L.	
„ 18		
„ 25	The Casuals *v.* Civil Service. I.L.	
Nov. 1	The Casuals *v.* Oxford University	
„ 8	The Casuals *v.* Woking. I.L.	
„ 15	The Corinthians *v.* The South Africans	
„ 19 (Wed.)	The Casuals *v.* Cambridge University	
„ 22	The Corinthians *v.* Cambridge University	
„ 29	The Corinthians *v.* Oxford University	
Dec. 6		
„ 10 (Wed.)		
„ 13	The Casuals *v.* Tufnell Park. I.L.	
„ 20		
„ 26 (Fri.)		
„ 27	The Casuals *v.* Ilford. I.L.	

1925

Jan. 3	First Round, F.A. Amateur Cup	
„ 10	First Round, F.A. Cup	
„ 17	The Casuals *v.* Nunhead. I.L.	
„ 24	The Casuals *v.* Old Malvernians	
„ 31	Second Round, F.A. Cup	
Feb. 7		
„ 14	The Casuals *v.* Northampton Nomads	
„ 21	Third Round, F.A. Cup	
„ 28	The Casuals *v.* St. Albans City. I.L.	
Mar. 7	Fourth Round, F.A. Cup	
„ 9 (Mon.)		
„ 14	The Casuals *v.* Leytonstone. I.L.	
„ 16 (Mon.)		
„ 21		
„ 28	Final, Arthur Dunn Cup	
Apl. 4		
„ 11		
„ 18	The Casuals *v.* Clapton. I.L.	
„ 25		
May 2	The Casuals *v.* Oxford City. I.L.	

(I.L. Denotes Isthmian League Match)

Ground Members Tickets admit to the Ground and Seats for all Corinthian and Casuals Matches (Cup Ties excepted). **PRICE, ONE GUINEA** (No Tax). All enquiries and applications for Tickets, which must be accompanied by a remittance, must be made to—

The Assistant Secretary, Corinthian F.C., Crystal Palace, S.E. 19

The Corinthian F.C. will take part in the F.A. Cup Competition and the Casuals F.C. in the F.A. Amateur Cup, Surrey Senior Cup, and the London Charity Cup Competitions.

Other Corinthian Matches with Prominent League Clubs will also be arranged
E. C. BAMBRIDGE, Hon. Sec., Corinthian F.C.
S. F. HEPBURN, Hon. Sec., The Casuals F.C.

ISTHMIAN LEAGUE.

ILFORD (2) v. THE CASUALS (0).

The Casuals have made a very uncertain start in the Isthmian League, and on Saturday they dropped both points at Ilford. Their visit attracted about 4,000 spectators. Excellent combination by the Casuals was allowed to go by without reward as the visiting forwards were weak in front of goal. During an attack by Ilford Bower conceded a corner, and this produced a goal, Oldershaw's place kick being so well directed that the ball curled under the bar. Packenham-Walsh carried through a run in fine style and registered Ilford's second goal. Ilford were subjected to heavy pressure in the second half, but the Casuals' forwards had a bad day when it came to shooting or sweeping the ball into goal, and the home defence prevailed. Result: Ilford 2, Casuals 0.

Next Saturday the Casuals visit Clapton in the first round of the London Charity Cup.

ISTHMIAN LEAGUE.

	P.	W.	D.	L.	F.	A.	Pts.
Clapton	6	5	0	1	19	7	10
Dulwich Hamlet	7	4	1	2	21	15	9
St. Albans City	5	4	0	1	21	11	8
London Caledonians	6	4	1	1	12	9	9
Ilford	7	4	0	3	18	15	8
The Casuals	4	2	0	2	9	9	4
Tufnell Park	5	2	0	3	9	10	4
Leytonstone	5	2	0	3	11	16	4
Civil Service	2	1	1	0	3	1	3
Nunhead	5	1	1	3	8	11	3
Wycombe Wanderers	5	1	1	3	9	18	3
Wimbledon	6	1	0	5	11	18	2
Oxford City	1	0	1	0	1	1	1
Woking	4	0	0	4	2	13	0

THE CASUALS

EARLY HISTORY

A team called Casuals existed as early as the 1870s but by 1883 arrangements seem to have been put on a firmer footing. A few months after the Corinthians were formed in 1882, T W Blenkiron, a Cambridge Blue and Old Carthusian, and F Buckley, an Old Etonian took the steps to set up the organisation and the club adopted Buckley's racing colours of chocolate and pink.

The players were drawn mainly from the old boys of public schools and over the next 50 years, Casuals became a well-respected amateur club, among the pioneers of competitive amateur football. They played in the first Amateur Cup Final in 1894, losing 1 – 2 to the Old Carthusians. They were the founder members of both the Isthmian League in 1905 and, after the amateur/professional split, of the Southern Amateur League in 1907. The Casuals were, in effect the chief nursery for the Corinthians with players often members of both clubs.

CASUALS COME TO THE PALACE

When the Crystal Palace ground became available it was G N Foster (honorary secretary of Corinthians) and S F Hepburn (honorary secretary of Casuals) who negotiated with the Crystal Palace Company for their two teams to move there. When all was agreed, they set about renovating the pavilion, stands and dressing rooms.

The Sportsman announced: *"With reference to the recent announcement to the effect that from next season onwards*

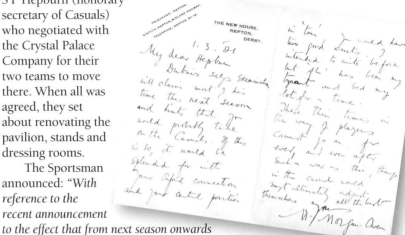

BELOW: LETTER FROM M MORGAN-OWEN, PRESIDENT OF THE CASUALS, IMPLORING SIDNEY HEPBURN TO BECOME HON. SECRETARY OF THE CLUB.

ABOVE: M MORGAN-OWEN.

LEFT: THE CRYSTAL PALACE GROUND. INSET: G N FOSTER AND S F HEPBURN.

After the Great War, Corinthians and Casuals agreed to work together and at a meeting in 1921, they jointly passed a resolution proposed by C Wreford Brown, *"that this meeting is of the opinion that efforts should be made to obtain a suitable ground in the London area which might be used by both the Corinthians and Casuals Football Club, with a view to a mutually beneficial arrangement being arrived at for the future"*. Corinthians members were also invited to support Casuals by accepting invitations to play for the Casuals whenever possible.

the Corinthian and Casuals Football Clubs will play at the Crystal Palace, it is requested that all communications on business matters be addressed to the Assistant Secretary, Corinthians FC, Crystal Palace, S E 19. All communications for the Corinthians FC should be addressed to Mr G N Foster, Corinth, Foxgrove Road, Beckenham.

With reference to the Casuals FC, all communications should be addressed to Mr S F Hepburn, Heathcroft, Putney Hill, S W 15".

Corinthians had the honour of playing the first game on the ground – against Tottenham. So it was not until Casuals met Kingstonians on October 21st in the second round of the FA Amateur Cup, and drew 1 – 1 with them at Kingston, that Casuals had their first opportunity to play at the Crystal Palace. The replay turned out to be an exciting game ending in another draw (2 – 2). Four thousand people, including a large contingent from Kingston, turned up to the old Cup Final ground.

CASUALS: H B Kidd; H G Payne, A G Bower; F H Ewer, A H Butcher, H H Low; M Howell, R L Holdsworth, H F Dubuis, E Martin, R G Pinfield.

BELOW: THE CASUALS ELEVEN FOR 1922.

should be played. Last season they had one disappointment after another. When they played and lost their first match none of the players had kicked a ball by way of practice. They were right out of the match-winning condition and circumstances prevented them from developing a strong side.

The practices on Monday and Wednesday served to bring their speed into operation, but several of the players still require to work hard at ball practice.

Many of those taking part came from long distances in order to participate in the games. For instance, one came from Bath and another from Brighton. That is a proof of their enthusiasm.

PINFIELD'S BRILLIANT GOAL

Wednesday's teams were practically arranged to represent the first attack against the first defence. The first attack won easily, and the finest goal of the evening was scored by R G Pinfield, almost from the touch line. It was a goal similar to that which beat Alderson, the Crystal Palace goalkeeper, in the replayed Cup-tie at Millwall. That this goal by Pinfield was no more accident is shown by the fact that he has scored many similar goals. The most sensational goal of the kind he has ever scored was of a like character. It was scored by him while he was playing for Reading in 1913. The match in question was the second round of the English Cup against

KINGSTONIAN: C Warner; E W Rassell, R Blaber; G Scott, J A Rowe, S C Edwards; W G Soper, T Fulton, H Rassell, W J Wright, F S Brown.

It was assumed that there would be sufficient following in the Crystal Palace, Norwood and Penge area for both Corinthians and Casuals to thrive. The reputation of Casuals had spread far and wide and they gained considerable publicity in the local press. The Penge Advertiser sent a reporter to early practice matches:

RIGHT: MILES HOWELL.

Tottenham Hotspur, who were the visitors to Reading. His goal sufficed for Reading to win the match by 1 – 0.

The practice matches were played on the cycle track. Mr Frank Smith, who is the groundsman at the Palace, rendered assistance to the players in the dressing rooms. It will be remembered that for several years Mr Smith was the assistant trainer to the Crystal Palace FC.

"The Casuals FC have been hard at it this week and two fast practice matches have been played at the Crystal Palace.

The Casuals hold a prominent position in amateur football circles, but there are thousands of lovers of the great winter game within a ten mile radius of the Crystal Palace, who, having had no opportunity to witness their play, only know of the club by name.

The members of the club are all University men, and that fact alone constitutes a guarantee that they have a sound knowledge of the game and how it

The Casuals open their Isthmian League programme on Saturday when they visit West Norwood......".

Thus, the Casuals blended into the scene at the People's Palace. Miles Howell (Casuals' captain) and Sidney Hepburn (Hon Secretary) even entered as a pair for the Crystal Palace Badminton Club's handicap doubles.

CASUALS' FIRST SEASON

In the first season, Casuals decided to concentrate their efforts on the Isthmian League, in which the Reserves also participated. Their only other interest was in the FA Amateur Cup, the first time since 1907.

They had a good run in the FA Amateur Cup. After beating Redhill in a replay, their next opponents were Kingstonians. Again, a replay was necessary and this gave Casuals the opportunity to play their first game at the Crystal Palace on October 21st. As this match also ended in a draw (2 - 2), a second replay ensued before Casuals went through.

In the fourth round, Casuals' opponents were local rivals Wimbledon. Unfortunately, after drawing with the Dons at Plough Lane, Casuals were unable to hold the replay at the Crystal Palace as the ground was already booked for a Corinthian match (against Cambridge University). Consequently, Casuals were forced to go to Wimbledon again and lost.

Restrictions on the use of the Crystal Palace facilities were not the only limitations that Casuals had to endure. Being an amateur club, there were not the funds to provide the sort of conditions for players that their professional counterparts might have experienced. Players were expected to provide their own boots, socks and shorts but when selected to play were given a Casuals shirt in the club colours of chocolate and pink. In addition to competitive games, players were invited to attend practice sessions on Tuesday's and Thursday's.

That first season was an indifferent one but there were some successes. The midweek team, known as Casuals Wednesday, scored some outstanding victories over lesser opposition, for instance Gipsy Hill Police were beaten 16 – 1 in a very one-sided game.

On Easter Monday in 1923, something like 10,000 holiday-makers took a look at the football served up by Casuals when they played a friendly against Luton Clarence. Casuals were evidently the better side but it was a well-contested match ending in a win for Casuals by five goals to three.

The following Saturday the home team found themselves in a much more serious encounter in the Isthmian League. Civil Service were the top side in that league at the time with 26 points out of 22 games. The Casuals were weakened by the absence of A G Bower, K R G Hunt, M Howell and A G Doggart (Corinthians all!). They were therefore struggling to hold the Civil Service forwards. Despite some spirited shooting by Pinfield, the Civil Service ran out winners by 2 – 0.

CASUALS: H B Kidd; H G Payne, F H Plaistowe; W Shillcock, F H Ewer, A Platts; S F Hepburn, E Martin, H F Dubuis, J H Lockton, R G Pinfield.

CIVIL SERVICE: F J Hayne; W N Armstrong, G Jones; T C Culpeck, C W Harbridge, A F Orchard; D M Hallett, O L H Levy, A Gilbert, F Tait, A Perry.

1923 – 24 SEASON

With such fantastic facilities at the Crystal Palace, the Casuals ran a number of teams. By 1923, they were running five teams, including the mid-week side (Casuals Wednesday) and the secretary was keen to hear from young "old boy" players with a view to trials in the various teams.

ABOVE: ERIC MARTIN.

SIDNEY F HEPBURN

Sidney Hepburn was born on 16th September 1896. He was the son of Sir Harry Hepburn also a keen and respected sportsman with honours in golf, tennis and football. Sidney went to Rugby school where he played for the second rugby XV. After War service, he went up to Oxford and gained his Soccer 'Blue' in 1919-20 and his Lawn Tennis 'Blue' in 1920. It was here that he acquired his nickname of "Sprouts" the exact origin of which is lost in the mists of time but may have related to his consumption of the green vegetable at an undergraduate dinner.

Hepburn was unusual in that he wore glasses while playing football. He was an all-round athlete but he concentrated on football and represented the Isthmian League and the Southern Amateur League. Of course, his legacy is as a result of the fact that in 1921 he became Honorary Secretary of the Casuals and was largely responsible for the revitalisation of the Club and the old Cup Final ground at the Crystal Palace, which became the home of the Casuals in 1922. Hepburn also played for the Club at various levels.

The prospects for the 1923 – 24 season were high. Improvements were made to the ground; S F Hepburn wrote:

"I am glad to say our tenancy of the Crystal Palace ground – in conjunction with the Corinthian F C – will be continued... also improvements to the ground – particularly from the point of view of the popular side – are in hand. The playing pitch will be taken out to the old position.....".

Most of the old players were still available – Howell, Pinfield, Bower, Dubuis, Morris, Ewer, Lockton, Payne, Hunt, Martin, Hepburn, Platts, etc., but the drive was still on to recruit new "old boys".

So the club broadened their participation, this time getting involved in the Surrey Intermediate Cup and other local competitions. Also, the usual fixtures were organised, including friendlies with Oxford, Cambridge and London Universities, Northampton Nomads, Liverpool Ramblers and Ipswich Town amongst others.

On Easter Saturday 1924, with the Corinthians away in Glasgow (for the annual match with Queen's Park), Casuals entertained Northampton Nomads. The Nomads were reasonably well-known at the time, having had some success in the FA Amateur Cup competition. In the 1923 – 24 season they had reached the fourth round losing to Clapton. So it was surprising that Casuals had an easy victory by three goals to nil.

ISTHMIAN LEAGUE
v.
CORINTHIAN F.C.
To be played at
THE
CRYSTAL PALACE,
Sydenham, S.E.
On Saturday, 26th December, 1925,
Kick-off 2.15 o'clock.

ABOVE & RIGHT: TEAM CARD FOR THE ISTHMIAN LEAGUE V CORINTHIANS IN DECEMBER 1925. THE CASUALS HAD PLAYERS ON BOTH SIDES AND THE LINESMAN WAS S F HEPBURN.

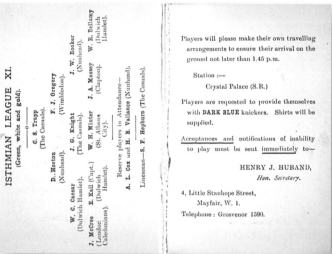

CASUALS: A M Wilkinson; H G Payne, F V Smith; C E Glenister, H F Dubuis, A Platts; S F Hepburn, F H Barnard, J Lockton, M Howell, F A Ryder.

NORTHAMPTON NOMADS: A F Wells; F H Holder, L C Hawtin; R A Shaw, E F Towell, J T Badham; R Goldie, N W Timms, I M Sorensen, R L Wright, J Tysoe.

The 1923-24 season ended in fine style on May 3rd 1924 when Casuals took two Isthmian League points off Wycombe Wanderers. The heavy rain which fell during the match meant that the ball became heavier and stuck in the mud.

Consequently, there was only one goal in the first half (to Casuals). In the second half seven goals were scored as more and more mistakes were made. Wycombe scored two and Casuals five leading to a 6 – 2 victory.

CASUALS: A M Wilkinson; H G Payne, A G Bower; C E Glenister, H F Dubuis, P A Sargeant; S F Hepburn, P J Boswell, J H Lockton, G S Cruikshank, T A Ryder.

WYCOMBE: J Kipping; R Walker, H Phipps; W J Smith, F Adams, F Gates; A Grace, A E Weaver, R G Hinton, A Smith, A W Fryer.

The Norwood News reviewed the 1923-24 season as follows:

"The Casuals have just completed a successful season. They hold the 7th position in the Isthmian League table, having won 13 matches out of 26 with an aggregate of 27 points. Generally speaking, they have played very good football, but a few displays have been disappointing. These have been due to fielding weak sides, but this is unavoidable in the Casuals Club, as so many players have interests elsewhere.

It speaks well for the spirit of the members when several have travelled long distances in order to play, and the fact that 152 different players have been called upon to fill the five weekly teams, is a great disadvantage if winning combinations are to be found.

However, the management of the club feel that they have fulfilled their object, which is to supply good, clean football to their patrons, and it is hoped that the Casuals will continue to give an exhibition of the highest class of amateur football at the Crystal Palace".

There was one sad addendum to the 1923 -24 season. It was reported in the Norwood News that Eric Martin, a very popular member of Corinthians and Casuals, had died in a mid-air collision at Duxford, when his Bristol fighter struck an Avro both of whom were involved in stunt flying.

CASUALS CONSIDER A MOVE

Unfortunately, despite all the interest and publicity, the Casuals found that they did not get the attendances that they had hoped for. By the start of the 1924-25 season the situation was becoming difficult. It was argued that one of the reasons was the shilling (5p) charged to view their matches. This was the admission price for all football matches at the Crystal Palace but at other clubs nearby, for example Dulwich Hamlet, Nunhead, West Norwood, fans paid only 8d (3p).

At the time, there was an intense debate about the reduction of one penny in Entertainment Tax and whether this benefit should be passed on to the spectators and not absorbed by the League clubs. Against this

LEFT: THE CASUALS FIRST TEAM SQUAD FOR THE 1923-24 SEASON.

background, the Casuals could not resist a reduction. So in 1924, the gate price was dropped to sixpence (2¹/₂ p).

Sidney Hepburn also enticed well-known players to the Casuals ranks, for instance, one Andrew Ducat, who had played for Arsenal, Aston Villa and Fulham, and one of the few who had played for England at cricket and football. After Ducat had relinquished the manager's role at Fulham, Hepburn persuaded the Football Association to re-instate him as an amateur. To this they finally agreed provided he played only for Casuals' mid-week side.

However, new players and reduced prices were insufficient to draw the crowds to the Crystal Palace ground. *"The fact is that there was not sufficient support in the Sydenham district for an Isthmian League club – even a winning one – so that the Old Boys had no option but to go elsewhere".*

Hepburn told members of the Club:

"During the last three seasons, although the standard of play in the club has steadily increased, as have its successes on the field, the lack of support (in spite of an introduction of a sixpenny gate this year) has steadily diminished, and the financial loss on the Casuals FC has been amazing.

The officials of the club have felt that in the interests of the club it is impossible to continue bearing this burden indefinitely, and it is with very great regret that they have felt obliged to move to a district where the possibility is that the local supporters will be very much greater.

The most important point, however, is that there is no reason to anticipate that the co-operation and close relations that have existed at the Crystal Palace between the Corinthians and the Casuals should in no way be affected; it is certainly to the great interests of both clubs that this relationship should remain as heretofore.

My Committee feel that some explanation is due

to our friends and supporters".

The last Casuals match, on May 2nd 1925, to be played at the Crystal Palace was an Isthmian League game against Oxford City. The Norwood News described it as *"a curious game, in which some good football was witnessed"*. Though at one stage, Casuals led 3 – 1, eventually Oxford ran out the winners by 4 – 3 with three goals by Rogers.

CASUALS: C S Trapp; H G Payne, J G Stevenson; C E Glenister, G B Partridge, H F Dubuis; C H Sleightholme, J G Knight, M Howell, J H Lockton, R G Pinfield.

OXFORD: A Meeson; B J Brooker, S Wyatt; S Bayliss, R Dorn, F V Spiller; S Cox, H Wackett, L Rogers, F Hartley, F Tobin.

The ground selected for their new home was that of Kingstonians at Richmond Road described as a *"well appointed enclosure"*. This arrangement suited the Kingstonian because at the time they were in need of money to buy the freehold of the ground.

BELOW: ROYAL AIR FORCE COMRADES ACT AS PALLBEARERS AT THE FUNERAL OF ERIC MARTIN IN 1924.

So, the Casuals left the Crystal Palace but their association with Corinthians continued, culminating in their amalgamation in 1939.

"SPORTY" FOOTBALL AT THE PALACE.

Crystal Palace and Corinthians Meet on the Old Cup Final Ground.

TOP: CARTOON FROM THE CROYDON ADVERTISER OF CRYSTAL PALACE V CORINTHIANS 3RD FEBRUARY1933.
BOTTOM: CORINTHIANS 1923. L TO R: A BOWER, A PHILLIPS, F CREEK, H DOUTHWAITE, H BELL, J MOULSDALE, C ASHTON, J MORRISON, L BLAXLAND, B PATCHETT.

138

"PLAY UP CORINTH"

Of course, the Corinthians had been in existence for many years. They had been formed out of the desire to give the best English players the opportunity of "playing together" and preparing for international matches. By 1882, England had been on the receiving end of a few defeats by the Scots (a fixture that had originally been proposed to improve the standard of the game in Scotland) and lack of practice was identified as the problem.

So N L Jackson, the Assistant Secretary of the FA, summoned a number of prominent players from the public schools to a meeting at Paternoster Row. The result of the meeting was the formation of the Corinthian Football Club.

From these beginnings grew one of the most respected amateur clubs in the country. With no ground of their own, they played their games on the grounds of their opponents until finally settling in 1895 at Queen's Club, West Kensington.

THE SITUATION AFTER THE GREAT WAR

The circumstances in which the Corinthians found themselves after the Great War were difficult indeed. The Club had been in decline since the amateur/professional split of 1907. For seven years (1907-1914) they were barred from playing against the big professional clubs and also lost the services of outstanding players such as Rev. K R G Hunt, H A Walden and others who preferred to join Football League clubs. The War itself also took the lives of young talent from the Public Schools who would normally have found their way into the Corinthian ranks.

As soon as the Great War ended, plans were prepared to restore the Club to its former standing. It was quickly decided that the Club should be continued and, more critically, that it should now be able to take part in a Cup competition. Though this was a highly contentious decision, (G O Smith was very critical!), it allowed the Club to enter for the FA Cup and thus again compete against the big professional clubs.

CORINTH COMES TO CRYSTAL PALACE

There remained the problem of finding a home ground. This issue was resolved with the decision to use the vast arena at the Crystal Palace. Their Hon. secretary Geoffrey Foster worked selflessly, with S F Hepburn of the Casuals to achieve this. He took up residence in Beckenham, buying a house at 12 Foxgrove Road and even called the house "Corinth". (This was later destroyed in the Second World War).

The ground prepared, the first match on the newly-acquired ground was played on Monday September 11th, 1922, against Tottenham Hotspur (who had won the FA Cup for the second time the previous year); and after a fine game in front of 10,000 spectators, the professionals won a narrow

victory by two goals to one, although they were a goal down at half-time. The Corinthians that day were:

B Howard Baker; A G Bower, J S F Morrison ; J R B Moulsdale, C B G Hunter, A E Knight; M Howell, H A Hambledon, F N S Creek, H F Dubuis, K E Hegan.

The honour of scoring the first goal on the new ground fell to Hegan, and it was generally agreed that a good start in the new era had been made.

In the Corinthian clubroom in the pavilion, the records, photographs and historical souvenirs of a great past were placed; and to these was added a memorial to those members who gave their lives in the Great War.

LEFT: THE MEMORIAL TO THE CORINTHIANS KILLED IN THE FIRST WORLD WAR.

The memorial was dedicated at a special service held before the Inter-varsity match on Wednesday, December 13th, 1922 (see chapter Ten). Rev. K R G Hunt led the service and Dr M J Rendall, the Headmaster of Winchester College and an old Corinthian himself, gave a brief address before unveiling the Memorial. G O Smith then laid a wreath in the name of the Corinthian Football Club.

Over the next ten years or so, the Corinthians played their home games either on the old Cup Final pitch or in the adjacent arena (for the smaller fixtures). The Corinthian fixture list was a mixture of matches against representative sides - the Army, Isthmian League; amateur touring sides - Northern Nomads, Yorkshire Amateurs; Football League sides - Birmingham, Stoke; international teams - South Africa; and foreign teams - Bohemians, Grasshoppers of Zurich; and the universities. There were also the annual tussles with old rivals Queen's Park. Above all, the years 1923 - 1933 were dominated by the Cup ties.

Against the amateurs, the Corinthians normally performed brilliantly, often with spectacular scores, and they also held their own against the League teams. In the Cup ties they had mixed fortunes but they were always crowd-pullers, with attendances of 30,000 - 40,000 typical for their tussles with the major League teams.

EARLY PROBLEMS

The conflicts of the past briefly threatened to explode again when the fixture list for the 1922-23 season was being prepared. Foster was approached by the secretary-manager of Plymouth Argyle, Bob Jack. Argyle were then riding high in the new Football League Third Division South. Due to their success in the previous season, they were exempt from the early rounds of the FA Cup and so had no game on Saturday November 18th. In the circumstances, what could be better for the young Argyle players than to play at the old Cup Final ground and against the best amateur team of the day.

Unfortunately, one of their fellow League members, Crystal Palace (now resident at the Nest, two miles away) objected as the alternative attraction would affect the attendance at their League game with Barnsley on the same day. Foster was furious and a very public row ensued. However, the Football League backed Crystal Palace and instructed the FA to cancel the fixture. The FA adjudged only that Argyle should pay Corinthians £10 in compensation. Once more, the amateur football world had been snubbed.

Despite this, Corinthians went ahead with their participation in the FA Cup and even played a friendly against Crystal Palace themselves later in the season. The final score: 3 - 3; the attendance 10,000.

FA CUP ENTRY 1922-23

Corinthians were exempt from the early rounds out of respect for their previous exploits; they joined the fray at the same time as the major League Clubs. So it was on the 13th January 1923 that the Corinthians participated in their first Cup game. Their first opponents were newcomers to the Football League; Brighton and Hove Albion who had joined the new Third Division when it was formed in 1921.

After a 1-1 draw at the Goldstone Ground, which attracted a record attendance, the two teams met again at the Palace four days later. Such was the interest that 20,000 turned up at the Palace but it was a wonder that the game took place at all. Two players (A E Knight and K E Hegan) were delayed on trains and so missed the start of the game, and J R B Moulsdale was unwell.

TEAM: B.Howard Baker; A G Bower, J S F Morrison; F H Ewer, C B G Hunter, L B Blaxland; M Howell, A H Phillips, C T Ashton, A G Doggart, A T Davies.

The referee was fog-bound, so the senior linesman had to officiate, and frosty conditions with a rockhard ground made ball-control very difficult. Nevertheless, it was a most exciting game. Brighton took the lead in the first half but midway through the second half, Phillips centred the ball to Ashton, who fired a shot at goal; the ball rebounded off a defender and fell to Howell who scored with a shot just inside the post.

The Corinthians had more chances during extra time but no more goals were scored. So, a further replay was needed and five days later the protagonists met again at Stamford Bridge before a massive 43,780 crowd (receipts £2,920). In a disappointing game, Corinthians finally lost to the only goal of the match. However, in the evening both sides attended a joint dinner.

The rest of the season was just as successful with games against amateur sides of all types. In one game, against the Army, F N S Creek had the distinction of scoring ten goals.

The Crystal Palace ground was alive again and with the success of the Corinthians, Casuals and the other amateur events, the future once more looked promising. When Everton visited the Palace on 24th March 1923, the programme notes stated:

"This season's arrangements on the ground were more or less in the nature of an experiment, but we feel that the experiment has been a great success and it will be continued next season.

It is hoped that during the summer, work will be carried out for banking on the east side of the ground, which will enable a large crowd to witness a match with a better view, and when this is effected, it is hoped that the ground may be used by the Football Association and other bodies for some of our big representative matches" (reported in the Croydon Advertiser).

CUP SUCCESS 1923-24

The next season (1923 -24) was the first full season and was notable for the record number of matches played. Queen's Park were beaten 4 - 1 on two occasions and Cambridge University were trounced 7 - 1. However, the highlight of the season was the historic victory over Blackburn Rovers. The game at the Palace on 12th January 1924 was a meeting of old rivals. On soft ground with a strong breeze

BELOW: THE CORINTHIAN TEAM, THAT BEAT BLACKBURN ROVERS 12TH JANUARY 1924.
BACK ROW L TO R: A H PHILLIPS, J R B MOULSDALE, B HOWARD BAKER, L B BLAXLAND, K E HEGAN.
FRONT ROW L TO R: F W H NICHOLAS, C T ASHTON, J S F MORRISON, A G BOWER, A G DOGGART, F N S CREEK.

blowing down the ground, the Corinthians raced to a 1 - 0 lead after 15 minutes. The goal, scored by Doggart, was followed by near misses by Creek and Phillips. In the second half, Rovers got much more of the game but the Corinthian defence held throughout; Morrison particularly had a superb game. As Norman Creek states in his book, 'History of the Corinthians':

"The victory was in fact, a triumph of determination, and, a great re-assertion of amateur football after many years of obscurity".

TEAM: B Howard Baker; A G Bower, J S F Morisson; J R B Moulsdale, C T Ashton, L B Blaxland; F W H Nicholas, A H Phillips, F N S Creek, A G Doggart, K E Hegan.

Unfortunately, Corinthians were brought down to earth in the next round when they lost by five goals to nil against West Bromwich at the Hawthorns.

DISAPPOINTMENT 1924-25

The following year the Corinthians were well and truly trounced by Sheffield United (5 - 0) at Bramall Lane in the FA Cup. In fact, it was a most disappointing season. Corinthians were without some of their best players for many of their games.

The exception was the visit of the South Africans on November 15th 1924. The tourists had already defeated Aston Villa, Liverpool and Chelsea. In fact, they had only lost to Brentford and Queen's Park, Glasgow. The Norwood News reported:

"Although the South Africans made eight changes in their team, it was generally admitted that they had practically their strongest side. A good crowd was present, and clever play was well applauded. The Upper Norwood Prize Band provided musical selections prior to the match and during the interval".

However, it was the Corinthians that ended on top. After an even first half with only one goal, the second half saw an equaliser for the South Africans but three more for Corinth: final score 4 - 1.

CORINTHIANS: B Howard Baker; A G Bower, J S F Morrison; A E Knight, C T Ashton, F H Ewer; A E Taylor, F Hartley, F N S Creek, A G Doggart, K E Hegan.

SOUTH AFRICANS: A J Riley; F C A Schwein, G W Brunton; G Parry, A Skene, B P Tuohy; J Green, A Maton, D Murray, G Hodgson, E T Stuart.

For the visit of Birmingham only 3,000 people turned up to watch a disappointing game. Although the Corinthian defence and the half-backs were sound, the forwards were incapable of making any impact on the Birmingham defence. Two goals in the second half were enough to give the visitors victory.

ABOVE: CARTOON OF CORINTHIANS HISTORIC VICTORY OVER BLACKBURN ROVERS, 1 - 0 IN JANUARY 1924.

OVERLEAF: PAINTING BY CHARLES CUNDALL OF 3RD ROUND CUP TIE CORINTHIANS V MANCHESTER CITY IN 1926.

F N S CREEK

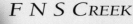

Norman Creek was a frail-looking player, a most unlikely build to stand up to strong physical defences but he had the ability to keep his balance and ride through tackles. Starting as a centre-forward he played at inside-right in most of the Cup-ties. He was both an amateur and a full international and holds the Corinthian record of scoring 10 goals in one match.

In later life, he became Assistant Director of Coaching at the FA, the England amateur team manager, a journalist and a BBC commentator.

Of course, he wrote the definitive history of the Corinthians.

CUP GLORY AGAIN
1925-26

The season that followed was much better for Corinthians and the 1925-26 season must rank as one of the best in Corinthian history. Only four matches were lost of the 31 matches played and that included the Cup replay against Manchester City. One of the reasons was that in this season there were the lowest number of members of the Club and therefore there were the fewest number of changes to the team. The Corinthians got their revenge over Birmingham with a 1 - 0 home victory.

Unfortunately, the game against the Royal Navy scheduled for 21st November 1925 was cancelled due to the death of Queen Alexandra.

TOP RIGHT: THE CORINTHIANS 1926-27. L TO R: K E HEGAN, A H CHADDER, F H EWER, A G BOWER, C T ASHTON, A E KNIGHT (CAPT.), B HOWARD BAKER, F N S CREEK, F HARTLEY, J R MOULSDALE, A E TAYLOR.

ABOVE & RIGHT: PROGRAMME COVER AND TEAMS FOR CORINTHIANS V MANCHESTER CITY IN JANUARY 1926.

FAR RIGHT: PROGRAMME COVER FOR CORINTHIANS V NEWCASTLE UNITED 1927.

BOTTOM LEFT & RIGHT: NEWSPAPER CUTTINGS OF CORINTHIANS V NEWCASTLE UNITED TELL OF AN HEROIC FIGHT BY CORINTHIANS.

CORINTHIANS V MANCHESTER CITY

The highlight of the season has to be the first Cup match against Manchester City at the Crystal Palace. The Corinthians team was a makeshift one but they combined effectively and it was not long before Creek scored. Manchester City equalised a minute before half-time and when they took the lead 15 minutes before full-time, it looked like the Corinthians were beaten. However, two goals from Hegan and Creek put the amateurs back in the driving seat. Then with only three minutes to go, confusion in the Corinthians penalty-area, when Baker took too many steps carrying the ball, led to a free kick for Manchester City only six yards from the goalmouth and the ball being prodded into the net.

With no further goals in the game, the teams adjourned to Maine Road five days later but this time Manchester City were too good for the amateurs and ran out 4 - 0 winners.

TEAM: B Howard Baker; A G Bower, A E Knight; C B G Hunter, C T Ashton, F H Ewer; R G C Jenkins, A H Chadder, F N S Creek, F Hartley, K E Hegan.

CORINTHIANS V NEWCASTLE UNITED

The 1926-27 season was dwarfed by the epic struggle with Newcastle United. After a resounding victory over Walsall (4 - 0), Newcastle were drawn in the next round. The Magpies were top of the League at the time (and eventual champions) but the first half of this game belonged to Corinthians. Chadder was particularly effective in neutralising Gallacher in the midfield. Corinthian pressure eventually led to the opening goal when Ashton scored from a centre by Hegan. This score was held until 15 minutes from the end and Newcastle must have been getting desperate (after all, they had never won a Cup game at the Crystal Palace!). At this point, as the Times reported:

HEROIC FIGHT BY THE CORINTHIANS.

Newcastle a goal behind only thirteen minutes from the end. Amateurs' heavy handicap. All three half-backs hurt. Chadder sits on Gallacher. Professionals get going at the eleventh hour.

A. H. CHADDER

"the professional team turned in their desperation to what the boxers call the 'rough stuff' - some of it fair enough, some of it decidedly not. They soon scored an

NEWCASTLE WIN AT THE PALACE AT LAST.

LONDON WILL HAVE TWO "CUP FINALS" this season. One was played at Crystal Palace on Saturday. Here, Howard Baker is saving the Corinthians, with Gallacher (stripes), Ewer, Knight, and Chadder anxiously watching events.

BROADCASTING OF FOOTBALL

The first football match to be broadcast was on 22nd January 1927 when Arsenal met Sheffield United at Highbury. The exercise was repeated a week later for the first Cup match to be covered by the BBC – Corinthians v Newcastle United.

For these early games, the BBC attempted to make it easy for the listener by printing a grid in the Radio Times dividing the pitch into eight squares. While the commentator described the game, a second voice would call out the square in which the play was taking place. It is claimed that the expression 'Back to square one' originated from this mechanism. (When the ball was transferred back to square one, it would have been returned to the goalkeeper and any attack would have to start again).

--- RADIO TIMES ---   203

THE CORINTHIANS v. NEWCASTLE UNITED.

Fourth Round Cup Tie to be broadcast on Saturday, January 29.

GALLACHER,
Captain of Newcastle United.

THE SCENE OF THE MATCH.
The Crystal Palace Ground, looking eastward.

Sport & General

A. E. KNIGHT,
Captain of the Corinthians.

WE print below a plan of the Crystal Palace Football Ground where, on Saturday, January 29, the Corinthians will meet Newcastle United in the Fourth Round of the fight for the coveted F.A. Cup. A running commentary on the match will be broadcast from London and Daventry, S.B. to many stations, between 2.35 and 4.20 on that afternoon, with a half-time interval of five minutes at 3.30.

Listeners will find our plan of the ground helpful in following the course of the match on their sets. It is to this plan that the announcer will refer in reporting the to-and-fro of the game. The sound-proof observation hut from which the broadcast-commentary is to be carried out is situated on the west side of the ground, about fifteen yards to the left of the centre-line on the accompanying plan.

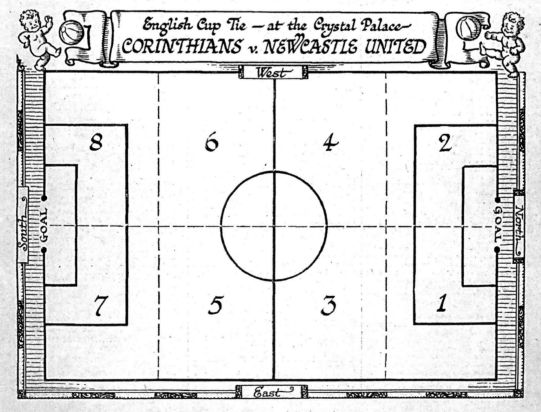

NEWCASTLE UNITED FOOTBALL CLUB, 1926-27.

Seated in Front.—W. Bradley, W. Wilson, I. Tate.
1st Row.—T. H. Urwin, W. Gibson, Noel. Mackenzie, F. C. Hudspeth, J. P. Gliner, H. Gallacher, D. Crawford, J. Low, T. McDonald, G. S. Seymour.
2nd Row.—S. F. Bates, (Director), A. Maitland, J. Harris, R. Mooney, Dr. R. W. Simpson, J. R. Clarke, W. Hampson, J. Graham, (Director), C. W. Spencer, L. Crown.
3rd Row.—J. G. McPherson, (Trainer), O. Park, G. Lowes, G. T. Rutherford, (Director), W. Curbon, T. M. Mitchell, E. Finlay, F. Nicholson, T. Oliver, (Director), J. Loughlin, Dr. B. B. Appleby.
4th Row.—W. L. Low, (Trainer), T. Curry (No. I), T. Curry, (No. 2), R. Keating, G. Robson, J. Hopf, F. G. Watt, Jun.(Asst. Sec.), Roy Mackenzie, A. McCombie (Trainer).

ABOVE: NEWCASTLE UNITED FOOTBALL CLUB, 1926-27, AS DEPICTED IN THE PROGRAMME.

RIGHT: PROGRAMME COVER FOR CORINTHIANS V MILLWALL IN JANUARY 1930.

RIGHT: CARTOON 'THE TALE OF A SHIRT', CORINTHIANS V MILLWALL.

equalising goal from a free kick and then Jenkins retired hurt. Against ten men Newcastle forced their advantage and ran out 3 - 1 victors.

Once again, it cannot be too strongly urged that the defence in these matches, strengthened as it was by A H Chadder, gave a display as good as any in the history of the Club".

TEAM: B Howard Baker ; A G Bower, A E Knight; J R B Moulsdale, A H Chadder, F H Ewer; A E Taylor, F N S Creek, R G C Jenkins, C T Ashton, K E Hegan.

Over the Christmas period, the Club went to North Wales (Wrexham) to play the newly-formed Welsh Dragons, and in March they went to Paris to play Red Star Olympic. In the game against the Isthmian League XI (at Wimbledon) on Boxing Day both sets of forwards played such fine football that 11 (perfect) goals were scored; many critics still consider this to have been the best game of amateur football since the Great War.

CHANGING TIMES

Good wins against League opposition early in the 1927-28 season and then high scoring games against amateur sides, may have convinced the Corinthians that their position was guaranteed. The game against the Northern Nomads was particularly notable. Both teams were somewhat weakened. There were four goals in the first half, three of them for the visitors. However, the second half led to a goal glut. In an exhilarating display, Corinthians scored ten goals, six of them by Ashton; final score 11 - 3.

TEAM: B Howard Baker; A G Bower, A E Knight; W T Whewell, C B G Hunter, L B Blaxland; R W V Robbins, F Hartley, C T Ashton, E A Ridgeon, K E Hegan.

But times were changing. An early exit from the FA Cup inflicted by New Brighton was followed, in 1928, by the Crystal Palace Company forcing the Corinthians to share the main football arena at the Palace. Taking advantage of the popularity of a new sport imported from Australia, a speedway track was built around the ground and for six years speedway events were interspersed with football.

An indifferent season in 1928-29 was followed by a classic. The 1929-30 season opened with the Corinthians in superb form. As usual, they were far superior to the amateur sides pitted against them. It must have been soul-destroying for the Sandhurst Cadets who played at the Palace on November 20th. The Corinthians put out a strong side including Howard Baker, Whewell, Glenister, and a forward line of Watson, Barber, Stone, Doggart and Parker but the Cadets were disappointing. The final score: 18 - 0.

CORINTHIANS V MILLWALL

When the Cup competition came around again, the Corinthians were drawn against Millwall, This was another of those occasions when the Corinthians justified the respect that they received. Three games were needed to separate the teams and in total 138,000 people watched the three matches.

The first game at the Crystal Palace attracted 45,000 spectators to watch what was a memorable match. The weather was unusual. Fifteen minutes before kick off there was bright sunshine but gradually the clouds gathered and before long players and spectators were battered by rain and snow. By the end, there was a blizzard.

F. J. MADGWICK
WHOLESALE AND RETAIL SPORTS AND GAMES OUTFITTER
151, Sydenham Road, Sydenham, S.E.26
ALL GOODS BY BEST MAKERS ONLY

CORINTHIAN F.C.
AT THE
CRYSTAL PALACE
Honorary Secretary :—
R C BAMBRIDGE, "The Elms," in, Merton Hall Road, Wimbledon, S.W.19.
Assistant Secretary :
G. C. BAMBRIDGE, Crystal Palace, S.E.19

OFFICIAL PROGRAMME

3rd Round F.A. Cup.
THE CORINTHIANS
v.
MILLWALL
Saturday, 11th Jan. 1930.
Kick off 2.30 p.m.
PRICE TWOPENCE

F. J. MADGWICK,
WHOLESALE AND RETAIL, SPORTS AND GAMES OUTFITTER
151, Sydenham Road, Sydenham, S.E.26
CONTRACTOR TO CLUBS AND SCHOOLS

THURSDAY, *The Daily Mail* JANUARY 16, 1930.

THE TALE OF A SHIRT. By TOM WEBSTER.

Daily Mail Copyright.

ALWYN HARVEY CHADDER (1903-1995)

Harvey Chadder epitomised the qualities of the Corinthians. In those twilight years between the Wars when the Corinthians could still match the big professional clubs, Chadder showed the style, grace and tenacity which had made the Corinthians the most respected football team in the country.

Educated at Taunton School, he went on to St John's College, Oxford and appeared in the varsity matches from 1923 to 1925 (as an inside forward). He spent most of his professional life as a housemaster at Malvern College and for 20 years he was Master in charge of football.

Harvey Chadder died in December 1995 at the age of 91.

LEFT: *A H IN 1921 AFTER RECEIVING HIS BLUE FOR OXFORD.*

TOP FAR LEFT: *WEDDING PHOTO, 9TH APRIL 1929.*

BOTTOM LEFT: *A H WITH HIS SON DICK CHADDER AFTER GAINING HIS BLUE FOR OXFORD IN 1956.*

BELOW: *DRAWING OF A H AS AN ENGLISH AMATEUR INTERNATIONAL BY HENRY COLLER 'SOCCER CELEBRITIES'.*

The Bridegroom of Corinth.

THE WELL-KNOWN CORINTHIAN, Mr. A. H. Chadder, with his bride, Miss Gwendoline James, after their wedding at Rusthall.

Chadder was ever-present in the Corinthian sides that appeared in the FA Cup and his most illustrious moment was in the game against Newcastle United in 1927. In the centre-half position, he so dominated the Newcastle centre-forward Hughie Gallacher that the Daily Telegraph described him as being "held in a vice". It was only when Newcastle adopted some dubious tactics and Chadder was injured that the professionals were able to score and win the game.

RIGHT: CARTOON 'AN EXCITING AFTERNOON' CORINTHIANS V MILLWALL 2ND REPLAY, AT STAMFORD BRIDGE.

AN EXCITING AFTERNOON. By TOM WEBSTER.

BELOW: A G DOGGART SCORES CORINTHIANS' GOAL IN THE REPLAY AT STAMFORD BRIDGE.

Daily Mail Copyright.

On the pitch, the Corinthians had a poor start and Millwall raced into the lead which they held until the interval. Soon after half-time, a combination of Creek, Hegan and finally Robins got the equaliser for the Corinthians, only for Millwall to score again. Then just before the end, the Corinthians equalised again with a blistering run and shot by Ashton.

Tom Addison, who now lives in Geelong, Victoria, Australia, went to this game. He still remembers the day: "*I went with father to the game. I used to follow the Corinthians and my old School team, Old Chigwellians. There was a good crowd. The stands were back at an angle. We were in the middle of the ground almost by the centre line. It was an old wooden stand.*

We could not see because of the fog and we thought it would be difficult to get home so we left in the middle of the second half.

I particularly remember Baker - he was a good goalkeeper".

Howard Baker was indeed a fine player. He played for England at both full and amateur levels. He was the British high-jump champion and appeared in the 1912 and 1920 Olympic teams. He also played for Chelsea and Everton. He could kick the ball the length of the field which, given the weight of the ball, was no mean feat.

Four days later, a replay was played at the Den in front of 33,000 only to see another draw (1 - 1). So the team reconvened on January 20th at Stamford Bridge. By this time, the battle had achieved some notoriety, so 60,000 attended only to see the Corinthians finally collapse when Millwall turned in a very physical performance in the second half; final score 5 - 1.

Later in the season, the Corinthians were less lucky against their old rivals, Queen's Park. These games could still pull in the crowds - or maybe it was as a result of that Cup marathon against Millwall - but 10,000 came and watched Queen's Park win by the odd goal in five.

CORINTHIANS V BOHEMIANS

The first game of the 1930-31 season was against Bohemians of Dublin. In a downpour, the pitch deteriorated making it difficult to play good football. Being without Howard Baker, Norman Creek deputised in goal and he put on a good performance even though he let in three goals. However, the Corinthian forwards were even more successful, eventually getting a goal tally of six goals; final score 6 - 3.

TEAM: F N S Creek; A H Chadder, C H J Hill; C T Ashton, W T Whewell, A T Barber; A H Fabian, A G Doggart, G D Kemp-Welch, W H Webster, K E Hegan.

The season's Cup opponents were Port Vale. Norman Creek stated that *"if the match had not been a Cup-tie, no game would have been played; for, apart from the thick fog, the Crystal* Palace ground was in its worst condition since the Corinthians took it over. It had been badly cut up on the previous Saturday and for some reason had not been rolled, and with a week's frost setting in, it was very uneven and rough"*. In the event, Port Vale adapted better to the conditions and ran out 3 - 1 winners.

EASY FOR CORINTH

SWISS TEAM POOR MARKSMEN

BRILLIANT CHADDER

Corinthians 3, Grasshoppers 1

The Grasshoppers of Zurich, who had beaten the Casuals in mid-week, found the Corinthians too much for them at the Crystal Palace.

Weak finishing was the Swiss team's trouble. Their forwards advanced on the Corinthian goal by means of really model footwork, but their marksmanship was deplorable.

Owing to the absence of Hegan, Creek, Ashton, Whewell, and Partridge, who were playing for England in the Amateur International at Swansea, the Corinthians had an experimental side, who played well enough to gain a sound win. The Grasshoppers, who have a great reputation in Continental amateur football, fielded the men who decisively defeated the Casuals.

Play throughout ran in the Corinthians' favour, for, whilst playing a well-combined, short-passing type of football which was very nice to watch, the Tourists lacked the more direct thrustful methods displayed by Corinth.

There was little to choose between the defences in the opening half, but the Corinthians' forwards crowded on the pressure so much in the second that the Swiss backs were rather leg-weary towards the finish.

F. Adam, at outside-right, was the Grasshoppers' outstanding player. He was both fast and tricky, and seldom lost control of the ball. The left-wing pair, A. Zwkovic and M. Abegglen, executed many fine movements, and incidentally gave L. G. Rumsey and W. H. L. Lister a busy afternoon.

For the Corinthians A. H. Chadder, back at centre-half, gave a great display, his tackling being faultless, and, particularly during the second half, he overshadowed I. Hitrec, the Swiss centre-forward. R. W. V. Robins, G. T. L. Ansell, and H. V. Benest were the pick of the forwards. R. S. Grant in goal was very safe, and made several brilliant clearances.

The play opened fast, the Corinthians having the advantage of a strong wind. The Grasshoppers attacked soon after the start, and Grant twice saved from Hitrec, while some centres from Adam were wasted. Robins, Chadder, Cornelius, and Cooper all shot wide when well placed, and later Hitrec hit the Corinthians' bar with a great shot. Chadder gave the home team the lead with a penalty kick awarded for pushing.

After Grant had saved from Adam, the Swiss pressed and Hitrec equalised with a shot at short range. Five minutes later some good passing by the Corinthians enabled Ansell to score. Both goalkeepers were then tested several times, Grant doing specially well in the Corinthians' goal. Ansell dribbled through the visitors' defence, and scored near the end.

LEFT: PROGRAMME COVER AND MATCH REPORT OF CORINTHIANS V GRASSHOPPERS OF ZURICH, FEBRUARY 1932.

BELOW: THE MATCH WAS ALSO REPORTED ON BY THE SWISS PRESS.

Tages-Anzeiger

Zürcher Fussballer in London
Corinthians - Graßhoppers 3:1 (1:0)

London, 27. Febr. w. Die gute Presse, welche die Graßhoppers für ihr erstes Spiel gegen Casuals fanden, hat die Londoner aufhorchen lassen. Einstimmig drückten sich die Berichterstatter der großen Blätter dahin aus, daß das Amateurteam kein vollkommeneres Spiel zeigen könne. Diese Meinungsäußerungen sind natürlich bei der Zürcher Expedition mit größter Befriedigung aufgenommen worden, und sie belebten die Stimmung im Hinblick auf die schwere Aufgabe des Samstags.

Die Corinthians mußten zwar zwei Spieler für das am gleichen Tage stattfindende Amateurtreffen Wales - England (1:3) abgeben, aber ihr ziemlich großes und ausgeglichenes Spielermaterial gestattete die Ausfüllung der Lücken durch absolut vollwertige Spieler. Der Verlauf der Partie zeigte, daß das Wort von der Ungewißheit im Fußballsport immer noch seine Geltung hat. Die Briten zeigten nämlich in der ersten Hälfte sehr wenig, gelangten aber kurz vor der Pause durch einen zu harten Elfmeterentscheid in Führung. Von der 20. Minute an hatten die Zürcher glatt dominiert, doch mußten sie sich mit mehreren Eckbällen und einem Lattenschuß zufrieden geben, während dem Gegner ein im Eifer des Gefechts begangener Schnitzer zu einem Tor verhalf. Zu Beginn der zweiten Hälfte wurden die Platzherren für eine volle Viertelstunde in ihre Hälfte zurückgedrängt. In der 12. Minute fiel durch Hitrec der Ausgleich. Schon die nächsten Minuten hatten den Kampf zugunsten der Zürcher entschieden können; aber einerseits Schußpech, andererseits glänzendes Können des Corinthians-Goalkeepers Grant verhinderten jeden Erfolg. Ein kurzer Moment des Nachlassens brachte dann in der 16. Minute den Briten neuerdings die Führung. Jetzt wurden sie auch wesentlich besser, im Feldspiel waren ihnen die Zürcher freilich weiterhin überlegen. Grant rettete seinem Team durch famose Abwehr den Sieg, der kurz vor Schluß noch eine zahlenmäßige Erhöhung erfuhr, indem ein Verfehlen mehrerer Zürcher Spieler zum dritten Tor führte. Mit einem wertvollen Sieg und einer unverdienten Niederlage kehrt die Graßhopper-Mannschaft am Sonntag in die Heimat zurück, nachdem sie den schweizerischen Fußball sehr ehrenvoll vertreten hat.

FAR LEFT: "R S GRANT, THE CORINTHIAN GOALKEEPER, TRAINS HIMSELF TO KEEP A COOL HEAD WHEN THINGS BEGIN TO WHIRL".

ABOVE: "THE CORINTHIAN TEAM HAVE BEEN TRAINING IN THEIR SPARE TIME AT A WEST END GYMNASIUM FOR THEIR CUP-TIE MATCH WITH PORT VALE AT THE CRYSTAL PALACE TO-DAY. IN THIS PICTURE DOGGART, THE CORINTHIANS CAPTAIN (LEFT), WITH CHADDER AND WEBSTER (RIGHT), ARE SEEN WITH THEIR INSTRUCTOR IN THE GYMNASIUM YESTERDAY".

ABOVE, RIGHT & BELOW: TICKET AND PROGRAMME FOR CORINTHIANS V WEST HAM UNITED, JANUARY 1933.

The loss of exemption from the early rounds of the FA Cup after the defeat by West Ham in 1933, led to a loss of status for the Corinthians. It was no longer felt that Corinthians could expect to draw large crowds but Corinthians argued that they would have difficulty in raising a team of sufficient standard before January as leading players were committed to their universities prior to this time. Partly in protest and partly the difficulty in getting players, Corinthians withdrew from the competition.

Further problems ensued, as it was only their share of the FA Cup gates which enabled the Club to lease the football enclosure in the Palace grounds. The Norwood News reported:

"By the courtesy of the management, the Corinthians will play their matches against Oxford and Cambridge at their old ground this season. No other home matches have been arranged, and no professional club at present figures on this season's fixture list.

Meanwhile, the Corinthians are looking for a new ground in the London district at which matches can be played".

Eventually, the Club selected Hurlingham but ultimately moved to Kingston. The writing was on the wall.

For the 1934-35 season, Corinthians swallowed their pride and re-entered the FA Cup but were now forced to join the minor clubs in the first round.

Being drawn away against Watford (lost 0 - 2) in 1934-35 and Reading (lost 3 - 8) in 1935-36, it was the beginning of the 1936-37 Cup campaign before the Corinthians played a Cup game at the Crystal Palace again.

COLLAPSE AND FALL

So, it was on 28th November 1936 with a game against Bristol Rovers that Corinthians re-visited the Crystal Palace. It is significant that this game drew the smallest attendance at any of the Cup matches played that day, just over 2,000. Corinthians were easily beaten 2 - 0.

Ironically, this was the last game that Corinthians played at the Crystal Palace before the Second World War. Two days later, at about 7pm on Monday 30th November, a fire began inside the building and despite the efforts of the Crystal Palace staff, and subsequently the local fire brigades, within two hours the building had collapsed in a heap of charred wood, molten glass, cracked stonework and mangled metal.

It seems a sad symbol not only of the fall of the Crystal Palace but also the decline of the Corinthians. No longer could the Corinthians compete successfully with the professional teams and the end was inevitable.

Edmund Grayson in 'Corinthians and Cricketers' sums up the sorry state of Corinthians when he describes his attendance at a match in 1937.

"I shall never forget a dull November afternoon in 1937 at the White City, itself a legacy of Edwardian London, when the Corinthians, themselves then nothing more than a legacy in name of Victorian and Edwardian soccer, made their final FA Cup appearance in London, against Southend United. Any resemblance to the old greatness, even of the twenties, had completely gone. A miserable crowd of 2,000 sprinkled round the empty stadium gave an eerie atmosphere to what resembled a memorial service rather than any parade of soccer talent, or at least of amateur soccer talent, by what had once been the country's premier amateur club. As the thumps of the ball echoed round the deserted stands, with the occasional whisper, 'Play up Corinth', filtering through the murky air like some haunting cry that one snatches to retain but always slides away.....".

The signs of the amateur times were reflected by the decision in June of 1937 that the Corinthians should join with the Casuals and the two Clubs should run under a joint executive committee for at least the next three seasons. Then, in 1939 a full merger took place to form Corinthian-Casuals FC.

The Crystal Palace park however did not die. Just four days after the fire, work began on creating a motor-racing circuit. When this opened in 1937 the football ground began to be used as a paddock for cars.

Football disappeared from the Crystal Palace and the vast slopes were covered with crowds cheering on cars and motor-cycles rather than football teams.

In 1939 even these contests were curtailed when war again diverted the nation to more pressing tasks.

PREVIOUS PAGE, RIGHT HAND COLUMN: S F HEPBURNS' INVITATION TO CORINTHIANS JUBILEE DINNER AT THE DORCHESTER HOTEL IN 1932. BELOW, JUBILEE DINNER MENU COVER.

BELOW: MOTOR-CYCLE FOOTBALL ON THE CUP FINAL GROUND.

BOTTOM: THE SOUTH TRANSEPT ENGULFED IN FLAMES DURING THE CATASTROPHIC FIRE THAT DESTROYED THE CRYSTAL PALACE ON THE NIGHT OF THE 30TH NOVEMBER 1936.

THE CRYSTAL PALACE GROUNDS IN 1950, THE 'SPORTS ARENAS' CAN BE SEEN NEAR THE TOP OF THE PHOTOGRAPH.

'EDUCATION AND RECREATION', A NEW BEGINNING

In the post-war world of the 1940s and early 1950s, the priority was national reconstruction. In the circumstances, the renovation of a dilapidated park with a heap of rusted metal at its most prominent position were low down on the list. The Crystal Palace and its environs were therefore left to decay further. The London County Council took on the role of custodian and some activities gradually returned.

A NEW ERA – NATIONAL SPORTS CENTRE

Though little was done immediately, in 1951 an Act of Parliament was passed to develop the site for the purpose of *"education and recreation, and the furtherance of commerce, art and industry"*.

Sir Gerald Barry, formerly the Director-General of the 1951 Festival of Britain, was invited to submit a scheme for the redevelopment and it was he who proposed the building of a National Youth and Sports Centre. This was to include an outdoor sports stadium and an indoor centre. Work was started in 1960 and the Centre, designed by Sir Isaac Hayward, was officially opened on 13th July 1964 by HRH the Duke of Edinburgh. The building cost £2,750,000.

So, the football stands and the pavilion were finally swept away to be replaced by a modern all-seater stand for a new audience to watch athletics. Initially, the ground seated 12,000 spectators with 4,500 under cover in a single cantilever stand on the exact site of the previous pavilion and football stands. In 1977, the Queen Elizabeth II Jubilee stand was built on the other side of the ground, which could accommodate a further 4,500 people. A new tradition was beginning. However, football had not quite ended its flirtation with the Crystal Palace.

CORINTHIAN-CASUALS

In 1950 the combined Corinthian-Casuals, now playing in the Isthmian League, had finally settled at the Oval. However, their season was restricted because of the need to prepare the cricket surface. So the Club returned to the Crystal Palace for some of their games each season. In 1957, they decided to make a more definite return and agreed to rent the ground for the sum of £200 per season. For three years, all Reserve and 'A' home games were played at the Palace. At the beginning and end of each season, the first team also made use of the ground. The last match was played on March 12th 1960.

Negotiations between Corinthian-Casuals continued through 1961 and 1962 with a view to the Club taking up a tenancy as the ground evolved

ABOVE: LOGO OF CORINTHIAN - CASUALS WHICH BECAME ONE CLUB IN 1939.

LEFT: NATIONAL SPORTS CENTRE.

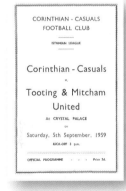

CORINTHIAN - CASUALS
FOOTBALL CLUB

ISTHMIAN LEAGUE

Corinthian - Casuals
v.
Tooting & Mitcham United

At CRYSTAL PALACE
ON
Saturday, 5th September, 1959
KICK-OFF 3 p.m.

OFFICIAL PROGRAMME · · · · Price 3d.

ABOVE: PROGRAMME COVER FOR AN ISTHMIAN LEAGUE MATCH PLAYED AT CRYSTAL PALACE, BETWEEN CORINTHIAN-CASUALS AND TOOTING & MITCHAM.

LEFT: CARTOON FROM THE NORWOOD NEWS OF OCTOBER 16TH 1964, WITH REFERENCE TO THE CORINTHIANS V ARSENAL GAME (SEE PAGE 155).

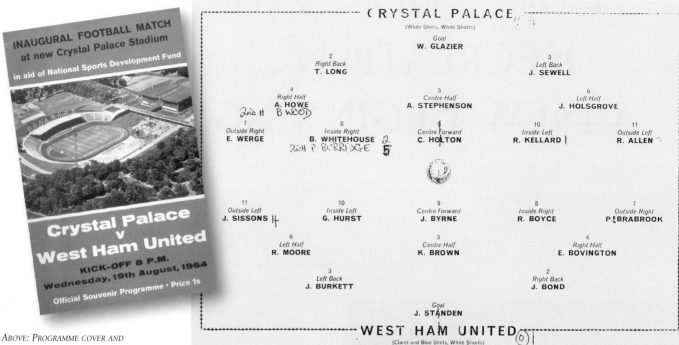

CRYSTAL PALACE
(White Shirts, White Shorts)

Goal
W. GLAZIER

| 2 Right Back **T. LONG** | | 3 Left Back **J. SEWELL** |

| 4 Right Half **A. HOWE** | 5 Centre Half **A. STEPHENSON** | 6 Left Half **J. HOLSGROVE** |

2nd H B WOOD

| 7 Outside Right **E. WERGE** | 8 Inside Right **B. WHITEHOUSE** 2 | 9 Centre Forward **C. HOLTON** | 10 Inside Left **R. KELLARD** | 11 Outside Left **R. ALLEN** |

2nd P. BURRIDGE 5

| 11 Outside Left **J. SISSONS** | 10 Inside Left **G. HURST** | 9 Centre Forward **J. BYRNE** | 8 Inside Right **R. BOYCE** | 7 Outside Right **P. BRABROOK** |

| 6 Left Half **R. MOORE** | 5 Centre Half **K. BROWN** | 4 Right Half **E. BOVINGTON** |

| 3 Left Back **J. BURKETT** | | 2 Right Back **J. BOND** |

Goal
J. STANDEN

WEST HAM UNITED
(Claret and Blue Shirts, White Shorts)

ABOVE: PROGRAMME COVER AND TEAM SHEET FOR CRYSTAL PALACE V WEST HAM UNITED ON 19TH AUGUST 1964.

INAUGURAL FOOTBALL MATCH at new Crystal Palace Stadium in aid of National Sports Development Fund

Crystal Palace v West Ham United
KICK-OFF 8 P.M.
Wednesday, 19th August, 1964
Official Souvenir Programme · Price 1s

ABOVE: LOGO OF CRYSTAL PALACE FC USED WHEN THEIR NICKNAME WAS THE 'GLAZIERS'.

into the National Sports Centre. but this was always rejected.

Ironically, by 1967 the Sports Council was prepared to agree to such an arrangement but Corinthian-Casuals had by then already reached an agreement with the Tooting and Mitcham to play home games at their ground.

Despite this, Corinthian-Casuals, Corinthians or Casuals alone, played a number of games at the Crystal Palace, especially after the National Sports Centre was built. For instance, on October 14th 1964, Corinthians, without the Casuals, revived the Sheriff of London Shield, the proceeds going to the Central Council for Physical Recreation and to the Corinthian-Casuals Trust Fund.

JOHN SEWELL

John Sewell was ever-present in the Crystal Palace team from 1963 until 1971. He was the only player to appear in all three pre-season friendlies at the Crystal Palace. Sewell was born in Brockley on 7th July 1936 and started his playing career with Bexleyheath. In July 1955 he signed for Charlton Athletic and became their regular full-back.

In October 1963 he was transferred to Crystal Palace and helped them win promotion to the Second Division. After five seasons, he became team captain and led the side into the First Division in 1969.

Sewell joined Orient in 1971 on a free transfer but soon moved to the United States where he played for and managed several clubs.

BELOW: PROGRAMME COVER AND TEAMS FOR CRYSTAL PALACE V CHELSEA ON 28TH JULY 1969.

CRYSTAL PALACE F.C. v. **CHELSEA F.C.**

at CRYSTAL PALACE NATIONAL SPORTS CENTRE NORWOOD , S.E.19
Kick-off 7.30 p.m.
MONDAY, 28th JULY, 1969
OFFICIAL PROGRAMME

ROYSTON DURBIDGE
ESTATE AGENTS
253 WESTWOOD LANE
SIDCUP
Tel: 01-304 0092

PROCTOR NETS LTD.
MANUFACTURERS OF ALL TYPES OF NETTING

TREND MINI CAR HIRE
Special Rates
Telephone: 778 2206 / 653 2227

CRYSTAL PALACE F.C. *(Claret and Light Blue Stripes, White Shorts)*	V	CHELSEA F.C. *(Royal Blue Shirts and Shorts, White Socks)*
From		From
J. JACKSON		P. BONETTI
J. SEWELL		T. HUGHES
J. LOUGHLAN		E. McCREADIE
D. PAYNE		J. BOYLE
R. HOY		R. HARRIS
J. McCORMICK	Referee: D. F. Pond (Chelmsford)	J. HOLLINS
R. HYND		S. HOUSTON
M. BLYTH		D. WEBB
M. LAZARUS	Linesmen: A. C. F. Turvey (Bedford)	A. DEMPSEY
S. KEMBER	C. C. Smith (Croydon)	T. BALDWIN
C. JACKSON		A. BIRCHENALL
B. WOODRUFF		C. COOKE
G. QUEEN		P. HOUSEMAN
T. TAYLOR		I. HUTCHINSON
C. TAYLOR		P. OSGOOD
		B. TAMBLING

We would like to record our appreciation to Mitre Sports for kindly donating the match ball.

KG SPORTS
FOOTBALL SPECIALISTS
For ADDIDAS, PUMA, GOLA, MITRE, LAWRENCE, BUCKTA, UMBRO ETC.
CLUB ENQUIRIES WELCOMED
312 SANGLEY ROAD, CATFORD, LONDON, S.E.6
Telephone: 01-697 2062

Come and see
MODERN BATHROOM & KITCHEN FITTINGS, at KNOWLES
New Showrooms
13-17 KNIGHT'S HILL
WEST NORWOOD, S.E.27.
Phone: 01-670 6171-6
(Early closing Saturday 12 o'clock)
ALL BUILDING MATERIALS

QUEENS HOTEL
CHURCH ROAD
CRYSTAL PALACE
S.E.19
Tel: 01-653 6622 (6 Lines)

In front of only 400 spectators, their opponents were Arsenal. The first half ended with Corinthians only one goal down. However, the second half was a disaster; Arsenal scored six further goals; final score 7 – 0. It is worth noting that the Arsenal team included their recent £80,000 signing Frank McLintock.

The last game was on November 28th 1970. Unable to play their fourth round FA Amateur Cup tie at Tooting and Mitcham (as Tooting and Mitcham also had a home game), the tie was

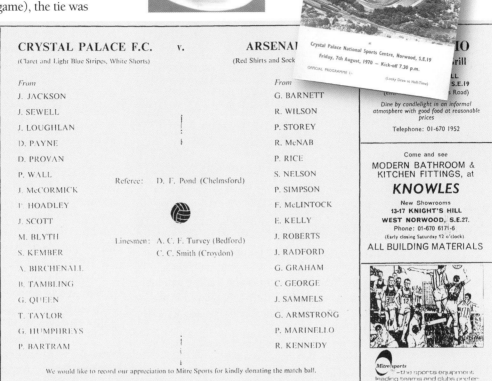

CRYSTAL PALACE F.C.   v.   ARSENAL
(Claret and Light Blue Stripes, White Shorts)   (Red Shirts and Socks)

From	From
J. JACKSON	G. BARNETT
J. SEWELL	R. WILSON
J. LOUGHLAN	P. STOREY
D. PAYNE	R. McNAB
D. PROVAN	P. RICE
P. WALL	S. NELSON
J. McCORMICK	P. SIMPSON
F. HOADLEY	F. McLINTOCK
J. SCOTT	E. KELLY
M. BLYTH	J. ROBERTS
S. KEMBER	J. RADFORD
A. BIRCHENALL	G. GRAHAM
R. TAMBLING	C. GEORGE
G. QUEEN	J. SAMMELS
T. TAYLOR	G. ARMSTRONG
G. HUMPHREYS	P. MARINELLO
P. BARTRAM	R. KENNEDY

Referee: D. F. Pond (Chelmsford)

Linesmen: A. C. F. Turvey (Bedford)
            C. C. Smith (Croydon)

We would like to record our appreciation to Mitre Sports for kindly donating the match ball.

CRYSTAL PALACE F.C.
v.
ARSENAL F.C.
(in aid of the National Sports Development Fund)

1004

Crystal Palace National Sports Centre, Norwood, S.E.19
Friday, 7th August, 1970 – Kick-off 7.30 p.m.

OFFICIAL PROGRAMME 1–   (Lucky Draw at Half-Time)

switched to the National Sports Centre at Crystal Palace. However, Casuals proved no match for their opponents Leyton. After Southam limped off with an injury after 24 minutes, their task was made extremely difficult. Leyton eventually won 2 – 0.

CASUALS: Lamb; Cairns, Jenkins; Southam (Wright), Hamer, Joy; Jones, Haywood, Elias, Payne, Dick.

FRIENDLIES

Initially as a celebration of the opening of the new complex, Crystal Palace Football Club were invited to play a friendly game against their East London rivals, West Ham. On August 19th 1964, Palace took on the then Cup-holders and trounced them 4 – 1 with goals from Kellard, Whitehouse, Allen and Burridge. Sissons got a consolation goal for West Ham.

CRYSTAL PALACE: Glazier; Long, Sewell; Howe, Stephenson, Holsgrove; Werge, Whitehouse, Holton, Kellard, Allen.

WEST HAM UNITED: Standen; Bond, Burkett; Bovington, Brown, Moore; Brabrook, Boyce, Byrne, Hurst, Sissons.

The match programme states that this game was the first all-seater football match.

This was followed over the next few years by other friendlies against Chelsea and Arsenal. The last was in 1970 when Crystal Palace took on the Arsenal – a team that was to win the double the following season. Two goals by John Radford aided by Ray Kennedy were enough to defeat the Palace on this occasion.

By 1975, Crystal Palace Football Club were making noises about a possible return to their original home. Representatives of the Club met with the Sports Council with a view to the stadium becoming Palace's home ground and the erection of large indoor arena on the upper terraces. The Club never came back with concrete proposals so nothing more happened.

ARTHUR DUNN CUP

At about the same time as the opening of the new Centre, it was suggested that the Arthur Dunn Cup would be a suitable competition to return to the Palace. Hence, in 1965, the Old Boys teams returned for the Arthur Dunn Cup Final where it continued to be held for the next 17 years. Once again, the Crystal Palace echoed to the sound of amateur footballers and their public school supporters. Old Malvernians were again dominant but the notable feature of the day was

TOP: FRANK McLINTOCK.

ABOVE: PROGRAMME COVER AND TEAM SHEET FOR CRYSTAL PALACE V ARSENAL ON 7TH AUGUST 1970.

ABOVE: THE CUP FINAL GROUND IN 1950.

RIGHT CENTRE: ORPINGTON & BROMLEY DISTRICT DIVISION TWO FINAL MEDAL RECEIVED IN 1956.

RIGHT:THE REFEREE CHECKS WHO HAS WON THE TOSS BEFORE THE START OF THE 1965 ARTHUR DUNN FINAL, WHILE THE TWO CAPTAINS R H CHADDER OF MALVERNIANS (RIGHT) AND B J HARE OF REPTONIANS MARSHALL THEIR TROOPS.

RIGHT: DICK CHADDER IS HELD ALOFT WHILE GRIPPING THE CUP IN CELEBRATION OF A MALVERNIANS VICTORY IN THE 1965 FINAL.

the friendly nature of the competition. Once again, football was "fun" at the Crystal Palace.

Tony Williams, editor of the leading national non-League magazine Team Talk, played in six Arthur Dunn Finals at the Crystal Palace, for Old Malvernians. He told us:

"I remember the main stands standing back from the pitch. There was lots of space and on the other side, people stood on the touchline. It was a good ground but an open ground.

Three to four hundred people would attend and the game would be reported in The Times and The Telegraph.

The best teams of my day were Old Reptonians, Old Brentwoods and Old Malvernians. The most exciting game I played in was the 1964-65 Final against Reptonians. We won 2 – 1 and I scored the winner. The matches were hard and tough.

The evenings after the game were fantastic. The party would start again on Sunday morning and go on all day. Everyone would stay in London for the weekend. Lots of teams would meet at and return to St Stephen's Tavern at Westminster".

LOCAL FOOTBALL

Evidently, the football ground has been used for football at all levels since 1945 much of it unreported. Alan Weldon, formally a local lad, discovered about one such game by accident. Twenty-odd years ago, he was watching the FA Cup Final on television, when his father turned to him and said:

"I've played at the Cup Final ground, y'know!. ... No, not Wembley!". His father then explained that FA Cup Finals had been played at another ground called the Crystal Palace in front of huge crowds and that Manchester United had won the Cup there.

He spoke of how he and his mates of Grove Park FC had won the Orpington and Bromley Sunday Football League, Division Two and Division One League and Cup doubles in successive seasons. The Division Two Final was played at the Crystal Palace in the 1955-56 season.

He said that he felt privileged to have played at a famous ground steeped in history, even though its biggest and best days had long gone. The size of the arena had struck him and he remembered the supporters, bedecked in rosettes who travelled to the game. The match itself, won 4 – 1 against rivals Coney Hall FC, went quickly but he kept the programme and the medal to remind him of the day he had lifted a trophy on the same spot that Manchester United, amongst others, had won the FA Cup.

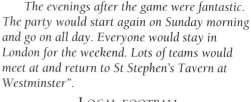

CONCLUSION

Football finally ceased at the Palace in 1982. The Crystal Palace had now become synonymous with athletics rather than football – a new history was in the making.

From time to time, it has been mooted that football should return. Crystal Palace Football Club have on occasions, the latest in 1993, continued to investigate the possibility of returning to their roots but local opposition to projected traffic congestion, noise and possible crowd trouble have stopped these proposals. So it would appear that the link of the Crystal Palace site and football may be broken.

Nevertheless, the Crystal Palace occupies a unique place in the history of football. It was a participant in the birth pangs of the new sport, the location of the FA Cup Final during those 20 years spanning the close of the nineteenth century and the beginning of the twentieth, which have been called the 'Golden Age of Football', a centre for the survival of amateur football and finally a ground where amateur footballers came to play for "fun".

We are sad to see its passing but its memory will endure in the name of Crystal Palace Football Club and in their logo which continues to show the Crystal Palace building and the twin towers.

POSTSCRIPT

It was announced in May 1999 that for the 1999-2000 season, Crystal Palace FC have come to an agreement with the Crystal Palace Sports Centre to use the facilities for the Club's Academy (youth) activities, training the Crystal Palace stars of the future. Also, Crystal Palace Academy matches and Reserve Team games will be played in the Stadium, the first game being against Tottenham Reserves on 1st September 1999.

Football is coming home to the Palace again?!

ABOVE: NATIONAL SPORTS CENTRE COMPLEX IN 1977, AFTER THE ADDITION OF THE QUEEN ELIZABETH II JUBILEE STAND.

BELOW: CRYSTAL PALACE FC LOGO DEPICTING THEIR CURRENT NICKNAME 'THE EAGLES'.

THE LADY FOOTBALLER.

HE : What are you, Half-back o Forward ?

SHE : Sir ! ! !

DEVELOPMENT OF THE RULES OF THE GAME

The FA was created with the aim of standardising the rules of the game. When the FA Cup Competition started in 1872, there were virtually no field markings, crossbars or goal-nets; a game could go on indefinitely, without an interval, without a referee, and without a referee, and with very few rules. It was still rare for a spectator to be charged admission and except when matches took place on well-established cricket grounds, he was not provided with a specific area to stand or sit. At best, he was prevented from encroaching on the field of play by a rope stretched along the imaginary touchline.

The game consisted primarily of individuals attempting to dribble the ball through the opposition, with possibly a team-mate *"backing up"* behind the dribbler to get the ball if it went loose, or to hustle and ward off opponents.

The only offences that were positively outlawed were hacking and playing the ball when *"offside"*, a rule based on the old Eton College term of *"sneaking"*, which meant loitering around your opponents' goalmouth until the ball arrived. At first, the FA ruled that *"any footballer caught between the ball and the opposing goal was 'out of play'"*, but by 1870 this had been amended to apply only if fewer than three opponents stood between him and his objective.

Hacking (the deliberate chopping-down of an opposing player) was illegal but still went on. In one match between Old Harrovians and Old Etonians, Charles Alcock was so severely bruised by Kinnaird that he asked him sharply: *"Look here, are we going to play the game, or are we going to have hacking?"*.

"Oh," Kinnaird replied, *"Let us have hacking by all means"*.

Technically, matches were controlled by two umpires, one provided by each side, but they were not expected to intervene unless specifically appealed to. In any case, there was no provision for penalising foul play, because gentlemen were not expected to commit fouls.

TOP LEFT: MR F J WALL, SECRETARY OF THE FOOTBALL ASSOCIATION IN 1895. TOP RIGHT: L RICHMOND ROOSE, STOKE'S FAMOUS AMATEUR GOALKEEPER AND WELSH INTERNATIONAL. CENTRE RIGHT: HEADING THE BALL FROM A WOODCUT BY W. RALSTON. BOTTOM LEFT: ILLUSTRATION OF THE OFFSIDE RULE. BOTTOM RIGHT: HOW THE FIELD WAS MARKED IN 1869.

GOALKEEPING

Initially, no importance was placed on goalkeeping. An injured player might be asked to go and defend the goal. It was only when handling was abolished that the goalkeeper position achieved any importance. But he got no further privilege or protection till 1893.

PASSING-ON

The rule in rugby and early forms of football had been that the ball should be passed back to a colleague but when passing forward was used in Scotland this was taken up quickly by the Northern English clubs, and became an integral part of the game.

HEADING

This was probably introduced in Sheffield as early as the 1860s. It was first used in the South by Lieutenant Sim, one of the Royal Engineers' full-backs in the 1875 Final. Charles Campbell, the Queen's Park half-back, was a good header of the ball. When his club met an Irish team in a friendly, one of his opponents was so astonished at the technique that he exclaimed: *"Bejabers, and that one kicks well with his head!"*.

HANDLING THE BALL

Though it was not acceptable to deliberately pick the ball up off the ground, the FA at first allowed a 'fair catch', but this was banned in 1866. Two years later, *"handling the ball under any pretext whatsoever"* was enforced, and accepted reluctantly.

LINE MARKINGS

The introduction of lines to mark the field of play brought about the need for legislation to decide how the game should be restarted. At first, when the ball went out of play behind the goal-line, if a defender touched it down, his side was awarded a free-kick from close to its goal; but if an attacker got there first, his team was awarded a free-kick from a position 15 yards along the goal-line (rather like a penalty corner in hockey).

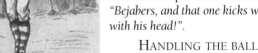
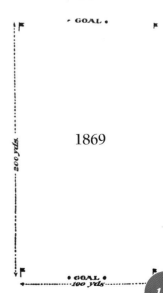

1869

In 1873, this changed to the modern concept of a corner-kick, awarded when the defender is the last to touch a ball that goes out of play.

Throw-ins originally went to the first player to touch the ball down after it left the field. Until 1898, it was possible to score from a throw-in. This was particularly advantageous up to 1882 because until then, a ball could be thrown in one-handed, which the cricketers/ footballers did with great success.

GOALPOSTS

The original rules provided for goalposts, but for three years there was no limit on the height at which a ball could pass between them and still counted as a goal. In 1866, the FA ordered a tape to be placed between the two posts, eight feet above the ground; and from April 1877, when the rules became standardised with the Sheffield Association, a crossbar became optional although not compulsory till 1882.

The Sheffield clubs had been using crossbars since about 1866, although the dimensions of their goals were a little bizarre - nine feet high and only four feet between the posts.

Goalnets were first introduced in 1885, but it was the Liverpool City Engineer, J A Brodie, who perfected and patented them in 1890. They first appeared in a Cup Final in 1892.

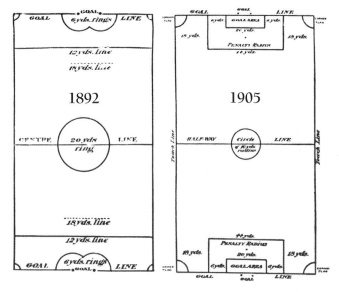

MARKING OF GOALMOUTH, PENALTY AREA AND CENTRE CIRCLE

Goalmouth markings did not arrive until 1892, the following words being added to the law:

"......*and lines defining six yards from the goal-lines shall also be marked out. The centre of the ground shall be indicated by a suitable mark, and a circle with a ten-yards radius shall be made round it*".

The original lines were in the shape of two semi-circles six yards from the goal, which marked the positions from which the goal kick was to be taken. The penalty area was marked by a continuous line twelve yards from the goal-line; within this area a penalty kick would be awarded if certain offences were committed. Some clubs also marked out a dotted line at eighteen yards behind which all players should stand when a penalty kick was being taken.

However, in 1902, the semi-circles, the dotted eighteen yard line, and the twelve yard line were abolished in favour of the rectangular goal area and the penalty box; the markings that are in use today.

NUMBER OF PLAYERS

For some time there were no hard and fast rules about the number of players: the FA favoured eleven but the Sheffield Association favoured twelve. Nor were teams always even numerically. When the Wanderers defended their unbeaten record against Upton Park, the game started with about eight on each side, latecomers joining as they arrived. It was only when the Wanderers found themselves losing 2 - 0 that Charles Alcock suggested a count, and discovered that while they had eleven players, their opponents had fifteen!.

TOP LEFT: THE FIELD IN 1883. CENTRE LEFT & RIGHT: THE FIELD MARKINGS IN 1892 AND 1905.
TOP RIGHT: FLIMSY GOALPOSTS AND A ROPE CROSSBAR IN 1878. BOTTOM RIGHT: ASTON VILLA V SUNDERLAND, 1893.

FA Cup - Original Crystal Palace Club record 1871 - 1876

Above: The Final between Old Etonians & Blackburn Rovers played at the Kennington Oval in 1882.

Below: Styles of football kit worn by the principal players in the 1880's.

1871 - 72

Nov	11	1st round	Hitchin	0 - 0*
Dec	16	2nd round	Maidenhead	3 - 0
Jan	20	3rd round	Wanderers	0 - 0*
Feb	17	Semi	Royal Engineers	0 - 0
Mar	9	Semi replay	Royal Engineers	0 - 3

1872 -73

Oct	19	1st round	Oxford University	2 - 3

1873 -74

Oct	9	1st round	Swifts	0 - 1

1874 -75

Nov	14	1st round	Cambridge Univ.	0 - 0
	21	1st round replay	Cambridge Univ.	1 - 2

1875 - 76

Nov	6	1st round	105th Regiment	0 - 0
	20	1st round replay	105th Regiment	3 - 0
Dec	11	2nd round	Wanderers	0 - 3

Rule 8   "whereby in case of a drawn match the clubs shall be drawn again in the next ties or shall compete again at the discretion of the Committee"

FA Cup Finals at the Crystal Palace - Match Statistics 1895 - 1914

20 April 1895

Aston Villa 1 West Bromwich Albion 0

Aston Villa: Wilkes; Spencer, Walford; Reynolds, James Cowan, Russell; Athersmith, Chatt, Devey, Hodgetts, Smith.

West Bromwich: Reader; Williams, Horton; Perry, Higgins, Taggart; Bassett, McLeod, Richards, Hutchinson, Banks.

Referee: J Lewis (Blackburn).

Scorer: Villa (Chatt 1).

Attendance: 42,560.

Gate Receipts: £1,545.

Guest of Honour: Lady Kinnaird.

18 April 1896

Sheffield Wednesday 2 Wolverhampton Wanderers 1

Sheffield: Massey; Earp, Langley; Brandon, Crawshaw, Petrie; Brash, Brady, Bell, Davis, Spiksley.

Wolves: Tennant; Baugh, Dunn; Owen, Malpass, Griffiths; Tanks, Henderson, Beats, Wood, Black.

Referee: Lieut. Simpson.

Linesmen: A G Hines, J Howcroft.

Scorers: Sheffield (Spiksley 1, 18); Wolves (Black 8).

Attendance: 48,836.

Gate Receipts: £1,824.

Guest of Honour: Lord Kinnaird.

10 April 1897

Aston Villa 3 Everton 2

Aston Villa: Whitehouse; Spencer, Reynolds; Evans, James Cowan, Crabtree; Athersmith, Devey, Campbell, Wheldon, John Cowan.

Everton: Menham; Meechan, Storrier; Boyle, Holt, Stewart; Taylor, Bell, Hartley, Chadwick, Milward.

Referee: J Lewis (Blackburn).

Scorers: Aston Villa (Campbell 18, Wheldon 35, Crabtree 44); Everton (Bell 23, Boyle 28).

Attendance: 65,891.

Gate Receipts: £2,162.

Guest of Honour: Lord Rosebery.

16 April 1898

Nottingham Forest 3 Derby County 1

Nottingham: Allsop; Ritchie, Scott; Forman, McPherson, Wragg; McInnes, Richards, Benbow, Capes, Spouncer.

Derby: Fryer; Methven, Leiper; Cox, A Goodall, Turner; J Goodall, Bloomer, Boag, Stevenson, McQueen.

Referee: J Lewis (Blackburn).

Scorers: Nottingham (Capes 19 and 42, McPherson 86); Derby (Bloomer 31).

Attendance: 62,017.

Gate Receipts: £2,312.

Guest of Honour: Lord Rosebery.

15 April 1899

Sheffield United 4 Derby County 1

Sheffield: Foulke; Thickett, Boyle; Johnson, Morren, Needham; Bennett, Beers, Hedley, Almond, Priest.

Derby: Fryer; Methven, Staley; Cox, Paterson, May; Arkesden, Bloomer, Boag, McDonald, Allen.

Referee: A Scragg (Crewe).

Scorers: Sheffield (Bennett 60, Beers 65, Almond 69, Priest 89); Derby (Boag 12).

Attendance: 73,833.

Gate Receipts: £2,747.

Guests of Honour: First Lord of the Treasury, A J Balfour, Lord Dalmeny.

21 April 1900

Bury 4 Southampton 0

Bury: Thompson; Darroch, Davidson; Pray, Leeming, Ross; Richards, Wood, McLuckie, Sagar, Plant.

Southampton: Robinson; Meechan, Durber; Meston, A Chadwick, Petrie; Turner, Yates, Farrell, Wood, Milward.

Referee: A Kingscott (Derby).

Scorers: Bury (McLuckie 9 and 23, Wood 16, Plant 80).

Attendance: 68,945.

Gate Receipts: £2,587.

Guests of Honour: Lord James of Hertford, Lord Rosebery, Lord Dalmeny.

20 APRIL 1901

Tottenham Hotspur 2 Sheffield United 2

TOTTENHAM: Clawley; Erentz, Tait; Morris, Hughes, Jones; Smith, Cameron, Brown, Copeland, Kirwan.

SHEFFIELD UNITED: Foulke; Thickett, Boyle; Johnson, Morren, Needham; Bennett, Field, Hedley, Priest, Lipsham.

REFEREE: A Kingscott (Derby).

SCORERS: Tottenham (Brown 23, 51); Sheffield United (Priest 10, Bennett 52).

ATTENDANCE: 110,820.

GATE RECEIPTS: £3,998.

GUESTS OF HONOUR: General Sir Redvers Buller, Lord Kinnaird.

REPLAY: Burnden Park 27 April 1901.

Tottenham Hotspur 3 Sheffield United 1.

19 APRIL 1902

Sheffield United 1 Southampton 1

SHEFFIELD UNITED: Foulke; Thickett, Boyle; Johnson, Wilkinson, Needham; Bennett, Common, Hedley, Priest, Lipsham.

SOUTHAMPTON: Robinson; C B Fry, Molyneux; Meston, Bowman, Lee; A Turner, Wood, Brown, Chadwick, J Turner.

REFEREE: T Kirkham (Burslem).

SCORERS: Sheffield United (Common 55); Southampton (Wood 88).

ATTENDANCE: 76,914.

GATE RECEIPTS: £2,893.

GUESTS OF HONOUR: Lord Kinnaird, Sir Thomas Lipton.

REPLAY 26 APRIL 1902

Sheffield United 2 Southampton 1

SHEFFIELD UNITED: Foulke; Thickett, Boyle; Johnson, Wilkinson, Needham; Barnes, Common, Hedley, Priest, Lipsham.

SOUTHAMPTON: Robinson; C B Fry, Molyneux; Meston, Bowman, Lee; A Turner, Wood, Brown, Chadwick, J Turner.

REFEREE: T Kirkham (Burslem).

SCORERS: Sheffield United (Hedley 2, Barnes 79); Southampton (Brown 70).

ATTENDANCE: 33,068.

GATE RECEIPTS: £1,625.

GUESTS OF HONOUR: Duc de Mandos (Spanish Ambassador), Sir Spencer Ponsonby Fane.

18 APRIL 1903

Bury 6 Derby County 0

BURY: Monteith; Lindsey, McEwen; Johnstone, Thorpe, Ross; Richards, Wood, Sagar, Leeming, Plant.

DERBY: Fryer; Methven, Morris; Warren, Goodall, May; Warrington, York, Boag, Richards, Davis.

REFEREE: J Adams (Birmingham).

SCORERS: Bury (Ross 20, Sagar 48, Leeming 56, 75 Wood 57, Plant 59).

ATTENDANCE: 63, 102.

GATE RECEIPTS: £2,470.

GUEST OF HONOUR: Lord Kinnaird.

23 APRIL 1904

Manchester City 1 Bolton Wanderers 0

MANCHESTER CITY: Hillman; McMahon, Burgess; Frost, Hynds, Ashworth; Meredith, Livingstone, Gillespie, A Turnbull, Booth.

BOLTON WANDERERS: Davies; Brown, Struthers; Clifford, Greenhalgh, Freebairn; Stokes, Marsh, Yenson, White, Taylor.

REFEREE: A J Barker (Hanley).

SCORER: City (Meredith 23).

ATTENDANCE: 61,374.

GATE RECEIPTS: £3,000.

GUESTS OF HONOUR: Hon. Alfred Lyttelton (Colonial Minister), A J Balfour, Lord Stanley (Postmaster General).

15 APRIL 1905

Aston Villa 2 Newcastle United 0

ASTON VILLA: George; Spencer, Miles; Pearson, Leake, Windmill; Brawn, Garratty, Hampton, Bache, Hall.

NEWCASTLE UNITED: Lawrence; McCombie, Carr; Gardner, Aitken, McWilliam; Rutherford, Howie, Appleyard, Veitch, Gosnell.

REFEREE: P R Harrower.

SCORER: Villa (Hampton 2 and 76).

ATTENDANCE: 101, 117.

GATE RECEIPTS: £7,785.

GUESTS OF HONOUR: Mrs Kenneth Kinnaird, Lord Kinnaird, Sir Walter Plummer MP.

21 April 1906

Everton 1 Newcastle United 0

EVERTON: Scott; Crelley, W Balmer; Makepeace, Taylor, Abbott; Sharp, Bolton, Young, Settle, H P Hardman.

NEWCASTLE UNITED: Lawrence; McCombie, Carr; Gardner, Aitken, McWilliam; Rutherford, Howie, Orr, Veitch, Gosnell.

REFEREE: F Kirkham (Preston).

SCORER: Everton (Young 75).

ATTENDANCE: 75,609.

GATE RECEIPTS: £6,625.

GUEST OF HONOUR: Lord Kinnaird.

20 April 1907

Sheffield Wednesday 2 Everton 1

SHEFFIELD WEDNESDAY: Lyall; Layton, Burton; Brittleton, Crawshaw, Bartlett; Chapman, Bradshaw, Wilson, Stewart, Simpson.

EVERTON: Scott; W Balmer, R Balmer; Makepeace, Taylor, Abbott; Sharp, Bolton, Young, Settle, H P Hardman.

REFEREE: N Whittaker.

SCORERS: Sheffield Wednesday (Stewart 21, Simpson 89); Everton (Sharp 38).

ATTENDANCE: 84,594.

GATE RECEIPTS: £7,053.

GUEST OF HONOUR: Lord Alverstone.

25 April 1908

Wolverhampton Wanderers 3 Newcastle United 1

WOLVERHAMPTON WANDERERS: Lunn; Jones, Collins; Rev. K R G Hunt, Wooldridge, Bishop; Harrison, Shelton, Hedley, Radford, Pedley.

NEWCASTLE UNITED: Lawrence; McCracken, Pudan; Gardner, Veitch, McWilliam; Rutherford, Howie, Appleyard, Speedie, Wilson.

REFEREE: T P Campbell.

SCORERS: Wolves (Hunt 40, Hedley 43, Harrison 85); Newcastle (Howie 73).

ATTENDANCE: 74,967.

GATE RECEIPTS: £5,998.

GUEST OF HONOUR: Sir John Bell.

24 April 1909

Manchester United 1 Bristol City 0

MANCHESTER UNITED: Moger; Stacey, Hayes; Duckworth, Roberts, Bell; Meredith, Halse, J Turnbull, A Turnbull, Wall.

BRISTOL CITY: Clay; Annan, Cottle; Hanlin, Wedlock, Spear; Staniforth, Hardy, Gilligan, Burton, Hilton.

REFEREE: J Mason (Burslem).

SCORER: United (A Turnbull 22).

ATTENDANCE: 71,401.

GATE RECEIPTS: £6,434.

GUESTS OF HONOUR: Lord Charles Beresford, Lord Derby, Lord Carnarvon, Earl Howe.

23 April 1910

Newcastle United 1 Barnsley 1

NEWCASTLE UNITED: Lawrence; McCracken, Whitson; Veitch, Low, McWilliam; Rutherford, Howie, Higgins, Shepherd, Wilson.

BARNSLEY: Mearns; Downs, Ness; Glendinning, Boyle, Utley; Tufnell, Lillycrop, Gadsby, Forman, Bartrop.

REFEREE: J T Ibbotson.

SCORERS: Newcastle United (Rutherford 83); Barnsley (Tufnell 37).

ATTENDANCE: 77,747.

GATE RECEIPTS: £6,898.

GUESTS OF HONOUR: Lord and Lady Gladstone. Lord Rosebery.

REPLAY: Goodison Park, Everton.

Newcastle United 2 Barnsley 0

22 April 1911

Bradford City 0 Newcastle United 0

BRADFORD CITY: Mellors; Campbell, Taylor; Robinson, Gildea, McDonald; Logan, Speirs, O'Rourke, Devine, Thompson.

NEWCASTLE UNITED: Lawrence; McCracken, Whitson; Veitch, Low, Willis; Rutherford, Jobey, Stewart, Higgins, Wilson.

REFEREE: J H Pearson (Crewe).

ATTENDANCE: 69,098.

GATE RECEIPTS: £6,512.

GUESTS OF HONOUR: Earl of Plymouth, Lord Kinnaird and Lord Portsmouth.

REPLAY: Old Trafford, Manchester.

Bradford City 1 Newcastle United 0

20 April 1912

Barnsley 0 West Bromwich Albion 0

BARNSLEY: Cooper; Downs, Taylor; Glendinning, Bratley, Utley; Bartrop, Tufnell, Lillycrop, Travers, Moore.

WEST BROMWICH ALBION: Pearson; Cook, Pennington; Baddeley, Buck, McNeal; Jephcott, Wright, Pailor, Bowser, Shearman.

REFEREE: J R Schumacher (London).

ATTENDANCE: 54,556.

GATE RECEIPTS: £6,057.

REPLAY: Bramall Lane, Sheffield.

Barnsley 1 West Bromwich Albion 0

19 April 1913

Aston Villa 1 Sunderland 0

ASTON VILLA: Hardy; Lyons, Weston; Barber, Harrop, Leach; Wallace, Halse, Hampton, Stephenson, Bache.

SUNDERLAND: Butler; Gladwin, Ness; Cuggy, Thomson, Low; Mordue, Buchan, Richardson, Holley, Martin.

REFEREE: A Adams (Notts.).

SCORER: Villa (Barber 75).

ATTENDANCE: 120,081.

GATE RECEIPTS: £9,406.

GUEST OF HONOUR: Earl of Plymouth.

25 April 1914

Burnley 1 Liverpool 0

BURNLEY: Sewell; Bamford, Taylor; Halley, Boyle, Watson; Nesbitt, Lindley, Freeman, Hodgson, Mosscrop.

LIVERPOOL: Campbell; Longworth, Pursell; Fairfoul, Ferguson, MacKinlay; Sheldon, Metcalfe, Miller, Lacey, Nicholl.

REFEREE: H S Bamlett (Durham).

SCORER: Burnley (Freeman 58).

ATTENDANCE: 72,778.

GATE RECEIPTS: £6,687.

GUESTS OF HONOUR: H M King George V, Earl of Derby, Lord Kinnaird.

LEFT: GENERAL SIR REDVERS H BULLER. V.C., G.C.B., K.C.M.G., P.C.. GUEST OF HONOUR AT THE 1901 FINAL.

BELOW: VIEW OF THE 1897 CUP FINAL.

ENGLAND V SCOTLAND INTERNATIONALS PLAYED AT CRYSTAL PALACE

APRIL 3 1897

England 1 Scotland 2

ENGLAND: Robinson (Derby County); W J Oakley (Corinthians), Spencer; Reynolds (Aston Villa), Crawshaw (Sheffield Wednesday), Needham (Sheffield United); Athersmith (Aston Villa), Bloomer (Derby County), G O Smith (Corinthians), Chadwick, Milward (Everton).

SCOTLAND: Patrick (St Mirren); N Smith (Rangers), D Doyle (Celtic); Gibson (Rangers), Cowan (Aston Villa), Wilson (Sunderland); Bell (Everton), Miller (Rangers), Allan (Liverpool), Hyslop (Rangers), W Lambie (Queen's Park).

SCORERS: England (Bloomer);
Scotland (Hyslop, Miller).

MARCH 30, 1901

England 2 Scotland 2

ENGLAND: Sutcliffe (Bolton Wanderers); Iremonger (Nottingham Forest), W J Oakley (Corinthians); Wilkes (Aston Villa), Forman (Nottingham Forest), Needham; Bennett (Sheffield United), Bloomer (Derby County), G O Smith, R E Foster (Corinthians), Blackburn (Blackburn Rovers).

SCOTLAND: Rennie (Heart of Midlothian); Battles (Celtic), Drummond (Rangers); Aitken (Newcastle United), Raisbeck (Liverpool), Robertson (Rangers); Walker (Heart of Midlothian), Campbell (Celtic), R McColl (Queen's Park), Hamilton, A Smith (Rangers).

SCORERS: England (Blackburn, Bloomer);
Scotland (Campbell, Hamilton).

APRIL 1, 1905

England 1 Scotland 0

ENGLAND: Linacre (Notts Forest); Spencer (Aston Villa), Smith (Reading); Ruddlesden (Sheffield Wednesday), Roberts (Manchester United), Leake (Aston Villa); Sharp (Everton), Bloomer (Derby County), V Woodward (Tottenham Hotspur), Bache (Aston Villa), Bridgett (Sunderland).

SCOTLAND: Lyall (Sheffield Wednesday); McCombie (Newcastle United), Watson (Sunderland); Aitken (Newcastle United), Thomson (Hearts), McWilliam (Newcastle United); Walker (Hearts), Howie (Newcastle United), Young (Everton), Somers (Celtic), Wilson (Hearts).

SCORER: England (Bache).

APRIL 3, 1909

England 2 Scotland 0

ENGLAND: Hardy (Liverpool); Crompton (Blackburn Rovers), Pennington (West Bromwich Albion); Warren (Chelsea), Wedlock (Bristol City), Lintott (Bradford City); Pentland (Middlesbrough), Fleming (Swindon), Freeman (Everton), Holley (Sunderland), Wall (Manchester United).

SCOTLAND: Brownlie (Third Lanark); Cameron (Chelsea), Watson (Middlesbrough); McNair (Celtic), Stark (Rangers), McWilliam (Newcastle); Bennett (Rangers), Walker (Hearts), Quinn (Celtic), Wilson (Newcastle), H Paul (Queen's Park).

SCORER: England (Wall 2).

CRYSTAL PALACE - FIRST TEAM FIXTURES PLAYED AT CRYSTAL PALACE 1905-1915

1905-06 MGR: J.R.ROBSON

Sat	Sep	2	Southampton Res	3 - 4
Sat	Sep	23	Leyton	0 - 0
Sat	Oct	14	Fulham Res	5 - 0
Sat	Nov	4	Grays United	9 - 1
Wed	Dec	13	Reading Res	3 - 0
Sat	Dec	23	Swindon Res	3 - 0
Tue	Dec	26	Portsmouth Res	1 - 0
Sat	Jan	20	St Leonards	3 - 1
Sat	Feb	10	West Ham Res	3 - 1
Wed	Feb	21	Southern United	4 - 0
Sat	Mar	3	Watford Res	4 - 0
Sat	Apr	14	Wycombe Wanderers	4 - 0

FINAL LEAGUE POSITION: 1st in Southern League, Division Two.
Palace also played in the United Counties League and won the Championship.

FA Cup

Sat	Oct	7	Clapham (1Q)	7 - 0
Sat	Nov	18	Chelsea (3Q)	7 - 1
Sat	Dec	9	Luton Town (4Q)	1 - 0
Fri	Jan	19	Blackpool (1R Replay)	1 - 1

1906-07 MGR: J.R.ROBSON

Sat	Sep	1	Northampton Town	3 - 0
Sat	Sep	15	Fulham	0 - 3
Wed	Sep	19	Reading	4 - 1
Sat	Sep	29	West Ham United	1 - 1
Sat	Oct	13	Swindon Town	3 - 2
Sat	Oct	27	Luton Town	0 - 1
Sat	Nov	17	Millwall	3 - 0
Sat	Dec	1	Portsmouth	1 - 0
Sat	Dec	15	Plymouth	0 - 2
Sat	Jan	5	Queen's Park Rangers	5 - 1
Sat	Jan	26	Southampton	1 - 1
Sat	Feb	9	Tottenham Hotspur	0 - 1
Sat	Mar	16	Brentford	0 - 3
Sat	Mar	30	Leyton	1 - 0
Mon	Apr	1	Watford	1 - 3
Sat	Apr	13	New Brompton	1 - 3
Wed	Apr	17	Bristol Rovers	3 - 3
Wed	Apr	24	Norwich City	0 - 1
Sat	Apr	27	Brighton & Hove Albion	2 - 2

FINAL LEAGUE POSITION: 19th in Southern League, Division One.
FA Cup

Wed	Feb	6	Fulham (2R)	1 - 0
Sat	Feb	23	Brentford (3R)	1 - 1
Sat	Mar	9	Everton (4R)	1 - 1

1907-08 MGR: EDMUND GOODMAN

Wed	Sep	4	Northampton Town	0 - 2
Sat	Sep	14	Plymouth Argyle	0 - 4
Sat	Sep	28	Queen's Park Rangers	2 - 3
Sat	Oct	12	Swindon Town	4 - 1
Sat	Oct	19	New Brompton	3 - 3
Sat	Nov	2	Brighton & Hove Albion	2 - 1
Sat	Nov	16	Bradford	1 - 1
Sat	Nov	30	Brentford	2 - 1
Sat	Dec	14	Leyton	3 - 0
Sat	Dec	28	Watford	3 - 1
Sat	Jan	4	Southampton	1 - 0
Sat	Jan	18	West Ham United	1 - 3
Wed	Feb	12	Tottenham Hotspur	0 - 2
Wed	Mar	4	Luton Town	4 - 2
Sat	Mar	7	Portsmouth	2 - 2
Sat	Mar	21	Millwall	2 - 0
Sat	Apr	4	Bristol Rovers	1 - 1
Sat	Apr	18	Reading	2 - 0
Mon	Apr	20	Norwich City	2 - 1

FINAL LEAGUE POSITION: 4th in Southern League, Division One.

1908-09 MGR: EDMUND GOODMAN

Sat	Sep	5	Leyton	5 - 1
Wed	Sep	16	Southampton	2 - 3
Sat	Sep	19	Brighton & Hove Albion	4 - 0
Wed	Sep	30	Norwich City	4 - 0
Sat	Oct	10	Luton Town	2 - 0
Wed	Oct	21	Queen's Park Rangers	3 - 0
Sat	Oct	24	Portsmouth	3 - 2
Sat	Nov	7	Northampton Town	2 - 3
Sat	Nov	21	Millwall	2 - 1
Sat	Dec	19	Watford	3 - 1
Sat	Jan	9	West Ham United	2 - 2
Sat	Jan	30	Plymouth	0 - 1
Sat	Feb	20	Swindon Town	1 - 1
Sat	Mar	6	Exeter City	0 - 0
Wed	Mar	17	Southend United	1 - 3
Sat	Mar	20	New Brompton	1 - 2
Wed	Mar	31	Brentford	3 - 1
Sat	Apr	10	Coventry City	0 - 1
Mon	Apr	12	Reading	0 - 0
Sat	Apr	17	Bristol Rovers	4 - 1

FINAL LEAGUE POSITION: 16th in Southern League, Division One.
FA Cup

Thu	Jan	21	Wolverhampton Wanderers (1R)	4 - 2
Sat	Feb	6	Burnley (2R)	0 - 0

1909-10 MGR: EDMUND GOODMAN

Wed	Sep	1	Brentford	1 - 0
Wed	Sep	8	Bristol Rovers	3 - 1
Sat	Sep	11	Watford	1 - 1
Sat	Sep	25	Southend United	6 - 0
Sat	Oct	9	Plymouth Argyle	3 - 0
Wed	Oct	13	Norwich City	4 - 0
Sat	Oct	23	Croydon Common	2 - 0
Sat	Nov	6	New Brompton	6 - 2
Sat	Nov	20	Queen's Park Rangers	0 - 1
Sat	Dec	4	Swindon Town	2 - 0
Sat	Dec	11	Exeter City	3 - 0
Sat	Jan	8	Coventry City	1 - 2
Sat	Jan	29	Reading	1 - 1
Sat	Feb	12	Leyton	1 - 2
Sat	Feb	26	Southampton	2 - 0
Wed	Mar	9	Portsmouth	4 - 2
Sat	Mar	12	Millwall	4 - 1
Sat	Mar	26	Northampton Town	1 - 0

Mon	Mar 28	West Ham United	2 - 4
Sat	Apr 9	Luton Town	1 - 3
Sat	Apr 30	Brighton & Hove Albion	0 - 0

FINAL LEAGUE POSITION: 7th in Southern League, Division One.

FA Cup

Sat	Jan 15	Swindon Town (1R)	1 - 3

1910-11 MGR: EDMUND GOODMAN

Sat	Sep 10	Bristol Rovers	1 - 0
Sat	Sep 17	Norwich City	0 - 3
Sat	Oct 1	Leyton	5 - 4
Wed	Oct 5	Portsmouth	0 - 1
Sat	Oct 15	Plymouth Argyle	6 - 1
Sat	Oct 29	Southend United	0 - 0
Sat	Nov 12	New Brompton	3 - 2
Sat	Nov 26	Queen's Park Rangers	2 - 1
Sat	Dec 10	Luton Town	3 - 1
Sat	Dec 24	Northampton Town	0 - 0
Tue	Dec 27	Brighton & Hove Albion	1 - 1
Sat	Dec 31	Swindon Town	2 - 5
Sat	Jan 28	Brentford	1 - 1
Sat	Feb 11	Watford	1 - 0
Sat	Feb 25	Southampton	2 - 2
Sat	Mar 11	Coventry City	2 - 0
Sat	Mar 25	Millwall	1 - 0
Sat	Apr 8	West Ham United	4 - 1
Mon	Apr 17	Exeter City	1 - 0

FINAL LEAGUE POSITION: 4th in Southern League, Division One.

FA Cup

Sat	Jan 14	Everton (1R)	0 - 4

1911-12 MGR: EDMUND GOODMAN

Sat	Sep 2	West Ham United	1 - 0
Sat	Sep 16	Swindon Town	2 - 2
Sat	Sep 30	Brighton & Hove Albion	1 - 1
Sat	Oct 14	Coventry City	3 - 0
Sat	Oct 28	Norwich City	6 - 0
Sat	Dec 16	Exeter City	5 - 0
Tue	Dec 26	Queen's Park Rangers	3 - 0
Sat	Jan 6	Bristol Rovers	4 - 1
Sat	Jan 27	Northampton Town	1 - 2
Sat	Feb 10	Stoke	1 - 2
Sat	Feb 24	Leyton	1 - 1
Wed	Feb 28	Plymouth Argyle	0 - 1
Sat	Mar 9	Luton Town	3 - 1
Sat	Mar 16	Southampton	3 - 1
Sat	Mar 30	Reading	1 - 1
Sat	Apr 6	Watford	2 - 0
Mon	Apr 8	Millwall	3 - 0
Sat	Apr 13	New Brompton	1 - 1
Sat	Apr 27	Brentford	2 - 0

FINAL LEAGUE POSITION: 7th in Southern League, Division One.

FA Cup

Wed	Jan 17	Brentford (1R)	4 - 0
Sat	Feb 3	Sunderland (2R)	0 - 0

1912-13 MGR: EDMUND GOODMAN

Wed	Sep 4	Brentford	3 - 1
Sat	Sep 14	Portsmouth	2 - 0
Sat	Sep 28	West Ham United	1 - 1

Sat	Oct 12	Coventry City *	3 - 0
Sat	Oct 26	Merthyr Town	2 - 1
Sat	Nov 2	Stoke	1 - 0
Sat	Nov 16	Southampton	8 - 0
Sat	Nov 30	Norwich City	1 - 0
Sat	Dec 14	Northampton Town	2 - 2
Thu	Dec 26	Millwall	2 - 0
Sat	Dec 28	Swindon Town	1 - 0
Sat	Jan 18	Exeter City	0 - 1
Sat	Feb 8	Brighton & Hove Albion	1 - 1
Sat	Mar 15	Plymouth Argyle	1 - 0
Mon	Mar 24	Bristol Rovers	3 - 0
Sat	Mar 29	Reading	4 - 2
Sat	Apr 12	Gillingham	0 - 1
Wed	Apr 23	Watford	2 - 1
Sat	Apr 26	Queen's Park Rangers †	1 - 2

FINAL LEAGUE POSITION: 5th in Southern League, Division One.

*H Collyer benefit match. † J Johnson benefit match.

FA Cup

Sat	Jan 11	Glossop (1R)	2 - 0
Sat	Feb 1	Bury (2R)	2 - 0

1913-14 MGR: EDMUND GOODMAN

Sat	Sep 6	Portsmouth	3 - 1
Wed	Sep 17	Northampton Town	3 - 0
Sat	Sep 20	Exeter City	0 - 0
Sat	Oct 4	Swindon Town	0 - 1
Sat	Oct 18	Merthyr Town	3 - 1
Sat	Nov 1	Plymouth Argyle	2 - 2
Sat	Nov 15	Reading	5 - 1
Sat	Dec 6	Watford	3 - 0
Sat	Dec 20	Gillingham	1 - 0
Fri	Dec 26	Southend	0 - 0
Sat	Jan 3	Millwall	3 - 0
Sat	Jan 24	Cardiff City	4 - 0
Sat	Feb 14	Bristol Rovers	5 - 3
Sat	Feb 28	West Ham United	1 - 2
Sat	Mar 14	Southampton	0 - 0
Sat	Mar 28	Queen's Park Rangers	2 - 1
Sat	Apr 4	Coventry City	3 - 1
Mon	Apr 13	Brighton & Hove Albion	0 - 0
Sat	Apr 18	Norwich City	3 - 0

FINAL LEAGUE POSITION: 2nd in Southern League, Division One.

FA Cup

Sat	Jan 10	Norwich City (1R)	2 - 1

1914-15 MGR: EDMUND GOODMAN

Sat	Sep 12	Brighton & Hove Albion	0 - 2
Sat	Sep 26	Cardiff City	0 - 2
Sat	Oct 10	Exeter City	0 - 0
Sat	Oct 24	Luton Town	2 - 3
Sat	Nov 7	Portsmouth	1 - 0
Sat	Nov 21	Swindon Town	3 - 0
Sat	Dec 5	Southend United	1 - 1
Sat	Dec 19	Queen's Park Rangers	2 - 2
Sat	Dec 26	Millwall	0 - 1
Mon	Dec 28	Norwich City	2 - 1
Sat	Jan 2	Bristol Rovers	1 - 0
Sat	Feb 6	Reading	4 - 1
Wed	Mar 3	Southampton	1 - 2

FINAL LEAGUE POSITION: 15th in Southern League, Division One.

The concluding games of the season were played at Herne Hill.

ARTHUR DUNN CUP FINALS PLAYED AT CRYSTAL PALACE

1903			
Old Carthusians (2 – 2)	2	Old Salopians (2 – 2)	2

1924			
Old Malvernians	2	Old Reptonians	0

1925			
Old Malvernians	2	Old Westminsters	1

1926			
Old Malvernians	3	Old Salopians	2

1927			
Old Salopians	6	Old Malvernians	3

1928			
Old Malvernians	3	Old Wykehamists	2

1929			
Old Wykehamists	3	Old Carthusians	0

1930			
Old Wykehamists	4	Old Salopians	1

1931			
Old Wykehamists	5	Old Citizens	1

1932			
Old Salopians	6	Old Reptonians	1

1933			
Old Salopians	3	Old Cholmeleians	1

1934			
Old Aldenhamians	6	Old Wykehamists	2

1935			
Old Salopians	3	Old Wykehamists	0

1936			
Old Carthusians	2	Old Bradfieldians	0

1965			
Old Malvernians	2	Old Reptonians	1

1966			
Old Reptonians	4	Old Malvernians	3

1967			
Old Brentwoods	3	Old Malvernians	2

1968			
Old Malvernians	1	Old Reptonians	1

1969			
Old Malvernians	1	Old Bradfieldians	0

1970			
Old Reptonians	2	Old Foresters	1

1971			
Old Malvernians	4	Old Brentwoods	0

1972			
Old Brentwoods	1	Old Salopians	0

1973			
Old Brentwoods	3	Old Malvernians	2

1974			
Old Foresters	2	Old Brentwoods	1

1975			
Old Malvernians	2	Old Foresters	1

1976			
Old Malvernians	5	Old Brentwoods	3

1977			
Old Carthusians	3	Old Brentwoods	0

1978			
Old Malvernians	4	Old Bradfieldians	1

1979			
Old Aldenhamians	1	Old Brentwoods	0

1980			
Old Chigwellians	4	Lancing Old Boys	2

1981			
Old Reptonians (3 – 3)	1	Old Malvernians	0

1982			
Old Carthusians	3	Old Malvernians	0

CASUALS FIRST TEAM FIXTURES PLAYED AT CRYSTAL PALACE 1922-1925

The following is a list of first team games known to have been played at the Crystal Palace while Casuals were resident. Due to the sporadic nature of the reporting of Casuals games in local newspapers and the fact that Casuals fixtures were altered on several occasions, some scores are not known.

HON SECRETARY: S F Hepburn, 61 Putney Hill SW15.
Telephone: Putney 889 (home); Sydenham 2180 (Ground).
CLUB COLOURS: Chocolate and Pink.

1922 - 23

Sat	Sep 16	West Norwood Reserves (Casual Reserves but the first team eleven)	2 - 3
Sat	Oct 21	Kingstonian (FA Amateur Cup replay)	2 - 2
Sat	Nov 4	Dulwich Hamlet	4 - 4
Sat	Nov 25	Wimbledon (FA Amateur Cup replay)	RNK
Sat	Dec 9	West Norwood	8 - 0
Sat	Dec 16	London Caledonians	3 - 0
Sat	Jan 6	Wycombe Wanderers	RNK
Sat	Jan 20	Wimbledon	1 - 2
Sat	Feb 10	Tufnell Park	7 - 1
Sat	Mar 3	Oxford City	2 - 0
Wed	Mar 7	Cambridge University	RNK
Sat	Mar 17	Ilford	3 - 2
Sat	Mar 31	Woking	0 - 0
Mon	Apr 2	Luton Clarence	5 - 2
Sat	Apr 7	Civil Service	0 - 2
Sat	Apr 14	Leytonstone	2 - 2
Sat	Apr 21	Nunhead	1 - 0

1923 - 24

Sat	Sep 15	Wimbledon	8 - 3
Sat	Sep 22	Clapton	1 - 3
Sat	Oct 13	Nunhead	3 - 0
Sat	Nov 3	Oxford University	6 - 1
Sat	Nov 17	London Caledonians	3 - 2
Sat	Dec 15	Oxford City	4 - 1
Sat	Dec 29	Ilford	6 - 2
Sat	Jan 26	Civil Service	5 - 2
Sat	Feb 9	Tufnell Park	4 - 1
Sat	Mar 1	Leytonstone	1 - 2
Sat	Mar 22	Dulwich Hamlet - cancelled as Casuals played Tooting Town Reserves in South London Charity Cup (lost 3 - 4)	
Sat	Mar 29	Northampton Nomads	3 - 0
Sat	Apr 12	Woking	5 - 1
Sat	Apr 19	St Albans City	0 - 4
Mon	Apr 21	Luton Clarence (Easter Monday fixture)	0 - 2
Sat	May 3	Wycombe Wanderers	6 - 2

1924 -25

Sat	Sept 13	Dulwich Hamlet	2 - 1
Mon	Sept 15	Great Eastern (Romford) London Charity Cup 1st Round	3 - 4
Wed	Sept 17	Wimbledon	3 - 1
Sat	Sept 20	London Caledonians	4 - 5
Sat	Oct 11	Wycombe Wanderers	5 - 3
Sat	Oct 18	Clapton (London Charity Cup)	2 - 1
Sat	Oct 25	Civil Service	4 - 2
Sat	Nov 1	Oxford University	2 - 4
Sat	Nov 8	Woking	RNK
Sat	Dec 13	Tufnell Park	0 - 2
Sat	Dec 27	Ilford	0 - 0
Sat	Jan 10	Woking	6 - 1
Sat	Jan 24	Old Malvernians	2 - 1
Sat	Feb 14	Northampton Nomads (cancelled due to state of pitch)	-
Sat	Feb 28	St Albans City	RNK
Sat	Mar 14	Leytonstone	2 - 1
Sat	Mar 28	Clapton	2 - 3
Sat	May 2	Oxford City	3 - 4

RNK = Result not known.

CORINTHIANS FIRST TEAM FIXTURES AT THE CRYSTAL PALACE

1897 - 98

Sat	Mar 19	Sheffield United	0 - 0
Mon	Apr 4	Sheffield United	1 - 1
Mon	Apr 11	Bolton Wanderers	3 - 3

1898 - 99

Sat	Feb 18	Everton	0 - 1
Sat	Mar 25	Southampton	2 - 2
Mon	Apr 3	Notts Forest	3 - 2

1899 - 1900

Wed	Nov 8	Aston Villa	2 - 1
Mon	Apr 16	Sheffield United	0 - 4

1900 - 1901

Sat	Mar 2	Aston Villa	0 - 1
Mon	Apr 8	Stoke	3 - 3

1904 - 5

Mon	Apr 24	Sheffield Wednesday	1 - 2

1922 - 23

Mon	Sep 11	Tottenham Hotspur	1 - 2
Sat	Nov 25	Cambridge University	5 - 2
Sat	Dec 2	Plymouth Argyle	0 - 2
Tues	Dec 26	Isthmian League	2 - 2
Wed	Jan 17	Brighton & Hove Albion	1 - 1
Sat	Feb 3	Crystal Palace	3 - 3
Sat	Feb 17	The Army	15 - 2
Mon	Feb 26	Queen's Park	2 - 1
Sat	Mar 24	Everton	3 - 2

1923 -24

Sat	Nov 24	Oxford University	2 - 0
Sat	Dec 1	Southampton	1 - 0
Sat	Dec 8	Cambridge University	7 - 1
Sat	Dec 22	Isthmian League	4 - 4
Sat	Jan 12	Blackburn Rovers	1 - 0
Sat	Feb 16	The Navy	4 - 1
Sat	Mar 8	Bolton Wanderers	0 - 0
Mon	Mar 31	Queen's Park	4 - 1

1924 - 25

Sat	Nov 15	South Africans	4 - 1
Sat	Nov 22	Cambridge University	7 - 0
Sat	Nov 29	Oxford University	3 - 3
Sat	Feb 28	Queen's Park	2 - 3
Sat	Mar 7	Birmingham	0 - 2
Wed	Apr 29	Crystal Palace	4 - 2

1925 - 26

Sat	Oct 17	Oxford University	6 - 2
Sat	Oct 24	Northern Nomads	4 - 2
Sat	Oct 31	Cambridge University	2 - 1
Sat	Nov 14	R.M.C	6 - 4
Sat	Dec 12	Derby County	1 - 1
Sat	Dec 19	The Army	3 - 2
Sat	Dec 26	Isthmian League	3 - 0
Sat	Jan 9	Manchester City	3 - 3
Sat	Jan 23	Royal Air Force	7 - 2
Sat	Mar 6	Queen's Park	4 - 2
Sat	Mar 13	Yorkshire Amateurs	3 - 0
Sat	Mar 20	Birmingham	1 - 0
Sat	Apr 10	Southern Amateur League	9 - 3
Sat	Apr 17	The Navy	3 - 1

1926 -27

Sat	Oct 16	Southern Amateur League	4 - 1
Sat	Oct 23	Oxford University	5 - 0
Sat	Oct 30	Cambridge University	2 - 1
Sat	Nov 6	Athenian League	1 - 9
Sat	Nov 20	R.M.C	14 - 2
Sat	Dec 18	The Navy	2 - 1
Wed	Dec 29	Tottenham Hotspur	0 - 2
Sat	Jan 15	Public Schools XI	11 - 2
Sat	Jan 29	Newcastle United	1 - 3
Wed	Feb 9	Surrey County	3 - 3
Mon	Mar 21	Queen's Park	1 - 3
Sat	Apr 9	R.A.F	8 - 4

1927 - 28

Sat	Oct 15	Southern Amateur League	10 - 1
Sat	Oct 22	Oxford University	10 - 3
Sat	Oct 29	Wiltshire	8 - 2
Sat	Nov 5	Cambridge University	5 - 3
Sat	Nov 12	United Hospitals	6 - 1
Wed	Nov 16	R.M.C	5 - 1
Sat	Dec 17	The Navy	3 - 3
Sat	Dec 24	Northern Nomads	11 - 3
Sat	Jan 7	Athenian League	4 - 1
Mon	Jan 9	Public Schools XI	6 - 1
Sat	Jan 21	Welsh Dragons	3 - 4
Sat	Jan 28	Southampton	5 - 0
Sat	Feb 4	R.A.F	9 - 4

Sat	Mar	3	Isthmian League	3 - 1
Mon	Mar	12	Queen's Park	5 - 1
Sat	Mar	24	The Army	4 - 4

1928 - 29

Sat	Oct	13	Southern Amateur League	4 - 4
Sat	Nov	10	Northern Nomads	3 - 0
Wed	Nov	14	R.M.C	8 - 2
Sat	Nov	17	Oxford University	7 - 2
Sat	Dec	1	Cambridge University	9 - 2
Sat	Dec	29	The Navy	4 - 5
Wed	Jan	2	Crystal Palace	4 - 1
Sat	Jan	5	Athenian League	5 - 0
Wed	Jan	16	Public Schools XI	3 - 0
Sat	Jan	19	The Army	15 - 4

1929 - 30

Sat	Oct	19	Cambridge University	1 - 2
Sat	Oct	26	Northern Nomads	6 - 3
Sat	Nov	2	Southern Amateur League	8 - 2
Wed	Nov	20	R.M.C	18 - 0
Sat	Dec	7	Oxford University	3 - 1
Sat	Dec	21	The Navy	4 - 1
Thu	Dec	26	Isthmian League	5 - 2
Sat	Jan	4	Athenian League	9 - 1
Sat	Jan	11	Millwall	2 - 2
Sat	Feb	1	The Army	4 - 2
Sat	Feb	22	Charterhouse School	3 - 1
Sat	Mar	15	Yorkshire Amateurs	8 - 1
Sat	Mar	22	Queen's Park	2 - 3

1930 - 31

Sat	Oct	11	Southern Amateur League	3 - 4
Sat	Nov	8	Northern Nomads	7 - 2
Wed	Nov	19	R.M.C	12 - 1
Sat	Nov	22	Cambridge University	3 - 4
Sat	Dec	6	Oxford University	2 - 5
Sat	Dec	13	Brighton & Hove Albion	4 - 1
Sat	Dec	20	The Navy	7 - 2
Sat	Dec	27	Bohemians (Dublin)	2 - 2
Sat	Jan	3	Athenian League	RNK
Sat	Jan	10	Port Vale (FA Cup)	1 - 3
Sat	Feb	21	Cambridge University	2 - 2
Sat	Mar	14	R.A.F	2 - 1
Sat	Mar	21	Yorkshire Amateurs	1 - 3

1931 -32

Sat	Sept	19	Old Malvernians	7 - 1
Sat	Sept	26	Old Bradfieldians	1 - 0
Sat	Oct	3	Old Wykehamists	3 - 4

Wed	Oct	14	R.M.A	15 - 1
Sat	Oct	24	Northern Nomads	4 - 2
Sat	Oct	31	Oxford University	6 - 1
Wed	Nov	18	R.M.C	2 - 4
Sat	Nov	21	Cambridge University	4 - 1
Sat	Dec	26	Isthmian League	2 - 5
Sat	Jan	2	Athenian League	1 - 2
Sat	Jan	16	R.A.F	4 - 2
Sat	Feb	6	The Army	3 - 4
Sat	Feb	27	Grasshoppers Club of Zurich	3 - 1
Sat	Mar	12	Yorkshire Amateurs	3 - 1
Wed	Mar	16	University of London	2 - 0
Sat	Mar	19	Old Salopians	0 - 3
Sat	Apr	9	Queen's Park	2 - 4

1932 - 33

Sat	Oct	8	Old Salopians	3 - 2
Sat	Oct	29	Cambridge University	4 - 3
Tue	Nov	1	Oxford University?	RNK
Sat	Nov	5	Yorkshire Amateurs	4 - 1
Sat	Nov	12	Oxford University	0 - 0
			Old Westminsters	RNK
Sat	Dec	10	Old Hurst Johnians	RNK
Sat	Dec	24	Royal Navy	6 - 4
Thu	Jan	12	AFA Public Schools XI	RNK
Sat	Jan	14	West Ham United (FA Cup)	0 - 2
Sat	Jan	21	Old Wykehamists	RNK
Sat	Jan	28	Old Cholmeleians	RNK
Sat	Mar	11	Lancing Old Boys?	RNK
Sat	Mar	18	St Thomas's Hospital	RNK
Sat	Mar	25	Northern Nomads	5 - 1
			London Hospital	RNK
Sat	Apr	8	London University	RNK
			Old Citizens	RNK

1933 - 34

Sat	Nov	18	Oxford University	2 - 5
Sat	Dec	2	Cambridge University	0 - 3

1934 - 35

Tue	Oct	30	Oxford University	1 - 0
Sat	Nov	3	Cambridge University	3 - 2

1935 - 36

Sat	Nov	16	Cambridge University	1 - 2
Sat	Nov	23	Oxford University	6 - 1

1936 - 37

Sat	Nov	28	Bristol Rovers (FA Cup)	0 - 2

THE CRYSTAL PALACE FOUNDATION

In May 1979, a group of local enthusiasts organised a photographic exhibition about the Crystal Palace. The exhibition was held at the National Recreation Centre in Crystal Palace Park and, despite the inclement weather, over 1000 people came along. As a result, the group decided to establish an organisation dedicated to preserving the history of the Crystal Palace; the Crystal Palace Foundation was born with about 1000 members.

From the outset, the Foundation had a number of aims. In the early days, considerable effort was spent in assisting the GLC, Bromley Council and English Heritage in excavating and renovating the Crystal Palace site – cleaning and restoring the statuary, rediscovering the Aquarium and a vaulted railway subway, the Tower bases, searching for a long-lost underground railway track. This work has continued and now extends to advising the appropriate bodies on historical accuracy when developments are planned.

A primary aim of the CPF was to establish a museum on the site. In 1982, the Foundation was allowed the use of the old Engineering School building and work began on the Museum project. This was completed in February 1988 and the Crystal Palace Museum

was officially opened by the Foundation president, the Duke of Devonshire, on 17th June 1990. The Museum is managed by the Crystal Palace Museum Trust and is staffed by volunteers. It is open every Sunday and Bank Holiday from 11am to 5pm and admission is free. The Museum has a shop which sells books and other items related to the Crystal Palace.

TOP RIGHT: EXCAVATING THE AQUARIUM SITE. LEFT: THE NAVE OF THE CRYSTAL PALACE AT THE TURN OF THE CENTURY.
RIGHT: THE CRYSTAL PALACE MUSEUM ON ANERLEY HILL. BOTTOM: THE SOUTHERN GRAND FOUNTAIN BASIN IN 1860, SITE OF THE CUP FINAL GROUND.

The Foundation created a Memories group to gather the recollections of those who had been to the Crystal Palace and remembered its demise. This has resulted in a vast collection of historical information some of which has led to publications on the subject. Notably, for the 50th anniversary of the fire which destroyed the Crystal Palace the Foundation published "The Crystal Palace is on fire!".

Over the last twenty years, members of the CPF have carried out extensive research into the infrastructure and various activities that took place at the Crystal Palace leading to a number of exhibitions and other publications. These have included "The Perfect Playground" (childhood memories of the Palace), "The Crystal Palace Dinosaurs"(a study of the antediluvian monsters in the Park), and an Education Pack for GCSE students.

Latterly, this research has included the sporting activities which have been a feature of the Crystal Palace scene for as long as the park has been in existence. The period during which the Crystal Palace dominated the top of Sydenham Hill was a time when sport in this country became organised and the Crystal Palace was at the centre of this expansion. When the two vast arenas were built in the 1890s, the Palace became the premier sporting venue (at least until the First World War) and today still continues to be an important sports centre.

The Foundation is at the heart of the community and has a voice on local issues where it affects the Crystal Palace site, regularly consulting its members for their views and influencing governing bodies and planners.

The CPF continues to arrange events to raise funds to support its activities and to finance the Crystal Palace Museum. There are also regular walkabouts around the Crystal Palace Park and talks about related subjects.

The CPF is always keen to have new members who are interested in the preservation of the heritage of the Crystal Palace site, wish to support the Foundation and maybe can contribute to its activities or can assist in the Museum.

If you are interested please contact the Secretary of the Crystal Palace Foundation at:

The Secretary,
The Crystal Palace Foundation,
c/o The Crystal Palace Museum,
Anerley Road, London SE19 2BA.

TOP CENTRE: SECTION OF THE LOWER TERRACE WHICH OVERLOOKS THE NSC.
TOP INSET: ARCHAEOLOGICAL RESEARCH WITH THE HELP OF THE PARK RANGERS.
LEFT: TWO SPHINXES FLANK A SET OF UPPER TERRACE STEPS, OVERSHADOWED BY
THE CRYSTAL PALACE RADIO & TV MAST. BOTTOM: THE CRYSTAL PALACE IN
ITS HEYDAY AT THE TURN OF THE CENTURY.

BIBLIOGRAPHY

Association Football and the men who made it – Gibson & Pickford 1906

Association Football – Caxton series (Caxton) 1960

Aston Villa Story

Bolton Wanderers – Percy M Young

Cassel Soccer Companion – David Pickering (Cassel) 1994

C B Fry – Iain Wilton (Richard Cohen Books) 1999

Corinthians and Cricketers – Edward Grayson

Cup Final Extra: A celebration for the 100th FA Cup Final – Martin Tyler

Crystal Palace: A complete record 1905-1989 – Mike Purkiss & Nigel Sands (Breedon Books)

Crystal Palace Centurions – Nigel Sands

Crystal Palace Football Club 1905 – 1995 – Nigel Sands (Sporting & Leisure Press), 1995

Daily Telegraph Football Chronicle – Norman Barrett 1993

Encyclopaedia of British Football – Phil Soar and Martin Tyler

Encyclopaedia of Sport – edited by Charles Harvey (Sampson Low, Marston and Co) 1959

England v Scotland – Brian James

English Football Internationalists' Who's Who – Douglas Lamming (Beverley) 1990

FIFA Museum Collection 1996

Football and the English – Dave Russell (Carnegie Publishing) 1997

Football Grounds of England & Wales – Simon Inglis (Willow Books) 1983

Football in Sheffield – Percy M Young

Guinness Record of the FA Cup – Mike Collett (Guinness Publishing), 1993

History of the Corinthians – F N S Creek (Longmans), 1933

How City won T'Cup – Mick Dickinson (City Gent Publications)

Manchester United – Percy M Young (Heinemann)

National Sports Centre Minute Books

News of the World Football Annual (various)

Non-League Club Directory (various) – Tony Williams

Official History of the FA Cup – Geoffrey Green

Palace Promotions – Nigel Sands (Sporting & Leisure Press)

Romance of the Wednesday – Richard A Sparling

Rothmans Football Yearbook (various)

Sheffield Football – a History – Keith Farnsworth

Soccer – A Pictorial History – Roger Macdonald (Collins)

Soccer in the Dock – Simon Inglis, 1985

Soccer: The World Game – Geoffrey Green

The Book of Football - A complete history 1905-06 (reprinted by Desert Island Books 1998)

The Crystal Palace – Patrick Beaver 1970

The Crystal Palace Story – Roy Peskett (Roy Peskett Publications) 1969

The Footballer (various)

The Official Centenary History of the Southern League – compiled by Leigh Edwards (Paper Plane Publishing Ltd) 1994

The Official Illustrated History of the FA Cup – Bryon Butler (Headline) 1996

The Phoenix Suburb – Alan Warwick 1972

Those Radio Times – Susan Briggs (Weidenfeld & Nicholson)

Total Sport – edited by A H Fabian and Geoffrey Green

We all follow the Palace (Eagle Eye Publications)

West Bromwich Albion – Percy M Young

West Norwood Cemetery's Sportsmen – Bob Flanagan 1995

50 Years of the FA Cup Finals (reprinted by Soccer Book Publishing Ltd)

100 Years of the FA Cup: The Official Centenary History – Tony Pawson

NEWSPAPERS AND PERIODICALS:

Athletic News, Birmingham Daily Post, Bolton Evening News, Bradford Daily Telegraph, Bury Guardian, Bury Times, Croydon Advertiser, Croydon Chronicle, Croydon Times, Crystal Palace Magazine, Crystal Palace Matters, Daily Mail, Daily Mirror, Daily Telegraph, Evesham Standard, Football: A weekly record of the Game, Football Echo and Sports Gazette, Glasgow Herald, Hampshire Chronicle and General Advertiser, Harmondsworth Magazine, Illustrated London News, Illustrated Sporting and Dramatic News, Liverpool Echo, London Evening News, Manchester Evening Chronicle, Neue Zürcher Zeitung, Northern Daily Telegraph, North-Eastern Daily Gazette, Norwood News, Norwood Review, Railway Magazine, Sheffield Daily Telegraph, Sheffield Independent, Sheffield and Rotherham Independent, South London Press, Sporting Sketches, Sunday Times, Sydenham & Penge Gazette, Tages Anzeiger, The Carthusian, The Daily Graphic, The Locomotive, The Sphere, The Sporting Life, The Sportsman, The Times, The Wykehamist, Uxbridge Gazette, Western Daily Press, Yorkshire Observer.

INDEX

Celtic, Glasgow 103, 105, 107, 109
Cercle de Bruges 99
Chadder, Alwyn Harvey (Oxford, Corinthians & England) 125, 144, 146, 147, 149, 150
Chadwick, A (Southampton & England) 31
Chadwick E (Everton & England) 103
Chapman (Sheffield Wednesday) 70
Chapman, Herbert (Arsenal Manager) 131
Charlton Athletic 129, 154
Charterhouse School 43, 97
Chatt, Bob (Aston Villa) 20
Chelsea 39, 85, 99, 109, 111, 112, 141, 148, 155
Chenery, Charles John (Crystal Palace) 16
Chesterfield Town 71, 99
Civil Service 135
Clapham Rovers 16, 93, 94, 112
Clapton Orient 93, 99, 111, 114, 127, 129, 136
Clawley (Tottenham Hotspur) 38
Cleaver, Ralph 49
Clegg, J C (FA President) 127
Cliftonville 127
Clyde 127
Coates, H L (Royal Navy) 128
Cobbold, W N (Old Carthusians) 99
Colclough, Horace (Crystal Palace) 116
Coles, Frank (Honorary Secretary of the London Banks FA) 131
Common, Alfred (Sheffield United) 43
Coney Hall FC 156
Cooper (Barnsley) 85
Corinthian Shield 99
Corinthian-Casuals 123, 151, 153, 154
Corinthian-Casuals Trust Fund 154
Corinthians 21, 43, 75, 93, 94, 95, 96, 97, 99, 103, 105, 116, 123, 124, 125, 127, 128, 129, 130, 133, 134, 135, 136, 137, 138, 139, 140, 141, 144, 145, 146, 147, 148, 149, 150, 151, 154
Cook (West Bromwich Albion) 84
Court Royal Hotel 28
Cowan, James (Aston Villa) 24
Cowan, John (Aston Villa) 25
Cozens, J H 111, 112
Crabtree, J W (Aston Villa) 95
Crawshaw (Sheffield Wednesday) 22, 61, 70, 71, 103

Cray Wanderers 94
Creek, F N S (Corinthians & England) 138, 139, 140, 141, 144, 146, 148, 149
Crewe Alexandra 116
Croydon 43, 68
Croydon Common 114, 115, 117
Crump, Charles 99
Crystal Palace Academy matches 157
Crystal Palace authorities 44
Crystal Palace Badminton Club 134
Crystal Palace Band 28, 64
Crystal Palace – Building and grounds, The 9, 10, 13, 25, 26, 51, 52, 55, 56, 59, 60, 81, 119, 126, 151, 152, 153, 157
Crystal Palace Company 10, 11, 16, 44, 63, 82, 106, 111, 123, 133, 146
Crystal Palace Concerts 22
Crystal Palace Engineering School 93
Crystal Palace FC 21, 75, 87, 110, 111, 115, 117, 119, 123, 134, 155, 157, Reserve Team 157
Crystal Palace fire 151
Crystal Palace football ground see Cup Final ground and Cycle track (Northern) ground
Crystal Palace High Level station 55
Crystal Palace Low Level station 40, 55, 56
Crystal Palace Magazine, The 11, 12, 111, 112
Crystal Palace, Original football Club 1871 15, 111
Crystal Palace Rovers 17
Crystal Palace staff team 93
Cundall, Charles 141
Cup Final (see FA Cup Final)
Cup Final ground 19, 35, 111, 112, 123, 139, 151, 156
Cycle track (Northern ground) 10, 93

D

Davis, A (Vice President of the FA) 127
Davies, John 77
Day, F 15
De Veen, R (Belgium) 99
Deptford Invicta 93
Derby County 19, 24, 26, 27, 28, 40, 44, 45, 46, 98
Derby, Lord 90
Derby Swifts 27
Derbyshire 39

Devey, John Henry George (Aston Villa & England) 20, 21, 24, 96
Dewar, Sir Thomas (Lord Mayor of London) 95, 96
Doggart, A G (Corinthians) 127, 128, 135, 140, 141, 146, 148, 149, 150
Dogherty, J (Portadown) 128
Douthwaite, H (Cambridge Univ) 124, 138
Drummond (Rangers) 105
Dubuis, H F (Casuals) 134, 135, 136, 137, 139
Dulwich Hamlet 68, 93, 128
Dundee 93
Ducat, Andrew (Casuals) 137
Dunn, Arthur Tempest Blakiston 92, 95, 96, 97, 129, 130 (see also Arthur Dunn Memorial Cup)
Dunn, Mrs Arthur 130

E

Earle S J T (Clapton) 127, 128
Eastbourne 131
Edwards (Old Salopians) 97
England 17, 23, 25, 27, 29, 39, 40, 43, 49, 63, 67, 69, 71, 75, 76, 77, 79, 87, 91, 94, 95, 97, 99, 100, 101, 102, 103, 104, 105, 106, 107, 108, 109, 114, 125, 126, 127, 128, 139, 141, 148
English League 30
Everton 26, 68, 69, 70, 91, 94, 95, 103, 107, 113, 117, 140, 148
Evesham Town 125, 126
Ewer, F H (Corinthians & Casuals) 127, 131, 134, 135, 136, 140, 141, 144, 146
Exeter City 116
Eyres-Monsell, Commander 127

F

FA Amateur Cup 97, 99, 125, 127, 133, 134, 135, 136, 155
FA Council 75, 77
FA Challenge Cup 16, 116, 139, 140, 141, 146, 147, 150, 151, 156
FA Cup Final 11, 19, 30, 39, 43, 51, 52, 60, 61, 63, 75, 85, 87, 91, 93, 94, 103, 109, 123, 156
Fairclough, Arthur (Barnsley) 79
Fallowfield (Manchester Athletic Ground) 19, 29

T

U

V

W

Y

PICTURE CREDITS

100 Years of FA Cup 71t, 79tr.

Aerofilms 122, 152, 156t.

Alan Weldon 156cr.

Alan (Fred) Pipes 30cl.

Andy George 12c, 19b, 21t, 25c, 29cl, 31c, 34t, 34c, 36t, 37, 38t, 38br, 39t, 40t, 40b, 43tl, 43b, 44cl, 46, 47b, 49t, 49b, 57br, 59t, 59br, 63cr, 67b, 69b, 70t, 71bl, 72tl, 76cr, 76cl, 78c, 78br, 79b, 84t, 84b, 85t, 85cl, 85b, 86b, 87b, 88c, 89t, 90t, 91tr, 91b, 91cr, 123cr, 130br, 133tr, 165c.

BBC Library 145.

Book of Football 16cr, 31b, 47t, 56b, 62, 64t, 64c, 66t, 66b, 67tl, 67tr, 67cr, 71b, 80, 94t, 95tl, 99, 100, 103tr, 105t, 106t, 106 & 107, 107tr, 107cr, 107br, 107b, 109b, 159tl, 159tr, 159bl, 159br, 160, 160t, 165b.

Bryon Butler 21t, 22cl, 28bl, 29tr, 44cr, 57bl, 75b, 77t.

Caxton press 14, 15t, 16t, 63tr, 92, 95tr, 95cr, 96br, 96bl, 133cr, 137t.

Charterhouse 94b.

Christies 18 inset, 23b, 27tr, 101b, 103b, 107cl, 109tl.

Croydon Advertiser 138t.

Crystal Palace Foundation 10b, 18, 55b inset, 59c, 82tl, 83bl, 82 & 83, 83br, 83tr, 118, 151cr, 153cl, 157t, 173, 174.

Crystal Palace Magazine 158.

Crystal Palace Museum 12b, 60c, 93b.

Daily Mirror 68, 69c, 70c, 70b, 72b, 75tl, 75tr, 87t.

Edward Grayson 95b, 103br.

Eric Price 55c, 56t.

Eric Spottiswoode 114br.

FA 69t, 96t, 139c, 140, 141.

Football Museum 11t, 16b, 16c, 17t, 25t, 25cr, 51c, 54, 61c, 73b, 79cr, 86tl, 94c, 159cr, 161b.

Harmondsworth Magazine 28cl, 39b, 40c.

Ian Bevan 13c, 20cr, 22bl, 25cl, 27bl, 29bl, 31b, 38bl, 43cl, 45br, 49c, 67b, 69b, 71br, 74t, 75c, 77b, 78bl, 81cr, 81br, 85cr, 85br, 87cr, 91br, 153tr, 161t.

Ian King 154t, 154b, 155tr.

Illustrated London News 8, 8 inset, 50, 80 & 81, 90c, 90bl, 90br, 97b.

Illustrated Sporting & Dramatic News 23, 24br, 26 & 27, 36b, 43cr, 45t, 48, 104 & 105.

John Blackmore 127.

Martin Tyler 79cl.

Melvyn Harrison 15b, 55t, 55c, 63b, 93cr, 112br, 119tr, 119b, 120, 121.

Michael Gilbert 9cl, 9cr, 9b, 13b, 51t, 52t, 57c, 61t, 89b, 123b, 132, 151b.

Mike Taylor 131b.

Museum of London 85bl, 88t.

Norman Barrett 21b.

Norman Epps 133cl, 134b, 135t, 137b, 139t, 150tr.

Norman Rosser (Malvern College) 129t, 129b, 156cl, 156b.

Norwood News 153b.

Norwood Society 57c.

Patrick Beaver 9tr, 94bl.

Penelope Bevan 19tr.

Peter Stanley 45b.

Phil Paine 153cr.

R Custance (Winchester School) 130tr.

Railway Magazine 52c, 52br, 52bl.

Replay Publishing 10t, 11b, 12t, 17b, 20t, 20tr, 20b, 24c, 26c, 34b, 35, 61b, 64b, 72tr, 73t, 76 & 77, 86tr, 88b, 101t, 111cl, 112tl, 125b, 138t, 141b, 160br.

Rev. Nigel Sands 111tr, 117, 154c.

Richard Chadder 125t, 130cl, 131t, 136, 144tr, 144tl, 144c, 144b, 145, 146tl, 146c, 146b, 147, 148tr, 148b, 149tl, 149c, 149bl, 150tl, 150bl.

Rob Marsden 75b, 110, 111c, 111br, 112tl, 113t, 113b, 114tr, 114c, 114b, 115t, 115c, 115br, 116br, 116cr, 116t, 116b, 117b.

Shrewsbury school 97tr, 97cr.

Sporting Life 124, 125c & b.

Sporting Sketches 29tl, 30b, 31tr, 32 & 33.

Stuart Hibberd 77b, 99t, 105br, 155tl.

Talbot Collection 55b, 60b, 130bl, 131t.

The Daily Graphic 27br, 42, 65, 87bl, 91c, 102, 108.

The Sphere 41.

Uxbridge Library 98.

Wolverhampton Wanderers 74t, 142 & 143.

Numbers refer to pages
t: top   b: bottom   r: right   l: left   c: centre

While every effort has been made to trace the owners of photographs used, this has sometimes proved impossible and copyright owners are invited to contact the publishers.

SUBSCRIBERS

1	Mrs Phyllis Hall	56	Dorothy & Dennis Butler (North Yorkshire)
2	The Football Association	57	Terry Rutter (London)
3	The Crystal Palace Foundation	58	Roy Turk (London)
4	The Crystal Palace Museum	59	Don Cain (London)
5	Crystal Palace FC	60	Dick Mott (Surrey)
6	Corinthian-Casuals FC	61	David Williams-Richardson (West Sussex)
7	Crystal Palace Sports Centre	62	Duncan Clark (London)
8	Bryon Butler	63	Ron & Edna Yates (North Yorkshire)
9	Ian Bevan (Kent)	64	Alice & Edward Johnson (North Yorkshire)
10	Michael Gilbert (London)	65	Betsy Graham (Surrey)
11	Stuart Hibberd (London)	66	Ian Smith (Kent)
12	Andy George (South Glamorgan)	67	Norman Shiel (Devon)
13	Eric Price (West Sussex)	68	Norman Shiel (Devon)
14	Gina Gilbert	69	Geoff Meredith (Kent)
15	Harvey Gilbert (Hong Kong)	70	Luke Ward (West Sussex)
16	Howard Gilbert (Essex)	71	Peter Ward (West Sussex)
17	Penelope Bevan	72	R C Robinson (London)
18	Siân Bevan	73	David & Marion Evans (Surrey)
19	Alisdair Bevan	74	Jon Weaver (Braintree Town FC - Essex)
20	Ruth Hibberd	75	Alan (Fred) Pipes (East Sussex)
21	Alice Hibberd	76	Ken Horsley (London)
22	Katherine Hibberd	77	Colin Paul Howlett (Hertfordshire)
23	Alison & Graham Wood (Buckinghamshire)	78	David Lancaster (Hertfordshire)
24	David Wood	79	David Keats (Surrey)
25	Owen Wood	80	Barry G Kitcherside (Surrey)
26	Michael D Lewis (Wiltshire)	81	Ian R King (Surrey)
27	Susan Thomas (Carmarthenshire)	82	Ron R Daughtry (Surrey)
28	Moya Beaty (Sussex)	83	Ron R Daughtry (Surrey)
29	Peter Stanley (London)	84	Michael E Wheaton (Kent)
30	Steve O'Riley (Kent)	85	Les Thompson (West Sussex)
31	Roger Jones (Pembrokeshire)	86	In memory of Geoffrey Andrews
32	Peter Jones (Carmarthenshire)	87	Bob Lilliman (London)
33	Ron Holton (London)	88	David London (Surrey)
34	Steve & Christine Dean (Dorset)	89	Chris Marsh (Derbyshire)
35	Richard Dean	90	Dennis Finch (Surrey)
36	David Dean	91	David Bennett (Surrey)
37	Rachel Dean	92	Andrew Hobson (Surrey)
38	Jim & Lynda Wade (Devon)	93	Jason Henderson (East Sussex)
39	Angela Wade	94	Keith & Kieron Coburn (Cambridgeshire)
40	Belinda Wade	95	Phil Ratcliffe (Kent)
41	Stuart & Vera Howard (Powys)	96	Rod Harrington (Somerset)
42	Bea Carter (Surrey)	97	Alistair J S Williams (Surrey)
43	John Hibberd (North Yorkshire)	98	John Ringrose (Essex)
44	Sue Hibberd (West Yorkshire)	99	Vince Taylor (Groundtastic Magazine - Essex)
45	Dave Evans (London)	100	L Allen (Essex)
46	Ian Beardall (London)	101	Wilfred Grove (London)
47	Gavin Graham (Toronto, Canada)	102	Peter Cogle (Grampian)
48	Sylvain Pierrot (Paris, France)	103	Mrs Audrey Godbold (Surrey)
49	Peter & Mamiran Haines (Kent)	104	Philip Paine (Kent)
50	Edward Graham (Toronto, Canada)	105	M Griffin (Kent)
51	Andre Zdrzalka (London)	106	Phil Brown (Lancashire)
52	Rick Fardell (Norfolk)	107	Tony Smith (Cheshire)
53	Neville & Betty Hill (Avon)	108	Phil Martin (Geneva, Switzerland)
54	Angela Warnock (Essex)	109	Ray Sacks (London)
55	Mary & Jimmy Harrison (North Yorkshire)	110	Andrew Elliott (London)

111	P Fenn	168	John Cartland (Surrey)
112	Anglo School (London)	169	Steven Raoul Roy (Kent)
113	Graham Cotterill (West Sussex)	170	Robert Tye (London)
114	Ron Hooper - Charlton Athletic Supporter (Oxfordshire)	171	Master R Wood (London)
115	Peter Hurn (Surrey)	172	Val Peckham (Avon)
116	Tony Brown (Hertfordshire)	173	Tom Addison (Victoria, Australia)
117	Jim Halliday (London)	174	Garth George Savin (London)
118	Fergus Pardis Milton (Hampshire)	175	Dr Cedric Demaine (Surrey)
119	John Northcutt (Essex)	176	Steve & Helen Yately (Surrey)
120	June Stewart (Kent)	177	Frank D Miles (Surrey)
121	Rev. Nigel Sands (Berkshire)	178	Roger & Matthew Browne (Kent)
122	John P Bottle (Surrey)	179	Elisabeth Thorburn (Essex)
123	Roger Lambert, Plumber (London)	180	Barry E Jones (London)
124	Mark James Bray (Somerset)	181	Michael J Dubus (Buckinghamshire)
125	David Kirkby (Leicestershire)	182	The Blundell Family (Surrey)
126	Stephen Metcalfe (Kent)	183	Christopher Dixey (Wiltshire)
127	Chris Wigginton (Leicestershire)	184	Neil Dyson (London)
128	John Friend (Lancashire)	185	Patrick Fuller
129	John W Brown - Local History Publications (London)	186	Jeanne Leach
130	Roy Sims, Bradford Park Avenue AFC (West Yorkshire)	187	Paul Claydon (Essex)
131	Martin Brunnschweiler (Isle of Man)	188	Ros Rackham (Kent)
132	Andrew Brunnschweiler (Isle of Man)	189	Norman F Epps (East Sussex)
133	Jack Merrifield (West Sussex)	190	Archie Starr - Charlton Supporter for 75 years
134	Paul Joannou - Newcastle Utd FC Official Historian	191	J Dodman (Surrey)
135	Gonzalo Gangoiti Uriguen (Bilbao, Spain)	192	Ian Lock - Ninety two Club Member 923
136	Gareth Protheroe (Shropshire)	193	David R Bottle
137	David George Barnett - Palace Supporter since 1945	194	Robert Stainforth (Middlesex)
138	John Grimme (Essex)	195	Dominic Cobby (Surrey)
139	Michael David Hersey (London)	196	Michael Petersen (Odense, Denmark)
140	Keith Cox (Illinois, USA)	197	Malcolm Taylor (Dorset)
141	Mark Evetts (Kent)	198	Alan Bowden (Dorset)
142	Derek Andrews (Surrey)	199	Mike Floate (Kent)
143	N Whitehead (Kent)	200	Alec Fleming (Middlesex)
144	Anne Elliott (Kent)	201	David Simpson (Kent)
145	Angus J Mackenzie (Kent)	202	Dave McManus (Kent)
146	Richard Saville (Essex)	203	Dave McManus (Kent)
147	Alan Weldon (Somerset)	204	Richard H Chadder (Oxfordshire)
148	Eric Richards (Herefordshire)	205	Simon Allison (Middlesex)
149	Graham E Lunn (Lancashire)	206	Steven Moles (Surrey)
150	Eric Pudney (London)	207	Geoff Kentfield (London)
151	John Gray (Nottinghamshire)	208	Robert Barnes (Kent)
152	Chris Overson (Middlesex)	209	Malcolm Bailey
153	Simon Inglis (London)	210	Alan Mason (Hinkley United, Leicestershire)
154	Allan Redding (London)	211	W A Malham (Kent)
155	Manchester United Museum and Tour Centre	212	Dink Poole (Kent)
156	Gerry Ryan (Surrey)	213	Steve Sadler (Bedfordshire)
157	Tom Bowden (Surrey)	214	Chris Preston (London)
158	David Murphy (Kent)	215	Trevor Enefer (Surrey)
159	Mr L T Oxley (Kent)	216	Keith Wyncoll (Kent)
160	Terry Morris (London)	217	Charles Baxter (Surrey)
161	Tony & Pam Jennings (Surrey)	218	Richard Dunning (Surrey)
162	Les Melluish (Surrey)	219	Dermot & Bridie Enright (Kent)
163	Jonathan Cotton (Surrey)	220	Alan Bennett (Middlesex)
164	Roy Hathaway (London)	221	Dave Collins (Welsh Football Magazine)
165	John Hugh-Jones (London)	222	Maria Grech (Surrey)
166	Owen C Morgan (Dorset)	223	Nancy Ruth Hibberd (North Yorkshire)
167	Hayden J Morgan (Dorset)	224	Mrs Ada Regan (Kent)